Moodle as a Curriculum and Information Management System

Beginner's Guide

Use Moodle to manage and organize your administrative duties, monitor attendance records, manage student enrollment, record exam results, and much more

Jason Hollowell

[PACKT] open source
PUBLISHING   community experience distilled

BIRMINGHAM - MUMBAI

Moodle as a Curriculum and Information Management System

Beginner's Guide

First published: January 2011

Production Reference: 1311210

Published by Packt Publishing Ltd.
32 Lincoln Road
Olton
Birmingham, B27 6PA, UK.

ISBN 978-1-849513-22-7

www.packtpub.com

Cover Image by Charwak A (charwak86@gmail.com)

Credits

Author

Jason Hollowell

Reviewers

Anthony Borrow, S.J

Brian Mattson

Kent Villard

Acquisition Editor

Sarah Cullington

Development Editor

Meeta Rajani

Technical Editor

Aditi Suvarna

Copy Editor

Laxmi Subramanian

Indexer

Tejal Daruwale

Editorial Team Leader

Aditya Belpathak

Project Team Leader

Lata Basantani

Project Coordinator

Leena Purkait

Proofreader

Mario Cecere

Production Coordinator

Melwyn D'sa

Cover Work

Melwyn D'sa

About the Author

Jason Hollowell is an English language teacher and educational program administrator. As a university student, Jason studied Political Science with the intention of proceeding to law school and becoming a lawyer. When he studied abroad in Japan, prior to his senior year in university, that plan changed and he returned to complete his university degree and then promptly headed back to Japan to learn more about its fascinating language and culture, never to consider law again. It was the beginning of a series of rewarding experiences that include working as a technical translator and interpreter for both Mitsubishi and Toyota Motors, earning a Masters Degree in Second Language Studies from the University of Hawaii, working for the University of Hawaii and then for Nihon University in Japan where he is now employed as an Associate Professor of English and the Director of the English Language Program. He has been involved in online education programs through the development of a SLOAN Foundation funded English writing program and, since 2004, has been an avid user of Moodle. Jason subscribes to the constructivist principles upon which Moodle was founded and has developed a working knowledge of PHP, MySQL, and Apache through many hours of experimentation and countless visits to online forums, especially those hosted on the `Moodle.org` website.

Acknowledgement

No book is the product of just the author—he just happens to be the one with his name on the cover.

Many people contributed to the success of this book, and it would take more space than I have to thank each one individually.

A very special thanks goes to Sarah Cullington, my editor, who is the reason that this book exists. Thank you, Sarah, for understanding the idea and helping me to develop it into something worthy of print, and for being a wonderful guide through this process. Thank you also to the entire Packt Publishing team for working so diligently to help bring out a high quality product.

I would also like to thank those people who helped me, with support, ideas, and feedback, as I experimented with Moodle as an educational program administration tool. They include Richard McMahon, Jason Myrick, George Harrison, and Yusuke Itamiya. A special thanks also goes out to Hiroko Nagasawa, without your help I would never have been able to get the grant funding that made the registration enrollment plugin, which was the final motivation to write this book, possible.

The many users of Moodle who participate in the forums on the `Moodle.org` site also deserve a very heartfelt thanks. You helped me discover the possibilities Moodle has to offer and rescued me when I got lost as I experimented and explored.

Finally, I must thank Martin Dougiamas for the amazing contribution he has made to education through his brainchild, Moodle!

About the Reviewers

Anthony Borrow, S.J is a Jesuit of the New Orleans Province who has been active in the Moodle community for the past five years. Anthony has an M.A. degree in Counseling from Saint Louis University and a Masters of Divinity from the Jesuit School of Theology of Santa Clara University. Anthony has worked on the design and implementation of various database systems since 1992.

Anthony serves the Moodle community as its CONTRIB Coordinator. In that role, Anthony has presented at various MoodleMoots (conferences) across the United States and provided in-house training opportunities for institutions learning how to implement Moodle. Anthony has taught at Dallas Jesuit College Preparatory and provides technical advise to the Jesuit Secondary Education Association (`http://jsea.org`) and the Jesuit Virtual Learning Academy (`http://jvla.org/`). Anthony is currently serving the community at Cristo Rey Jesuit College Preparatory of Houston (`http://cristoreyjesuit.org`) as their Campus Minister.

He is the co-author of the Honduras chapter of *Teen Gangs: A Global View*. He has also been the technical reviewer of various Packt books (0141, 1001, 1902, 4244).

> I am grateful to the Moodle community for continually inspiring me to learn more about educational technologies and fostering an environment where every voice contributes to building that community.

Brian Mattson is a history teacher from Lapeer, Michigan with a passion for Moodle and its use in both blended and remote learning environments. After teaching at an American school in Torreon, Mexico for four years he moved to Bulgaria where he and his colleagues pioneered the use of Moodle at the Anglo American School of Sofia. Currently he resides in Amsterdam, the Netherlands where he runs a Moodle consulting business that provides training and workshops for international schools throughout Europe and beyond. He can be contacted at `mattso13@iteach.org`.

I would like to thank two members of the Anglo American School of Sofia; Linda Dimitrov for her past and continued assistance with all things technical, and Jim Leahy who has provided me with constant encouragement in my professional endeavors. I am also grateful to all the students at the Anglo American School of Sofia who taught me as much as I taught them. Finally a special thanks to my wife Anette and my son Tijs for everything.

Kent Villard is a twenty-year veteran of the IT industry and currently is the E-Learning Coordinator for the University of Prince Edward Island. He has been administering Moodle for almost five years. Kent particularly enjoys the process of converting traditional curriculum to work in an online form. He has acted as a technical reviewer for Packt on *Moodle 1.9 for Design and Technology* and *Moodle 1.9 Teaching Techniques*.

When not administering Moodle or evangelizing the Mac platform, Kent can be found spending quality time with his beautiful wife Denise and awesome kids, Maxwell and Samantha.

Kent lives in Cornwall, Prince Edward Island in Atlantic Canada. He can be reached at `kent.villard@gmail.com`.

www.PacktPub.com

Support files, eBooks, discount offers, and more

You might want to visit www.PacktPub.com for support files and downloads related to your book.

Did you know that Packt offers eBook versions of every book published, with PDF and ePub files available? You can upgrade to the eBook version at www.PacktPub.com and as a print book customer, you are entitled to a discount on the eBook copy. Get in touch with us at service@packtpub.com for more details.

At www.PacktPub.com, you can also read a collection of free technical articles, sign up for a range of free newsletters and receive exclusive discounts and offers on Packt books and eBooks.

http://PacktLib.PacktPub.com

Do you need instant solutions to your IT questions? PacktLib is Packt's online digital book library. Here, you can access, read and search across Packt's entire library of books.

Why Subscribe?

- Fully searchable across every book published by Packt
- Copy and paste, print and bookmark content
- On demand and accessible via web browser

Free access for Packt account holders

If you have an account with Packt at www.PacktPub.com, you can use this to access PacktLib today and view nine entirely free books. Simply use your login credentials for immediate access.

My wife Hitomi, you fulfill me with peace, love, and happiness; my daughter Hana, you are my sunshine and my daily reminder of the beauty of life.

This book would not have been possible without your love and understanding.

Thank you from the bottom of my heart. 愛しているよ!

Table of Contents

Preface

Moodle is the most widely used Learning Management System in the world. Moodle is primarily used as an online learning course platform and few people know how to use it in any other way. However, Moodle can also be used as a management system. By adapting Moodle to become a curriculum and information management system, you can keep your administrative tasks in the same place as your lesson plans by managing student attendance records, recording grades, sharing reports between departments, and much more.

Moodle as a Curriculum and Information Management System will show you how you can use Moodle to set up an environment that enables you to disseminate information about your educational program, provide a forum for communication among all those involved in your institution, and even to control your course registration and enrollment.

This book will show you how to create courses and organize them into categories. You will learn to assign teachers to each course, which will greatly help you to manage timetables and student enrollment, which can otherwise be a very frustrating and time consuming task. You will learn how to display the different aspects of your Curriculum and Information Management System to make it easily accessible and navigable for staff and students alike, ensuring that everyone knows what they are doing and where they are meant to be.

This book is a practical step-by-step guide to expand the functionality of your Moodle Learning Management System.

What this book covers

Chapter 1, Welcome to Moodle as a Curriculum and Information Management System (CIMS)!, explains how to expand the use of the Moodle system to function as a portal for information exchange, professional collaboration, and curriculum management.

Chapter 2, Building the Foundation—Creating Categories and Courses, explains and demonstrates how to create and organize the courses offered in your curriculum, within Moodle.

Chapter 3, Student Account Creation and Enrollment, explains how to create student accounts in bulk and experiment with different ways of enrolling those students in courses on the Moodle site.

Chapter 4, Incorporating Educational Standards, introduces and explains some tasks that will enable you to incorporate educational standards in your Moodle CIMS site.

Chapter 5, Enabling your Moodle Site to Function as an Information Portal, explores some of the possibilities such as modifying display settings, removing course lists from the category page, increasing the detailed summary settings, and others, through discussion and experimentation.

Chapter 6, Customized Roles, explores various methods for monitoring and reporting on student access and performance in the Moodle site.

Chapter 7, Advanced Data Access and Display, explores the installation and use of several tools that allow for more advanced methods of accessing data generated and used by your Moodle site.

Chapter 8, Setting Up a Mini SIS, explores two different methods of setting up Moodle to function as an SIS.

Chapter 9, Promoting Efficient Communication, introduces and explains the strategies for establishing an efficient communication portal through your Moodle CIMS.

Chapter 10, Advanced Enrollment Plugin, covers how to enable your site to function as a registration and enrollment system that will allow you to regulate how students matriculate through the set of courses that make up your curriculum.

What you need for this book

- ◆ A web browser (Firefox preferred)
- ◆ A text editor

Who this book is for

If you are a teacher or head of a department in an institution and are interested in how Moodle can be used to streamline curriculum delivery and information flow in your institution, this book is for you. This book is also useful for Moodle administrators.

Conventions

In this book, you will find a number of styles of text that distinguish between different kinds of information. Here are some examples of these styles, and an explanation of their meaning.

Code words in text are shown as follows: "This will download a compressed package containing all of the files for the block called `myCourses.zip`."

A block of code is set as follows:

```
if (!defined('FRONTPAGECOURSELIMIT')) {
define('FRONTPAGECOURSELIMIT',    200);
```

New terms and **important words** are shown in bold. Words that you see on the screen, in menus or dialog boxes for example, appear in the text like this: "Select your language and click on the **Next** button found at the bottom of the screen."

 Warnings or important notes appear in a box like this.

 Tips and tricks appear like this.

Reader feedback

Feedback from our readers is always welcome. Let us know what you think about this book—what you liked or may have disliked. Reader feedback is important for us to develop titles that you really get the most out of.

To send us general feedback, simply send an e-mail to `feedback@packtpub.com`, and mention the book title via the subject of your message.

If there is a book that you need and would like to see us publish, please send us a note in the **SUGGEST A TITLE** form on `http://www.packtpub.com` or e-mail `suggest@packtpub.com`.

If there is a topic that you have expertise in and you are interested in either writing or contributing to a book, see our author guide on `www.packtpub.com/authors`.

Customer support

Now that you are the proud owner of a Packt book, we have a number of things to help you to get the most from your purchase.

Downloading the example code for this book

You can download the example code files for all Packt books you have purchased from your account at http://www.PacktPub.com. If you purchased this book elsewhere, you can visit http://www.PacktPub.com/support and register to have the files e-mailed directly to you.

Errata

Although we have taken every care to ensure the accuracy of our content, mistakes do happen. If you find a mistake in one of our books—maybe a mistake in the text or the code—we would be grateful if you would report this to us. By doing so, you can save other readers from frustration and help us improve subsequent versions of this book. If you find any errata, please report them by visiting http://www.packtpub.com/support, selecting your book, clicking on the **errata submission form** link, and entering the details of your errata. Once your errata are verified, your submission will be accepted and the errata will be uploaded on our website, or added to any list of existing errata, under the Errata section of that title. Any existing errata can be viewed by selecting your title from http://www.packtpub.com/support.

Piracy

Piracy of copyright material on the Internet is an ongoing problem across all media. At Packt, we take the protection of our copyright and licenses very seriously. If you come across any illegal copies of our works, in any form, on the Internet, please provide us with the location address or website name immediately so that we can pursue a remedy.

Please contact us at copyright@packtpub.com with a link to the suspected pirated material.

We appreciate your help in protecting our authors, and our ability to bring you valuable content.

Questions

You can contact us at questions@packtpub.com if you are having a problem with any aspect of the book, and we will do our best to address it.

1
Welcome to Moodle as a Curriculum and Information Management System (CIMS)!

You are on your way to learn how to expand the use of the Moodle system to function as a portal for information exchange, professional collaboration, and curriculum management.

This chapter will start with the basics by introducing the concepts and helping you to get your site installed and configured. The following topics will be addressed in this chapter:

- A brief explanation of Moodle, its underlying philosophy, and design
- Introduction of the CIMS idea
- Moodle installation
- Basic setup, configuration, and customization of your Moodle site

What is Moodle?

Moodle is a web-based software package that allows you to create an environment in which an educational program can be delivered. What does that mean? Moodle allows you to create course environments where all sorts of education can take place. Moodle is now the most widely used online learning software package with over 49,000 registered Moodle sites as of the first quarter of 2010. It is used by private and public educational institutions ranging from kindergartens to universities as well as by a wide range of businesses, non-profit organizations, governmental bodies, and healthcare facilities for virtually every training and educational program imaginable.

A VLE, LMS, and CMS

There are a multitude of acronyms out there today that claim Moodle as a member of their 'group'. Moodle is categorized as a **VLE (Virtual Learning Environment)** or **LMS (Learning Management System)** due to its focus on learning and education. Additionally, Moodle is described to be a **CMS (Course Management System)**, an **LCMS (Learning Content Management System)**, and sometimes even a **CMS (Content Management System)**.

Each of these categories of systems has its own unique and defining characteristics but for most of them, there are arguably more similarities than differences. Each is a software package that is installed on a server and set up to be accessed via the Internet or, in some business settings, through an intranet (an in-house network). The majority of them are designed to allow for the creation and maintenance of online learning environments. Two of the most widely used categories of systems that are used to describe Moodle, LMSs, and VLEs, are often used interchangeably, although the term LMS is generally used to describe a system of wider scope that includes the ability to perform administrative tasks involved in education such as reporting, documenting, and analyzing. Moodle's flexibility, in terms of how it can be set up and maintained, is one of the main reasons for its inclusion in virtually every category of online learning software package. In this sense, Moodle is similar to a chameleon that is capable of 'changing its color', or shifting its focus, in order to meet the needs of each institution and user.

Using Moodle as a CIMS

In most institutions, there is a need to maintain data and information related to the education taking place as well as to perform various peripheral tasks that are not directly related to, or are at a macro level to the education itself.

Some examples of this type of peripheral work are:

- Monitoring of student attendance records
- Presenting information of course offerings to students in order that they may make decisions about what courses to take
- Assigning courses to students in programs where students are not allowed to select their own courses
- Controlling which courses, and how many courses, students can register for or enroll in
- Establishing limits on how many students can enroll in a single course
- Delivering and analyzing standardized tests to students within a school or other type of educational or training program and various other educational, administrative, and collaboration-type tasks and activities

As Moodle is designed to be extremely flexible and is provided as an open source package, it is fairly easy to extend, and even stretch Moodle through imaginative uses, installation of third-party contributed plugins, and minor code manipulations to enable it to function as a system that helps to manage an educational curriculum and to support the flow and use of information that is accumulated and digested in such educational settings. As such, Moodle will function as what I call a **Curriculum and Information Management System (CIMS)**, while simultaneously functioning as an LMS. The CIMS idea encapsulates the various tasks that surround an educational institution and includes functions that are often performed by Portals, **Student Information Systems (SIS)**, and Content Management Systems (CMS). As a CIMS, Moodle can perform all of the tasks listed in the previous paragraph as well as a host of others that will be introduced in subsequent chapters. Get ready for an exciting adventure in setting up Moodle as your core CIMS and LMS!

Installing Moodle

Moodle installations can be roughly categorized into the following three categories:

- Installation of the XAMPP or MAMP packages
- Simple installation on a hosted web server
- Installation of a LAMP package on an in-house server

For the purpose of demonstrating how Moodle can function as a CIMS, we will walk through the installation and use of Moodle in MAMP and XAMPP packages. It is strongly recommended that you do not use a MAMP or XAMPP Moodle site as a production site (a site that is publicly accessible via the Internet). The MAMP or XAMPP environment is the ideal solution however, for being able to quickly experiment with Moodle on your own computer. If you prefer to experiment on a hosted server or dedicated LAMP installation, please make sure that your site is not available to the public and is not being used by students to ensure that you do not accidentally corrupt data or render your site inaccessible. Once you are comfortable with the methods presented in this book, you can implement them on a live production site. Additionally, the following information is provided as introductory information about preparing an environment in which Moodle can be served. Please visit the documentation area on the Moodle website (http://docs.moodle.org/en/Main_Page) for a wealth of information about getting a Moodle site up and running.

Installing MAMP and XAMPP packages

One of the quickest and easiest ways to get a Moodle site up and running for experimental purposes is to install a MAMP or XAMPP package. These packages consist of web server software (Apache), database server software (MySQL), and PHP and Perl programming language 'interpreters', that all run on your personal computer. This will allow you to run Moodle locally on your own computer. The following instructions will help you get one of these prepackaged local servers running on your desktop or laptop computer.

Time for action – installing the Mac OS X package

We will install the MAMP variety for Macintosh OS X because it is much more portable than the XAMPP variety. This means that once you have the MAMP folder in your **Applications** folder, all you need to do to use the MAMP package on a different computer is to copy the contents of the directory to the **Applications** folder of another machine running OS X. To install the Mac OS MAMP package, follow these steps:

1. First, go to `www.moodle.org` and move your mouse over the **Downloads** menu item.

2. Mouse over and click on the **Moodle for Mac OS X** link.

3. Then click on the **MAMP package** to start the download as shown in the following screenshot:

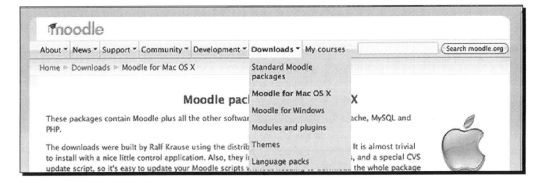

4. Once the download has completed, you will have a `Moodle4Mac-MAMP-19.dmg` file to work with. Double-click the file to decompress it. The following screenshot is of the window that will open when the dmg file has been mounted as a folder on your desktop.

5. Copy the contents of the MAMP package to your **Applications** folder, as instructed in the window.

6. Once all of the contents of the MAMP folder have been copied to your **Applications** folder, double-click on the **MAMP** application, shown in the following screenshot to launch the server control tool:

7. Click the **Start Servers** button to start the servers on your local computer. The Moodle instance contained in the MAMP package is preconfigured to use these servers.

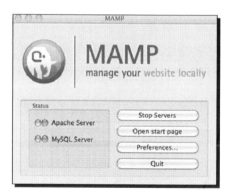

8. The red light, to the left of the server name, will turn green signifying that it is running. The MAMP control tool will automatically open the MAMP startup page in your browser. Click on the **Moodle** tab, shown in the following screenshot, to open your Moodle site in a new page:

What just happened?

You have now installed all of the components necessary to turn your computer into an experimental server for your Moodle site. You also have a prepackaged instance of Moodle that is ready to use the servers you have installed and turned on. You can now jump forward to the *Basic setup and customization of your Moodle site* section in this chapter.

Time for action – installing the Windows package

If you want to install a local instance of Moodle and the required server on a Windows machine, the XAMPP package is the only prepackaged variety available. The installation involves a few more steps than the Mac version but it is a straightforward process. To download and install the Windows version, follow these steps:

1. Click on **Moodle for Windows** from the **Downloads** drop-down menu from Moodle.org, and download the latest version. *Moodle V 2.4 Jan 10/2013*

2. Expand the contents of the package that is downloaded, to the location where you want your Moodle package. You will see a total of four items from the expanded package, as shown in the following screenshot. There will be a **Stop Moodle** icon, a **Start Moodle** icon, a **README** file, and a **server** folder. Detailed instructions can be found in the **README** file.

3. Double-click on the **Start Moodle** icon to start the Apache and database servers. A command prompt window with the message "Starting XAMPP" will appear and then after a few seconds the window will disappear. This means the servers are now running. Then proceed to the next step.

4. Navigate to your Moodle site by entering `http://localhost/` into your browser address window.   http:// 127.0.0.1 worked

5. After having started the servers by clicking on **Start Moodle** and typing the local host address into your browser address window, you may get a warning from Windows depending on the browser you are using and how the operating system is configured, about firewall protection. Go ahead and allow the content and bypass any warnings in order to access the site. You have installed the site and are the only one accessing it, so there is no need to worry about it containing possibly malicious content.

6. You will now be taken to the Moodle installer script. This installation process is the biggest difference between the Mac OS and Windows XAMPP package installations for Moodle. In Windows, you will go through the exact same installation process that you would go through if you were setting up a Moodle site on a hosted or dedicated server. The first screen will prompt you to select a language and provide information about the XAMPP package being used.

7. Select your language and click on the **Next** button found at the bottom of the screen.

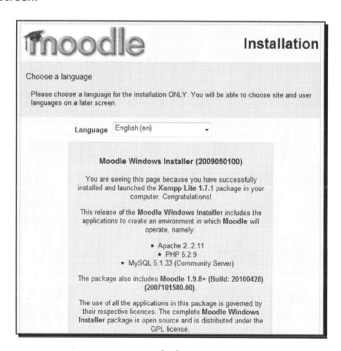

8. The next screen, shown in the following screenshot, will display the results of a PHP settings check. Everything should be OK as evidenced by the **Pass** message in green text to the right of each check item. If you get a **Fail** message in red text, you will need to determine the cause of the problem and fix it before you may proceed.

9. Click on the **Next** button to proceed with the installation.

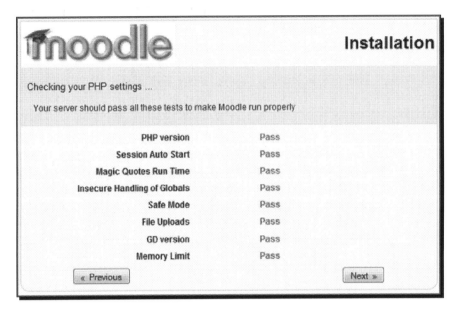

10. The next screen, shown in the following screenshot, will ask you to confirm the locations of the Moodle installation. These will include:

 - The web address
 - The Moodle directory (where Moodle files are contained)
 - The data directory (where Moodle will store data files)

These should be automatically filled in and it is not recommended to change the locations of the two directories unless you know what you are doing

11. If you are using Windows Vista, change the web address setting however, to `http://127.0.0.1`. While localhost and 127.0.0.1 are the same, there is an issue in Windows Vista that sometimes prevents localhost from working properly. As an additional note, once you have these locations set you should not move the Moodle directory or data directory. Doing so will make your site inaccessible until you move the directories back or change the paths in the `config.php` file, which contains directory paths and other fundamental settings for Moodle and is found in the Moodle directory.

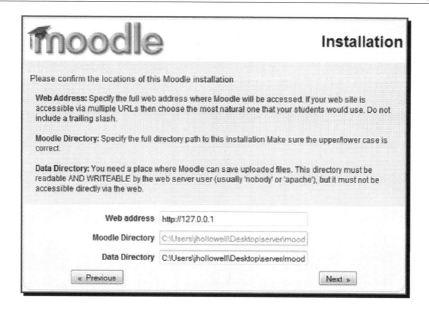

12. The screen that will appear after the locations have been correctly entered is a screen that allows you to enter settings for the database. The only field that should be altered on this screen is the password for the database. Even though this site is only going to be used for experimental purposes, it is a good idea to establish the habit of always selecting a password for your database. Enter a password and click on the **Next** button.

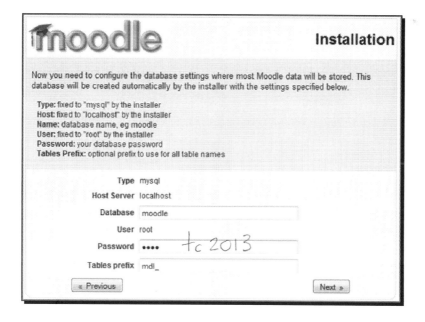

13. The next screen you will be presented with is a **Server Checks** screen informing you of the results of a check that was performed to ensure that the environment necessary for hosting Moodle is complete. These should all pass with a status of **OK** in the case of a XAMPP installation, as shown in the following screenshot:

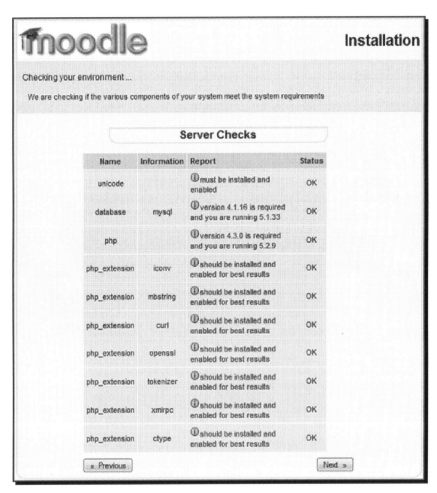

14. Click on the **Next** button to proceed to the next screen, which is a language pack download message screen. There is nothing to be done at this screen aside from reading the information presented.

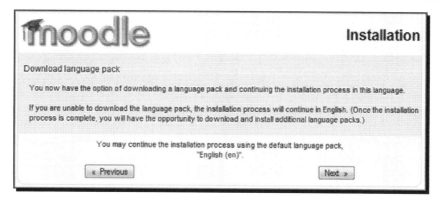

15. Click on the **Next** button and you will be presented with a **Configuration completed** message informing you that the `config.php` file was successfully created.

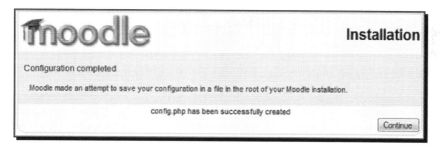

16. Click on the **Continue** button, which will display the copyright notice. Read quickly through the open source GNU public license message and then acknowledge that you understand, by clicking on the **Yes** button.

17. The final screen is a current release screen, which provides information about the Moodle version you have installed. Leave the **Unattended operation** tick box unticked and click on the **Continue** button.

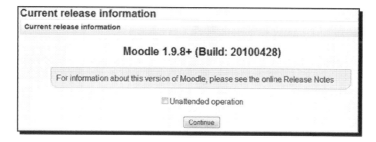

18. Click on the **Continue** button found at the bottom of this screen to start the database table creation process. This may take several minutes as all of the tables, in which Moodle stores data, are created in the database.

19. Scroll down in your browser window to watch as the tables are created and then click on the **Continue** button found at the bottom of the page when the creation process is completed. You will see tables being created again, this time for the various activities that come prepackaged in Moodle. Click **Continue** at the bottom of the page when the table creation process is finished. This process will be repeated multiple times before the database table creation portion of the installation is complete. Click on **Continue** at the bottom of the screen each time the option appears.

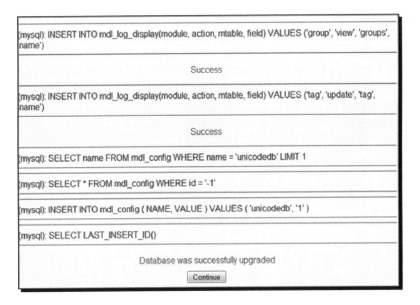

20. When the database table creation process has been completed you will be presented with a screen, shown in the following screenshot, that allows you to set the password and other profile settings for the administrator account. For our experimental server, leave the username **admin** and enter a password. The default on the Mac OS version is a very simple `12345` but you will need to create a more complicated password for this Windows install as the Moodle password policy is turned on by default in a standard Moodle Windows XAMPP install. Your password should:

- ❑ be eight characters long
- ❑ have one lower case letter and one upper case letter
- ❑ have at least one non-alphanumeric character (a symbol)

21. You can change the password settings once you have finished the installation process, if you want to use a simpler password. You will also need to enter the required fields for creating Moodle user accounts, which are:

- an e-mail address
- a city/town
- a country

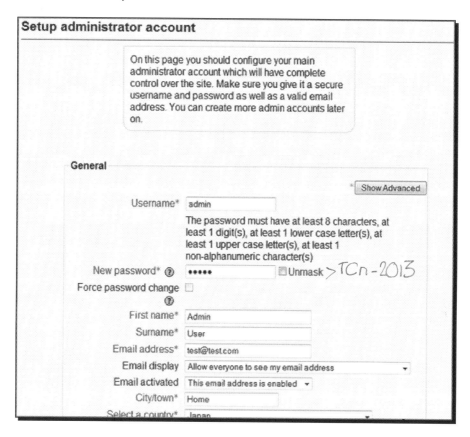

22. After entering information in the required fields, click on the **Update Profile** button found at the bottom of the page.

23. After setting up the admin account, the final page you will see before being taken to your Moodle site's front page is a page that allows you to enter information about the site. Enter some temporary information here, we'll change it later in this chapter, and click on the **Save Changes** button found at the bottom of the page. You have completed the installation process and will be taken to the front page of your site and logged in as the admin.

What just happened?

You have successfully installed and configured your XAMPP package to run on your Windows machine. By following the process that has been explained here, you have:

◆ Set the default language for your Moodle site

◆ Confirmed that your version of PHP is up-to-date

◆ Set the site address and locations for Moodle and its data

◆ Specified settings for the database

◆ Checked to make sure your server environment is sufficient to run Moodle

◆ Created all of the primary tables in the database required by Moodle

◆ Set up login information for the admin account

◆ Entered preliminary front page information for your site

Basic setup and customization of your Moodle site

Once you've managed to get your site up and running, you are ready to log in to your Moodle site and begin the initial customization process. As stated earlier, we'll be using the XAMPP package in Mac OS with Moodle 1.9.8+ installed for screenshots and explanation. So if you are using a Windows version, a hosted server, or have installed on your own server, the screen you see may be slightly different. The process however, will be identical as long as you are using the same version of Moodle. The latest 1.9 version is recommended and will look the same.

The first screen you will see after navigating to the front page of your Moodle site will look something like this:

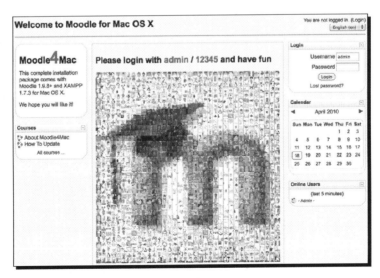

In the MAMP package for the Mac, you will see the **Username** and **Password** for the administrator account on the front page of Moodle. This is only acceptable because this site is not being served to the public and is only accessible by the user of the machine it is installed on. If you install Moodle on a hosted server, or on your own server, you will select a user name and password for the admin account when installing the system. In all public server situations, make sure you protect the privacy of your administrator login information. Access to the admin account is one of the easiest ways for an individual with malicious intent to abuse your site.

Time for action – basic customization

We'll start with some basic customization by changing some settings on and adding some of our own content to the front page. One of the uses we are proposing for Moodle is as a curriculum management system, so we should start by customizing the front page of Moodle so that it can better function as an "entry way" for students and teachers who will be interacting with our curriculum. To change the appearance of the front page follow these steps:

1. Assuming you have logged in to your site as the administrator, click on the **Turn editing on** button. This reveals various editing tools that allow you to create much of the content displayed on the page as well as allowing you to add activities and other resources such as web pages via drop-down menus. At the bottom of blocks that have content areas, which can be edited, you will see a small icon that looks like a hand holding a pencil. The **editing** icon found at the bottom-left of the center block below the Moodle logo picture has been enlarged and circled in the following screenshot:

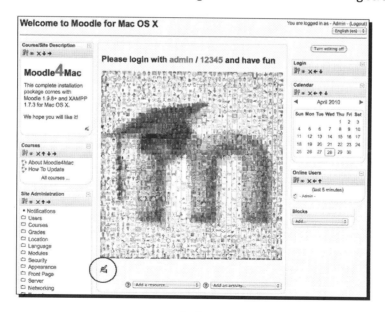

2. There are actually two ways to customize much of the content you see from the front page. The first is by turning on editing, as we have just done, and then by clicking on the editing icon mentioned earlier. The second method we are going to use is to click on the **Front Page** link found in the **Site Administration** block located on the left side of the screen when you log in as admin.

3. Next, click on the **Front Page settings** link as shown in the following screenshot:

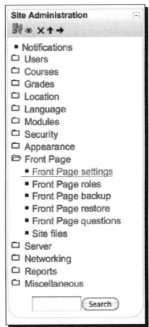

4. This will take you to a page that allows you to modify various settings that govern how the front page looks and also allows you to change content that is presented on the front page. A description of the settings, followed by a screenshot of the **Front Page settings** window, is as follows:

   □ **Full site name** is the name that appears at the top-left of the front page of your Moodle site. Enter Welcome to Moodle as a CIMS for our test site.

   □ **Short name** is the name that is used as the leftmost breadcrumb when navigating away from the front page. This should be kept as short as possible so as not to clutter the breadcrumb path. Use CIMS for our site.

- **Front Page Description** is what is displayed in the **Course/Site Description** block that is installed by default and displayed at the top-left of the front page. This information can be edited by clicking on the editing icon after turning editing on from the front page but we are editing it here from the **Front Page settings** in order to show the other settings that can be modified. We'll use, **This is the demonstration site for the Packt book "Moodle as a CIMS".**

- **Front Page** is for selecting items that are to be displayed to individuals who are not logged in to your Moodle site. There are four different items to choose from and thus four drop-down menus. The display order from top to bottom is determined by the order you place them in using the drop-down menus.

- **Front page items when logged in** is, just as it is written, for selecting items that you want to be displayed to the users after they have logged into the site. This allows you to customize how information will be displayed based upon whether an individual is logged into Moodle or not. We are going to use our Moodle front page to post news that is relevant to our curriculum and thus, have set **News Items** to be visible to both users who are logged in and to those who are not.

- **Maximum Category Depth** allows you to set how much category depth will be displayed on the front page. If you have many categories embedded within categories you may want to consider limiting this to keep your front page's appearance clean. Notice that I have not opted to have courses displayed via the front page, so this unlimited setting will have no impact on the appearance of the front page.

- **Include a topic section** provides us with a block at the top of the front page that can be used for posting a picture, logo, or textual information. In the MAMP package, there is a large picture of the Moodle logo, which was made from many small user pictures, in this topic section. We'll remove that and replace it with our own custom logo later.

- **News items to show** can also be selected here. This controls how many news items will be displayed on the front page. News items will be displayed in the order of posting, from the most recent one. Items beyond the number chosen here can be easily accessed by, for example, adding a **Main Menu** block to your front page, which we will do shortly.

- **Courses per page** allows you to set the number of courses that will be displayed on one page within a category. This is nice if you want to be able to allow students to see all courses on one page by simply scrolling down. Alternatively, you may want to reduce the number if your course list is extremely long so as to distribute the course list across several pages.

v.2.4
not
incl.

- **Allow visible courses in hidden categories** allows you to force courses that are inside categories that have been hidden, to show up on the front page, if you have opted to have courses displayed. The default here is **No** because it is assumed that the reason for hiding a category is to hide courses contained in that category but, as was stated earlier, Moodle is a very flexible tool and as there may be cases where you want courses contained in a hidden category to be displayed, you have the option here.

- **Default frontpage role** changes the default role setting for the front page and has an impact on how users will be able to interact with content made available on the front page. We have changed this to **Authenticated user** in order to allow students to access activities added to the front page.

Front Page settings screenshot showing fields: Full site name (Welcome to Moodle as a CIMS), Short name for site (eg single word) (CIMS), Front Page Description with editor (This is the demonstration site for the Packt book "Moodle as a CIMS".), Front Page (News items / None / None), Front page items when logged in (News items / None / None / None), Maximum Category Depth (Unlimited), Include a topic section (Default: Yes), News items to show (3, Default: 3), Courses per page (50, Default: 20), Allow visible courses in hidden categories (Default: No), Default frontpage role (Authenticated user, Default: None).

v 2.4
Default 15

v 2.4
not
incl.

5. Once you have made all the desired changes, click on the **Save Changes** button at the bottom of the page and then navigate back to your front page using the leftmost breadcrumb at the top of the page. In the following screenshot this would be **CIMS**:

CIMS ▶ Administration ▶ Front Page ▶ Front Page settings

6. You should notice that the breadcrumb has changed to the short name you entered in the **Short name for site** field and, once back to your front page, that the changes you just made have been updated on the front page.

What just happened?

You have just successfully changed the appearance of your front page by simply changing some of the content via the front page settings. We have just started to scrape the surface and will continue to customize our site with our own content and appearance.

Time for action – customizing the label area of the front page

Next, let's get rid of that big Moodle logo and replace it with a different graphic. Follow these steps to edit the image that appears on the front page:

1. Click on the editing icon located at the bottom-left of the picture we want to remove and before clicking, notice that hovering your mouse over this icon makes the message **Edit summary** appear.

2. After clicking you will see a screen titled **Summary of Site** with an HTML editor window that contains the information you saw on the front page. The image will probably not be visible but you can delete the text and image by selecting everything and deleting it.

3. Next, enter the information you want to display on the front page. Use `Welcome to the "Moodle as a CIMS" Demonstration Site` for our test site.

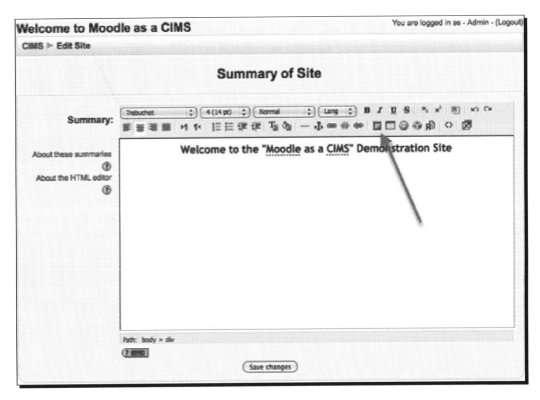

4. To add an image, click on the picture frame icon located in the menu bar of the HTML editor. The blue arrow is pointing to the insert image icon in the preceding screenshot. Hovering over this icon will make the **Insert Image** message appear. Clicking on the picture icon will make the **Insert Image** tool appear. You can provide an URL for the image you want to appear here but, unless you have a repository of images already up on the Internet, the easiest way to use this tool is to click on the **Browse...** button located at the bottom of the window and then locate and select an image from your computer.

5. After selecting the image, click on the **Upload** button. The image file name will now be displayed in the **File Browser** list and clicking on the file name will make the image appear in the **Preview** pane on the right.

6. Clicking on the file name will also automatically enter the URL. Below the URL enter alternative text to be displayed when hovering over the image.

7. Finally, click on **OK** and the image will appear in the HTML editor window as shown in the following screenshot. Click on the **Save changes** button and you will be redirected back to the front page of your site and will be able to see the new description and image.

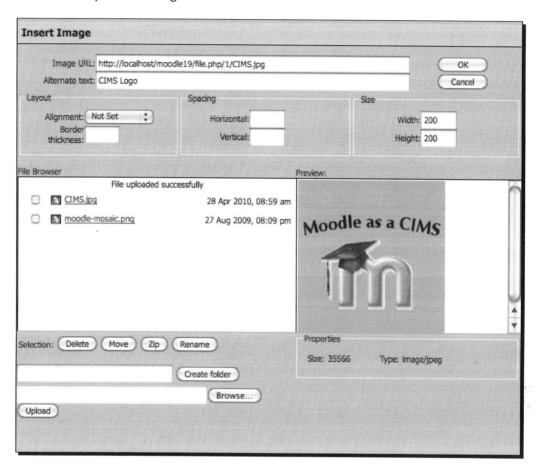

What just happened?

You just changed the image that appears in the top-center section of your Moodle site by deleting the old image and uploading a new image in its place. We did this by accessing the **Summary of Site** page and it also gave us a chance to use the **Insert Image** tool.

Time for action – adding the Main Menu block

We'll finish out this very basic customization of the front page by adding a block that provides access to activities that appear on the front page. This will allow you easy access, via HTML links, to all of the activities and resources that appear on the page. To add the **Main Menu** block to your Moodle front page, follow these steps:

1. Turn editing on and on the lower right side of the page a drop-down menu titled **Blocks** will appear.

2. Click on the **Add...** drop-down menu and select **Main Menu**.

3. The **Main Menu** block will be installed on the lower right side of the page so now click on the arrows at the top of the block just below the Main Menu title to move the block over to the left side of the page below the **Course/Site Description** block. Now the front page that we saw earlier looks like this:

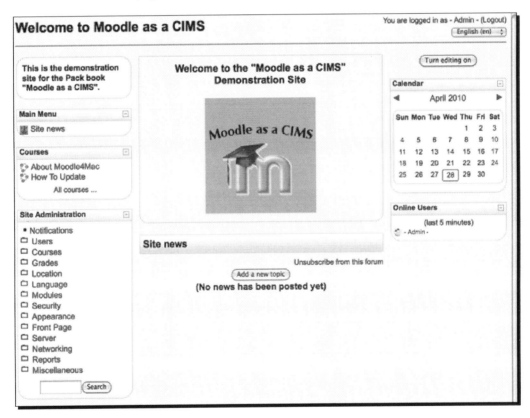

What just happened?

You have just added the **Main Menu** block to the front page of your Moodle site. As you add activities to the front page, they will be easily accessible via the **Main Menu** block. News items, for example, can all be viewed by clicking on the **Site News** link from within the **Main Menu**. Therefore, if you set your front page to display only three news items and regularly post news items, all past news items will be accessible from the **Main Menu** block.

Installing third party contributions

As mentioned earlier, one of Moodle's strengths is the ease with which you can install and use third party add-ons. There are a multitude of blocks, modules, and other plugins available from the Moodle.org download area that you can use to enable Moodle to perform all sorts of tasks. One word of caution on third-party blocks, modules, and other plugins; they are not maintained by Moodle headquarters and as such you should check the forums on Moodle.org for any known issues the plugin you are planning to install might have. Likewise, it is a good idea to install these types of plugins on a test site, like the one we've set up in this chapter, to experiment with them and make sure they function as desired. Once you are confident in using the features offered by a plugin and assured that it is what you want, you can install it on your production site.

Blocks and modules

As mentioned at the beginning of this chapter, blocks and modules comprise the majority of feature add-ons available for Moodle. They are also almost always very easy to install provided that you have the necessary level of access to the system that your Moodle site is being served from. Installation on a local XAMPP or MAMP package is extremely easy as it simply involves downloading the add-on from Moodle.org, decompressing it, and placing the folder of components into the appropriate folder/directory within the Moodle directory.

We will install the following block and module to continue to build our CIMS and to demonstrate the installation process:

- **My Courses block**: This provides students with an easy way to navigate to courses in which they are enrolled, and more importantly from the CIMS perspective, it provides an administrator with easy access to all of the courses on the site.

- **Attendance package**: This package actually consists of both a block and a module. The module is the main component, especially from the CIMS perspective and the block is used primarily to present personal attendance data to students in a block that appears in the course area.

Time for action – installing the My Courses block

To install the **My Courses** block, which is a block that allows users and the site administrator to access the courses they are enrolled in or are permitted to access, follow these steps:

1. First go to **Modules and plugins** in the **Downloads** tab of Moodle.org and search for **My Courses**.

2. If the search does not return an entry for *My Courses* and instead only lists *My Courses 2* and other similar items, navigate to the forum found at the following link and download the block from the forums. A packaged version will appear towards the bottom of the forum dated sometime in October 2010.

    *   Forum thread title: New myCourses block released
    *   Link: http://moodle.org/mod/forum/discuss.php?d=67494

3. If the **My Courses** block, contributed by *Rosario Carcò*, is listed in the **Modules and plugins** area, proceed to step 4. (Note—The **MyCourses** block is scheduled to appear in the Modules and plugins database on Moodle.org sometime in December 2010).

4. Click on **My Courses** and then click on the **Download latest version** link to download the block files.

5. This will download a compressed package containing all of the files for the block called myCourses.zip. To install the block on your local MAMP package, expand the package with a compression/expansion tool.

6. Expanding the package will create a folder titled myCourses that must be placed in the blocks folder located in your Moodle directory. For a MAMP package on the Mac OS, you can find the appropriate folder by opening the folder that contains your MAMP directory and then navigating to the blocks folder. The path is as follows: Applications/MAMP/htdocs/moodle19/blocks.

7. Drag-and-drop or copy the myCourses folder into the blocks folder.

8. After copying the contents to the blocks folder in your Moodle directory, your blocks folder will contain folders for the standard blocks plus the newly installed myCourses folder, as shown in the following screenshot:

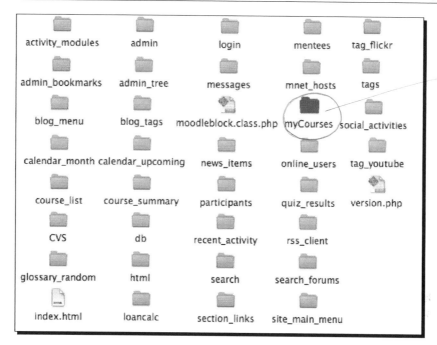

replaced by
- *course_list*
- *course_summary*
- *course_overview*

9. Next you must log in to your site as admin and click on the **Notifications** link found in the **Site Administration** block. This will start the installation of the block components and create tables in the database that will be used by the block.

10. You will see a message informing you that the tables have been set up correctly. Click the **Continue** button, shown in the following screenshot, to proceed:

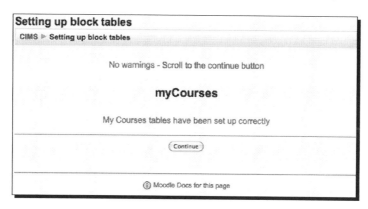

11. The next screen will be the main **Notifications** page. From this point, you can get back to the front page by clicking on the leftmost breadcrumb on the top-left side of the browser window.

12. Now that the **My Courses** block has been installed it can be inserted into the front page by turning on editing and selecting it from the drop-down **Blocks** menu. Our front page, with the **My Courses** added and moved to the top-left of the page, now looks like the following screenshot:

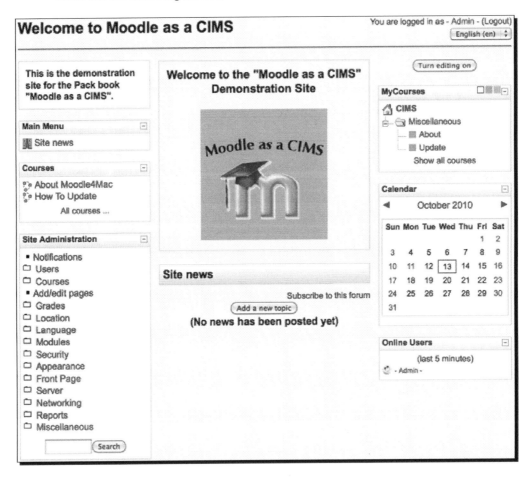

13. Finally, we can access the configuration settings for the **My Courses** block by clicking on the **Modules** link found in the **Site Administration** block.

14. Next, click on **Blocks** and then on the **MyCourses** link. The various configuration settings are modifiable from this screen. You can toggle these settings at any time to see how they affect the appearance of the **My Courses** block by returning to this page. Use the following settings for our test site:

- **Show scrollbars**: Untick this because we will set up the site with the categories that house our courses and won't need them.

- ❑ **Show all courses**: Tick this to provide a link at the bottom of the block for easy access to all of the courses on the site.

- ❑ **Show long names**: Leave unticked to keep long course names from cluttering the block.

- ❑ **Show category links**: Tick to make each category title a link that will take you to the list of courses offered in that category.

- ❑ **Show flat list**: Untick this or your courses will not be displayed in their categories.

- ❑ **Show course search box**: Leave this unticked as we won't use the **Course Search** box.

- ❑ **Toggle own courses**: Tick this to allow the admin to toggle between his or her own courses and all courses.

- ❑ **Toggle active courses**: Tick this to allow the admin to toggle active course visibility off and on.

- ❑ **Toggle inactive courses**: Tick this to allow the admin to toggle inactive course visibility off and on.

15. Return to the front page of your site to view the block. Note however, it will not fill with categories and courses until we have them, which we will work on in *Chapter 2, Building the Foundation—Creating Categories and Courses* and *Chapter 3, Student Account Creation and Enrollment*.

What just happened?

We have just installed the **My Courses** block and modified the settings that control how it will display categories and courses to the site administrator. As we fill our site with both categories and courses in subsequent chapters, the convenience of this block will become more and more obvious as we'll be using it regularly to access specific courses in the site.

Time for action – installing the Attendance package

Module installation is basically the same process as that for blocks with the obvious difference being in where the package contents are installed. In the case of modules, the package contents are placed in the `mod` folder. Next, we will install the `Attendance` package, which is actually a combination of both a module and a block so we'll be placing items in both of these folders. To install the package, follow these steps:

1. Using the same process that was explained for the **My Courses** block, from the **Modules and plugins** download page on `Moodle.org`, search for **Attendance**.

2. Click on the item with the one word title, **Attendance**.

3. From the detailed explanation menu click on the **Download for Moodle 1.9** link to download the package. The resulting download will be a zipped package titled `attendance_package.zip`.

4. Decompress this package and note that there are both `blocks` and `mod` folders contained in the package. This is because, as previously mentioned, this package contains both a block and a module.

5. Place the `Attendance` folder found in the `blocks` folder of your Moodle instance the same way you did with the `My Menu` package.

6. In the same manner, place the **attforblock** folder in the **mod** folder in your Moodle directory. The paths for installing the two components on the Mac OS MAMP are as follows:

    `attendance` **goes to** `MAMP/htdocs/blocks`.

    `attforblock` **goes to** `MAMP/htdocs/mod`.

7. Log in to your site as admin after placing the two folders in their appropriate places and click on the **Notifications** link. You will receive a series of **Success** messages and should click on **Continue** after everything is successfully installed.

8. Navigate to a course and turn editing on to add an Attendance activity to the course area. Add the Attendance activity by using the **Add an activity** drop-down menu. You will be presented with a screen that allows you to customize some of the settings for the Attendance activity, as shown in the following screenshot. Unless you want to change the name, the maximum grade, or some of the other settings, it is easiest to click **Save and display**.

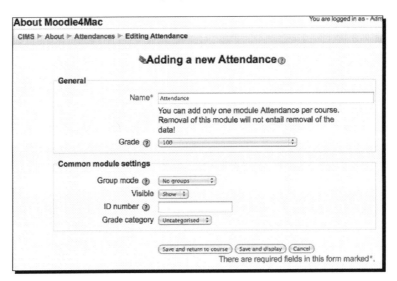

9. The subsequent screen is the **Sessions** display and will indicate that there are no sessions for the course. You can add sessions one at a time or in bulk by clicking on the **Add** tab. Other features of the **Attendance** module can be accessed by clicking on the corresponding tabs.

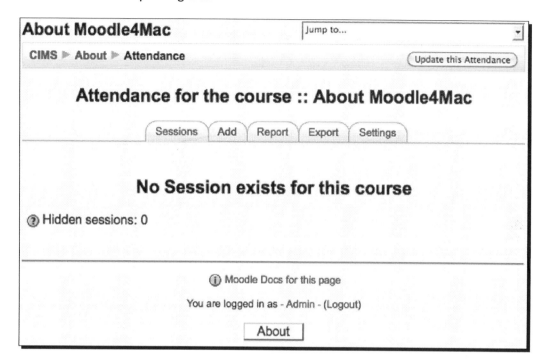

What just happened?

We have just installed the **Attendance** package, which includes both a module and a block. This tool, along with the **My Courses** block, will be utilized as we position our Moodle as a CIMS. Detailed explanation of the use of these tools in this context will be presented in *Chapter 4, Incorporating Educational Standards* (Attendance module) and *Chapter 6, Customized Roles* (My Courses block).

Installing other plugins (themes)

The process for installing themes is basically the same as for modules and blocks with, again, the difference being in the location that the package is installed. In the case of some plugins, there may be a need to make minor, or in the case of some contributed plugins, even major modifications to files in the Moodle directory. If the changes are minor and you are comfortable experimenting, then give it a try. This is why you are using a test site right! Some plugins however, require a patch, which is a modification to a core Moodle file or files. In addition to being undesirable, because it makes upgrading to a new version of Moodle more difficult, it can also be technically demanding. You can determine whether a plugin is a patch or not and also determine the installation requirements by viewing its entry in the Modules and plugins database found on the `Moodle.org` website. If the plugin requires a major patch or some other type of manual modification of code, and you are not a professional programmer, please proceed with caution. Make sure you have tested everything thoroughly on your experimental site before moving it over to your live server.

Time for action – installing the Aardvark Pro original theme

Now let's walk through the installation of a theme before bringing this introductory chapter to a close. Themes allow you to customize the look and feel of your Moodle site to an almost endless degree. In order to effectively utilize Moodle as a CIMS, we will need to install a theme that provides us with more content display capabilities. There are several themes that use a menu bar at the top of the screen that can include links to all sorts of content on your site. The current `Moodle.org` theme is a good example of one such theme. For our experimental site, we are going to download a flashy theme available from the **Themes** download area on `Moodle.org` called the "Aardvark Pro Original". It is a theme created by *Shaun Daubney* of Newbury College in the U.K. Follow these steps to download and install the theme:

1. Access `www.Moodle.org` from your browser and navigate to the **Themes** area of the **Download** section using the menu bar.

2. From the **Themes** section, the easiest way to find the theme we are looking for is to use the search string **Shaun Daubney**. This search will return several themes. Find the **Aardvark Pro Original** theme and download it to your computer. This will download a zipped package called `aardvar_pro1_2.zip`. Note that the version may be different by the time this book goes to print.

3. Decompress the package to get the `aardvark_pro` folder.

4. Place the `aardvark_pro` theme folder in the **Theme** folder found inside your Moodle directory.

5. After moving the theme into your theme folder, visit your site as admin and click on the **Appearance** link found in the **Site Administration** block.

6. Next click on **Themes** and then **Theme Selector**. The path can be seen in the **Site Administration** block and in the breadcrumb trail as shown in the following screenshot:

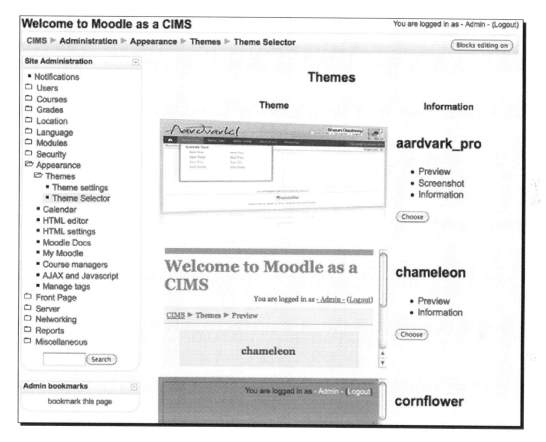

7. You are now viewing the theme selector window. It allows you to scroll through all of the themes that have been installed in the **Theme** folder in your Moodle main directory. You can click on the **Preview** link found beside each theme prior to selecting it if you want to see what it is going to look like before making changes.

8. The themes are in alphabetical order so the `aardvark_pro` theme should appear at the top of the list. Click on the **Choose** button found to the right of the small theme preview.

9. You will see some information about the theme's creator and notes about changes that have been made as the theme has progressed from version to version. Scroll down and click on **Continue** to return to the front page of your site that should now look something like the following screenshot:

What just happened?

We have just installed and selected the Aardvark theme for our Moodle site and as a result you can now see the menu bar located at the top of the screen just below the Aardvark theme title. Through the use of this menu bar, this theme will allow us to provide quick access to much more information than was possible with the standard default theme. We will explore all the possibilities of this and other information portal capabilities in *Chapter 5, Enabling your Moodle Site to Function as an Information Portal*, so if you cannot wait to continue polishing the appearance and more importantly the informational value of the front page, then take a quick peek ahead.

Summary

In this chapter, you have learned the basics about how Moodle is most commonly used and about the underlying constructivist ideology upon which Moodle is founded. The idea of structuring a Moodle site with the goal of enabling it to function as a Curriculum and Information Management System (CIMS), while also performing its core Learning Management System (LMS) role, was presented and we began to work on setting up an experimental site to demonstrate this idea. You learned the basics for getting a default site up and running and started the process of expanding that site via the addition of third party contribution plugins such as blocks, modules, and themes. In the following chapters of this book, I will continue to explain and demonstrate how you can use your Moodle site as a Curriculum and Information Management System.

2
Building the Foundation—Creating Categories and Courses

Now that you have explored the basics of Moodle, developed a concept of how it is designed and most often used, and walked through the installation process and initial customization process, it is time to work on further building Moodle into a CIMS. The C in CIMS stands for curriculum and the fundamental unit within curriculum, as I will use it in this chapter, is the course.

This chapter will explain and demonstrate how to create and organize the courses offered in your curriculum, within Moodle. The following topics will be covered in this chapter:

◆ The creation of course categories

◆ Creation of teacher accounts

◆ Installing and using the bulk course creation tool

Course categories

Categorization is an innate human behavior that allows us to perceive and understand the environment that surrounds us. Moodle designers must have recognized our tendency to categorize, because Moodle contains a flexible categorization system that allows for the creation of categories in which you may house additional categories and courses. Any educational program that offers courses of various varieties will invariably be using a categorization system like this for grouping courses into specific categories. A language program, for example, might group courses into skill-specific categories such as those of listening, speaking, reading, and writing. A larger entity, such as a college, would likely group courses into content-specific categories such as literature, sciences, speech communications, and the like, with additional subcategories used inside each of those main categories. No matter what the categorization system, Moodle is well-equipped to accommodate via its intuitive user-friendly course category creation interface.

Manual creation of course categories

We will quickly walk through the manual creation of a simple categorization system in the next few pages. It should be noted however, that course categories can be created automatically via the use of the Bulk Course Upload tool that will be introduced later in this chapter. While the automated creation process is certainly a more efficient one, it is a good idea to understand how to create, edit, and adjust categories manually as the need to make adjustments may arise after categories have been created automatically, and at that point, the only practical method may be via the manual process.

Using the language program sample as an example, we will set up a categorization system that uses the traditional language skills (listening, speaking, reading, and writing) as the highest level in the categorization system with subcategories for levels. In our example, our program will have four levels: Advanced, Intermediate, Beginner, and Basic, so we will set up each skill category such that it contains subcategories that coincide with the four levels.

Time for action – manually creating course categories

Let's get started by first taking a look at the courses and categories that exist in the default installation of our MAMP package. We'll proceed by manually creating the categories and subcategories we need for our language program example.

1. Log in to your Moodle site as admin, or as a user with administrative permissions, and click on the **All courses** link found at the bottom of the **Course categories** block from your front page.

An alternative method for accessing the **Course category** window is to simply type the word 'course' into your browser at the end of your website address from the front page of your Moodle site. This will direct your browser to the default file, `index.php`, located in the course directory (for example, for the XAMPP package, it will look like this `http://localhost/moodle19/course`).

2. The block should look like the following screenshot if you followed all the instructions from *Chapter 1, Welcome to Moodle as a Curriculum and Information Management System (CIMS)!* The following screenshot is of a default MAMP installation. For Windows XAMPP installations, no courses or categories will exist.

3. You will see the two default courses that are created in the MAMP package and no category. As shown in the following screenshot, the full name of the course will appear on the left side of the screen with a small icon of a person, below it. The icon, shown with an arrow pointing to it in the following screenshot, signifies that the course is set to allow guest users to access it. On the right side of the screen is the course summary.

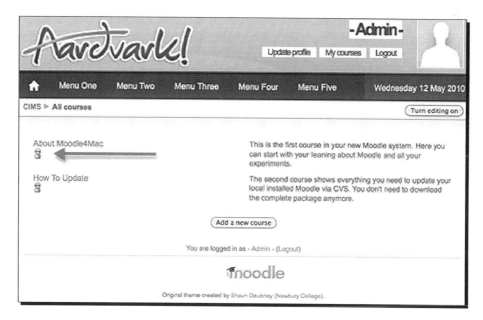

4. Click on the **Turn editing on** button from the **All courses** screen, shown in the previous screenshot, to reveal the course category as shown in the next screenshot. This editing screen displays the categories and the number of courses contained in each category. The category was not listed in the course view window in the previous screenshot because there is currently only one category.

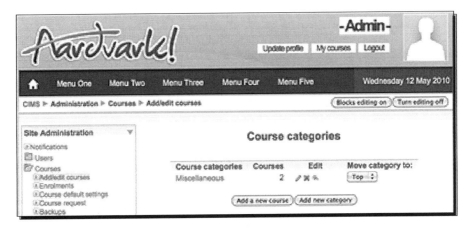

5. With editing on, now click on the **Add new category** button and, on the subsequent screen, type in the desired category title. For this example, we are going to enter the four skills mentioned previously. Also, as we want these to be our four main categories, we will set the **Parent category** to **Top**. Enter a category description and click on the **Create category** button to finish the process. The following screenshot shows our setup prior to creating the category:

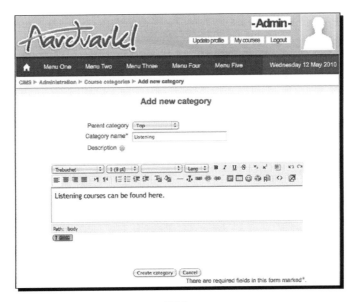

6. After clicking on the **Create category** button, the screen that you will see next will be an editing screen that will allow you to edit from within the Listening category you just created. As a result, you will not see the **Add new category** button. Instead, you will see an **Add a sub-category** button. Click on this button to access the screen that allows you to create a new category. After doing so, you will simply need to change the **Parent category** to **Top**. Repeat this process until you have created all of your top-level categories. After you have created all categories, turn the editing feature off and click on the **Course categories** breadcrumb link, found at the top-left of the screen, to see the result. It will look like the following screenshot:

Create top-level categories

 If you wish to change the order in which the categories appear, you can turn editing back on and use the up and down arrows to move categories.

7. In the following screenshot, which is the same screen as the previous one, with editing turned on, we have moved the **Miscellaneous** category to the bottom and rearranged the main categories into a different order.

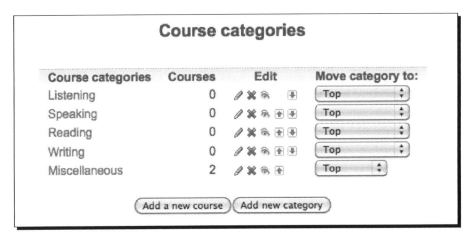

8. Next, we will create the four level categories using the same process explained for the main categories. The only difference is that we will create each of the four levels inside the main categories by designating the main category as the **Parent category**. From the editing screen shown in the previous screenshot, click on one of the categories and then on the subsequent **Add a sub-category** button, as shown in the following screenshot. Creating the category in this fashion will result in the parent category being automatically set to the main category to which you are adding the sub-category.

9. In the same fashion as earlier when we created multiple categories in succession however, after adding the first sub-category, if you click on **Add a sub-category** again, you will need to then adjust the **Parent category**. If you do not do so, you will be effectively burying sub-categories within sub-categories. The alternative is to click on the **Course categories** pull-down menu prior to clicking on **Add a sub-category**. Create all four levels, **Advanced**, **Intermediate**, **Beginner**, and **Basic**, using this process, for each of the four skills (**Listening**, **Reading**, **Speaking**, and **Writing**).

10. When you have finished adding all of the subcategories to the main categories and have returned to the main **Course Categories** window, your screen should look like the following screenshot:

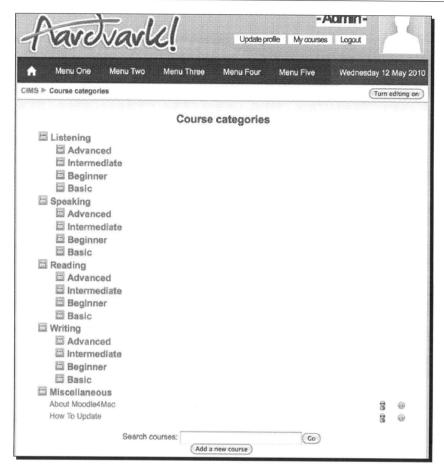

What just happened?

You have just created a simple categorization system with four main skills (Listening, Speaking, Reading, and Writing). Next you created four subcategories—levels, inside each of the main categories (Advanced, Intermediate, Beginner, and Basic).

As you followed the example used here or maybe created an even more intricate categorization scheme, you may have felt that the process was a bit time consuming and required quite a few mouse clicks. As mentioned in the beginning of this explanation, creating categories via the Bulk Course Upload tool is much more efficient and recommended when possible. There will be times however, when you need to create new categories after courses have already been made or to edit or rearrange categories. On these occasions, you may find it necessary to use the manual procedure so it is a good idea to be familiar with the process.

Teacher account creation

We could, at this point, jump to an explanation of the Bulk Course Upload tool. Unfortunately however, the Bulk Course Upload tool will not automatically create user accounts for us. Therefore, if we want to make the most of the tool, we will need to first create the accounts that we will label as teachers in the file used by the Bulk Course Upload tool.

Time for action – creating teacher accounts

We will create twenty users that are each going to be assigned to teach four courses. If you are only creating one user on your site, you may decide to create the account manually by clicking on the **Add a new user** link found via the following path: **Site Administration | Users | Accounts | Add a new user**. When adding multiple users however, it is a much more efficient process to use the **Upload users** feature found in the same list under **Accounts** where the **Add a new user** feature is located. To create the new teacher accounts, follow these steps:

1. Click on the **Upload users** link as previously described. The following screenshot shows the path visually:

2. After clicking on **Upload users** you will be presented with a screen that allows you to browse your computer and select the file that contains the information necessary to create the accounts. The file must be formatted as a CSV (Comma Separated Values) file and can be created in any text editor or in a Microsoft Excel or Open Document spreadsheet file and then saved as a CSV document. We will use Excel or an Open Document spreadsheet because there are often fields that are repeated and dragging a cell in a spreadsheet application allows for quick replication of values that are the same.

When using special characters and/or foreign language fonts, Open Document format, created using the Open Source productivity package Open Office, provides more accurate and reliable options for using UTF8, a character encoding method that allows for the use of virtually all languages and special characters.

3. Click on the question mark icon located to the right of the **Upload users** title to access detailed information about formatting of the file used to create users. The icon can be seen circled in the following screenshot of the **Upload users** screen.

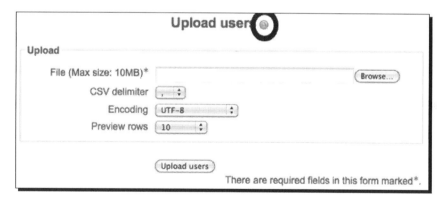

4. Following is a screenshot of the file used to create our twenty accounts that will be designated as teachers. This file is accessible from the Packt website at `www.packtpub.com/support`.

◇	A	B	C	D	E	F
1	username	password	firstname	lastname	email	emailstop
2	Teacher1	1234	Teacher	One	Teacher1@Moodle_As_A_CIMS.COM	1
3	Teacher2	1234	Teacher	Two	Teacher2@Moodle_As_A_CIMS.COM	1
4	Teacher3	1234	Teacher	Three	Teacher3@Moodle_As_A_CIMS.COM	1
5	Teacher4	1234	Teacher	Four	Teacher4@Moodle_As_A_CIMS.COM	1
6	Teacher5	1234	Teacher	Five	Teacher5@Moodle_As_A_CIMS.COM	1
7	Teacher6	1234	Teacher	Six	Teacher6@Moodle_As_A_CIMS.COM	1
8	Teacher7	1234	Teacher	Seven	Teacher7@Moodle_As_A_CIMS.COM	1
9	Teacher8	1234	Teacher	Eight	Teacher8@Moodle_As_A_CIMS.COM	1
10	Teacher9	1234	Teacher	Nine	Teacher9@Moodle_As_A_CIMS.COM	1
11	Teacher10	1234	Teacher	Ten	Teacher10@Moodle_As_A_CIMS.COM	1
12	Teacher11	1234	Teacher	Eleven	Teacher11@Moodle_As_A_CIMS.COM	1
13	Teacher12	1234	Teacher	Twelve	Teacher12@Moodle_As_A_CIMS.COM	1
14	Teacher13	1234	Teacher	Thirteen	Teacher13@Moodle_As_A_CIMS.COM	1
15	Teacher14	1234	Teacher	4teen	Teacher14@Moodle_As_A_CIMS.COM	1
16	Teacher15	1234	Teacher	Fifteen	Teacher15@Moodle_As_A_CIMS.COM	1
17	Teacher16	1234	Teacher	6teen	Teacher16@Moodle_As_A_CIMS.COM	1
18	Teacher17	1234	Teacher	7teen	Teacher17@Moodle_As_A_CIMS.COM	1
19	Teacher18	1234	Teacher	8teen	Teacher18@Moodle_As_A_CIMS.COM	1
20	Teacher19	1234	Teacher	9teen	Teacher19@Moodle_As_A_CIMS.COM	1
21	Teacher20	1234	Teacher	Twenty	Teacher20@Moodle_As_A_CIMS.COM	1

There are a couple of things that should be noted in this screenshot:

◆ Although it does not appear in the help file accessed by clicking on the question mark found next to the **Upload users** page title, the use of the **emailstop** field name allows you to set the user's **Email activated** setting, that appears in a user's profile, to **This email address is disabled**. We are using it because the domain we have specified for these dummy accounts is not a domain name that actually exists. This will prevent the system from attempting to send e-mails to these addresses. This is important if you will be creating users without knowing their e-mail addresses because Moodle requires that users have an e-mail address entered when accounts are created.

◆ Notice the way last names for users sixteen to nineteen have been formatted using the number (for example, **6teen**) instead of spelling out the name. This is because the **Bulk Course Creation** tool, which we will use later in this chapter, uses a search function built into Moodle that will return multiple users if one user's name is contained within the name of another user. For example, 'John Smith' and 'John Smithson' would both be returned from a search for 'John Smith'. The **Bulk Course Creation** tool can only assign a teacher when the search for that teacher returns a single user. Although it may be rare for this type of *name overlap* to occur in your system, you should be aware of the issue. You can also use usernames in place of full names when assigning teachers to courses, but will have the same problem with overlap. In our example, shown previously, a search for a teacher with the username 'Teacher1', would return eleven results. Why, you say? Because, not only would it return 'Teacher1', but it would also return teachers 10 through 19 as they all contain 'Teacher1' in their username.

♦ Additionally, the help file accessed from the **Upload users** page is a bit vague about the fields required in the file utilized to create accounts. Let it suffice to say that, generally, the more information you include in your user account creation file, the better. The six fields included in the file shown here are a minimum for quick and easy account creation. Of course, you may opt not to use the **emailstop** field if you are using legitimate e-mail addresses.

♦ Once you have formatted your file and saved it in the CSV format, you can then click on the **Browse** button to locate your file and then click the **Upload users** button to start the account creation process.

♦ You will be presented with a preview screen in which the first ten records from your file are displayed and you are given the option to adjust various settings. The following screenshot is of this **preview** screen. Under the **Settings** heading, the default values will be appropriate for creating new accounts if you have formatted your file in the same manner as the one we are using.

♦ Under the **Default values** heading, click on the **Show Advanced** button to display other settings that can be adjusted. You should change the default country here using the **Select a country** pull-down menu and possibly even the **City/town** setting, if you want to standardize this setting to the city or town in which your school or program is located.

You can change the default country by clicking on the **Location settings** link found under the **Location** directory in the **Site Administration** block found on the front page of your site. Even if you have set the default country via the **Location** settings, you will still need to specify the country when creating new accounts.

5. Generally, when creating accounts in bulk, you will not need to change any of the other default values unless so desired. Click on the **Upload users** button once you are finished and the accounts will be created. The following screenshot is of the **Upload users preview** screen with the **Show Advanced** menu toggled off:

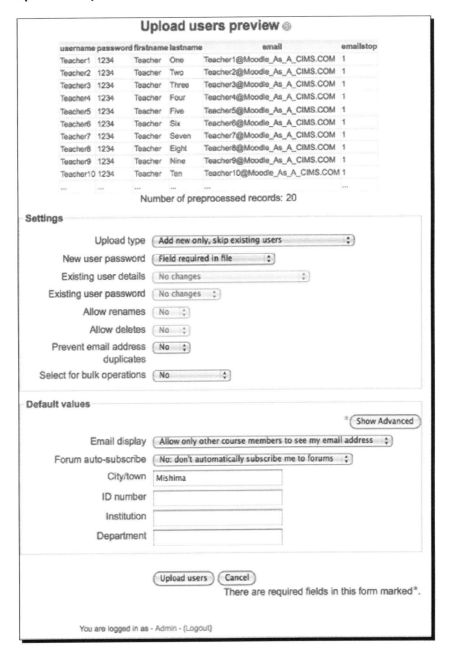

6. After clicking on **Upload users**, the next screen you will see will be a results screen displaying all of the accounts created. Summarized details are presented at the bottom of the screen just above the **Continue** button. If you receive any errors you may need to go back and correct formatting errors in your CSV file or you may be attempting to create two users with the same username. You will receive an error message that will help you trace the root of your problem. The results of the users with a weak password check, in our case, is zero because we have turned off the password policy in the **site policies security** settings.

Upload users results

Status	CSV line	ID	Username	First name	Surname	Email address	Password	Authentication	Enrolments	Delete
New user	2	45	Teacher1	Teacher	One	Teacher1@Moodle_As_A_CIMS.COM				
New user	3	46	Teacher2	Teacher	Two	Teacher2@Moodle_As_A_CIMS.COM				
New user	4	47	Teacher3	Teacher	Three	Teacher3@Moodle_As_A_CIMS.COM				
New user	5	48	Teacher4	Teacher	Four	Teacher4@Moodle_As_A_CIMS.COM				
New user	6	49	Teacher5	Teacher	Five	Teacher5@Moodle_As_A_CIMS.COM				
New user	7	50	Teacher6	Teacher	Six	Teacher6@Moodle_As_A_CIMS.COM				
New user	8	51	Teacher7	Teacher	Seven	Teacher7@Moodle_As_A_CIMS.COM				
New user	9	52	Teacher8	Teacher	Eight	Teacher8@Moodle_As_A_CIMS.COM				
New user	10	53	Teacher9	Teacher	Nine	Teacher9@Moodle_As_A_CIMS.COM				
New user	11	54	Teacher10	Teacher	Ten	Teacher10@Moodle_As_A_CIMS.COM				
New user	12	55	Teacher11	Teacher	Eleven	Teacher11@Moodle_As_A_CIMS.COM				
New user	13	56	Teacher12	Teacher	Twelve	Teacher12@Moodle_As_A_CIMS.COM				
New user	14	57	Teacher13	Teacher	Thirteen	Teacher13@Moodle_As_A_CIMS.COM				
New user	15	58	Teacher14	Teacher	4teen	Teacher14@Moodle_As_A_CIMS.COM				
New user	16	59	Teacher15	Teacher	Fifteen	Teacher15@Moodle_As_A_CIMS.COM				
New user	17	60	Teacher16	Teacher	6teen	Teacher16@Moodle_As_A_CIMS.COM				
New user	18	61	Teacher17	Teacher	7teen	Teacher17@Moodle_As_A_CIMS.COM				
New user	19	62	Teacher18	Teacher	8teen	Teacher18@Moodle_As_A_CIMS.COM				
New user	20	63	Teacher19	Teacher	9teen	Teacher19@Moodle_As_A_CIMS.COM				
New user	21	64	Teacher20	Teacher	Twenty	Teacher20@Moodle_As_A_CIMS.COM				

Users created: 20
Users having a weak password: 0
Errors: 0

(Continue)

7. Click on **Continue** from this screen to return you to the **Upload users** page. From this point you can click on the **Users** folder found in the **Site Administration** block and then on **Browse a list of users** to view and confirm the existence of the accounts you just created.

What just happened?

You have just created twenty user accounts inside your Moodle site. These users have not yet been assigned any roles. They are simply registered users at this point but that will change shortly when we assign them to teach courses that we'll be creating with the Bulk Course Upload tool.

Using the Bulk Course Upload tool

Rather than creating course categories and then courses one at a time and assigning teachers to each course after the course is created, we can streamline the process through the use of the Bulk Course Upload tool. This tool allows you to organize all the information required to create your courses in a CSV (Comma Separated Values) file that is then uploaded into the creation tool and used to create all of your courses at once.

Limitations of the Bulk Course Upload tool

Due to its design, the Bulk Course Upload tool only works with MySQL databases. Our MAMP package uses a MySQL database as do the LAMP packages explained in *Chapter 1, Welcome to Moodle as a Curriculum and Information Management System (CIMS)!* If your Moodle site is running on a database of a different variety you will not be able to use this tool.

Time for action – installing the Bulk Course Upload tool

Now that we have our teacher's accounts created, we are ready to use the Bulk Course Creation tool to create all of our courses. First we need to install the tool as an add-on admin report into our Moodle site. The steps for the installation process are virtually the same as those explained in *Chapter 1, Welcome to Moodle as a Curriculum and Information Management System (CIMS)!* for installing Modules, Blocks, and Themes. To install this tool, do the following:

1. Go to the **Modules and plugins** area of `www.moodle.org`.

2. Search for **Bulk Course Upload** tool.

3. Click on **Download latest version** to download the tool to your computer.

4. If this does not download the package to your hard drive and instead takes you to a forum in the **Using Moodle** course on `Moodle.org`, download the package that was posted in that forum on Sunday, 11 May 2008.

5. Expand the package, contained within, and find the `uploadcourse.php` file.

6. Place the `uploadcourse.php` file in your **admin** directory located inside your main Moodle directory.

7. When logged in as admin, enter the following address in your browser address bar: `http://localhost:8888/moodle19/admin/uploadcourse.php`. (If you are not using a MAMP package, the first part of the address will of course be different.)

8. You will then see the Upload Course tool explanation screen that looks like the following screenshot:

Upload an RFC4180-Compliant CSV file.
Valid fields for each course are:

Field	Value
category	[Forward]Slash-Delimited Category "Path" String (new categories are created as necessary) OR Integer Database Category ID
cost	String(10)
enrolperiod	Integer/Seconds
enrollable	0=FALSE,1=TRUE
enrolstartdate	String Date Literal
enrolenddate	String Date Literal
expirynotify	0=FALSE,1=TRUE
expirythreshold	Integer Value Between 10-30
format	String('social','topics','weeks')
fullname	String(254)
groupmode	0=NOGROUPS,1=SEPARATE GROUPS,2=VISIBLE GROUPS
groupmodeforce	0=FALSE,1=TRUE
guest	0=NO,1=YES,2=WITHKEY
idnumber	String(100)
lang	String(10)
maxbytes	Integer(Site Max)
metacourse	0=FALSE,1=TRUE
newsitems	Integer(10)
notifystudents	0=FALSE,1=TRUE
numsections	Integer(52)
password	String(50)
shortname	String(15)
showgrades	0=FALSE,1=TRUE
showreports	0=FALSE,1=TRUE
sortorder	Integer
startdate	String Date Literal
student	String(100)
students	String(100)
summary	Text
teacher	String(100)
teachers	String(100)
teacher[1,2,...]_account	Search String that returns only one User Account (as used in Administration » Edit user accounts OR Integer Database User ID
teacher[1,2,...]_role	String(40)
template	String
theme	String(50)
timecreated	String Date Literal
timemodified	String Date Literal
topic0 [main heading], topic1 ... topic52 [topic/week headings]	Text
visible	0=FALSE,1=TRUE

Upload Courses

Choose: (Browse...) (Upload)

9. The screen, shown in the previous screenshot, lists the thirty-nine different fields that can be included in a CSV file when creating courses in bulk via this tool. Most of the fields here control settings that are modified in individual courses by clicking on the **Settings** link found in the **Administration** block of each course. The following is an explanation of the fields with notes about which ones are especially useful when setting up Moodle as a CIMS:

- **category**: You will definitely want to specify categories in order to organize your courses. The best way to organize courses and categories here is such that the organization coincides with the organization of your curriculum as displayed in school documentation and student handbooks. If you already have categories in your Moodle site, make sure that you spell the categories exactly as they appear on your site, including capitalization. A mistake will result in the creation of a new category. This field should start with a forward slash followed by the category name with each subcategory also being followed by a forward slash (for example, /Listening/Advanced).

- **cost**: If students must pay to enroll in your courses, via the PayPal plugin, you may enter the cost here. You must have the PayPal plugin activated on your site, which can be done by accessing it via the **Site Administration** block by clicking on **Courses** and then **Enrolments**. Additionally, as this book goes to print, the ability to enter a field in the file used by the Bulk Course tool that allows you to set the enrolment plugin, is not yet available. Therefore, if you enter a cost value for a course, it will not be shown until the enrolment plugin for the course is changed manually by navigating to the course and editing the course through the **Settings** link found in the course **Administration** block. Check Moodle.org frequently for updates to the Bulk Course Upload tool as the feature should be added soon.

- **enrolperiod**: This controls the amount of time a student is enrolled in a course. The value must be entered in seconds so, for example, if you had a course that ran for one month and students were to be unenrolled after that period, you would set this value to 2,592,000 (60 seconds X 60 minutes per hour X 24 hours per day X 30 = 2,592,000).

- **enrollable**: This simply controls whether the course is enrollable or not. Entering a 0 will render the course unenrollable and a 1 will set the course to allow enrollments.

- **enrolstartdate** and **enrolenddate**: If you wish to set an enrollment period, you should enter the dates (start and end dates) in these two fields. The dates can be entered in the month/day/year format (for example, 8/1/10).

- **expirynotify**: Enter a 1 here to have e-mails sent to the teacher when a student is going to be unenrolled from a course. Enter a 0 to prevent e-mails from being sent when a student is going to be unenrolled. This setting is only functional when the **enrolperiod** value is set.

- **expirythreshold**: Enter the number of days in advance you want e-mails notifying of student unenrollment sent. The explanation file included calls for a value between 10 and 30 days but this value can actually be set to between 1 and 30 days. This setting is only functional when the **enrolperiod** value and **expirynotify** and/or **notifystudents** (see below) is/are set.

- **format**: This field controls the format of the course. As of Moodle 1.9.8+ there are six format options included in the standard package. The options are lams, scorm, social, topics, weeks, and weeks CSS, and any of these values can be entered in this field.

- **fullname**: This is the full name of the course you are creating (for example, History 101).

- **groupmode**: Set this to 0 for no groups, 1 for separate groups, and 2 for visible groups.

- **groupmodeforce**: Set this to 1 to force group mode at the course level and 0 to allow group mode to be set in each individual activity.

- **guest**: Use a 0 to prevent guests from accessing this course, a 1 to allow guests in the course, and a 2 to allow only guests who have the key into the course.

- **idnumber**: You can enter a course ID number using this field. This number is only used for administrative purposes and is not visible to students. This is a very useful field for institutions that use identification numbers for courses and can provide a link for connecting the courses within Moodle to other systems. If your institution uses any such numbering system it is recommended that you enter the appropriate numbers here.

- **lang**: This is the language setting for the course. Leaving this field blank will result in the **Do not force** language setting, which can be seen from the **Settings** menu accessed from within each individual course. Doing so will allow users to toggle between languages that have been installed in the site. To specify a language, and thus force the display of the course using this language, enter the language as it is displayed within the Moodle lang directory (for example, English = en_utf8).

- **maxbytes**: This field allows you to set the maximum size of individual files that are uploaded to the course. Leaving this blank will result in the course being created with the site wide maximum file upload size setting. Values must be entered in bytes (for example, 1 MB = 1,048,576 bytes). Refer to an online conversion site such as www.onlineconversion.com to help you determine the value you want to enter here.

- **metacourse**: If the course you are creating is a meta course, enter a 1, otherwise enter a 0 or leave the field blank.

- **newsitems**: Enter the number of news items you want to be displayed in your course in the news box that appears on the right-hand side of the page in each course. This value can range from 0 to 10.

- **notifystudents**: This controls whether students are to be notified if they are going to be unenrolled from a course. (See **expirynotify** and **expirythreshold** explained earlier) Enter a 0 to prevent students from being notified and a 1 to have notification e-mails sent to students.

- **numsections**: The number of weeks or topics that are displayed can be set using this field. The value entered must be between 1 and 52. If this field is left blank, only one section will be created.

- **password**: To set a password that controls access to this course, enter a value here. Teachers assigned to this course will have access to the password via the **Settings** area of the course. Setting the password to a randomly generated number is therefore one way to keep students, who have not been assigned to a course, from accessing the course. This is useful for programs that assign students to courses based upon enrollment data obtained from an external system. If courses are to be accessed via a predetermined password, that value can be entered here or if teachers will set their own passwords that are to be distributed to students in a classroom setting, the teacher can change the value via the course settings, if he or she so desires. It is important to consider all of your options and goals in terms of how courses within your Moodle site will be used in conjunction with the use of this field, and course setting, as it has the capability of helping you to position your Moodle site as a curriculum management system.

- **shortname**: This is the course short name setting that is used for display in the breadcrumb path.

- **showgrades**: Set this field to 1 to allow students to view the grade book and 0 to prevent them from accessing the grade book.

- **showreports**: This setting only pertains to students. Entering a 0 here prevents students from accessing their individual activity reports and a 1 allows them to access these reports.

- **sortorder**: This allows you to presort the courses within categories. For example, if you have five courses in the **Advanced Listening** category, you can enter a value of 1 to 5 in this field for each course. The course with 1 will be displayed at the top of the list, the course with a 2, below the first course, and so on.

- **startdate**: Enter the date the courses start here in the month/day/year format (for example, 6/1/10).

- **student** and **students**: These fields allow you to enter the default role title for student and students. For example, if you want students to be displayed as 'Employees', enter that value here.

- **summary**: Enter the summary for the course here. Unfortunately, you cannot use commas in your summary in this file as the comma is interpreted as a field separation point and corrupts the course creation process. Future versions of this tool will hopefully allow for the use of commas.

- **teacher** and **teachers**: These fields allow you to enter the default role title for teacher and teachers. For example, if you want teacher to be displayed as 'Manager', enter that value here.

- **teacher1_account**: Enter either the full name or the user name of the user to be assigned as the teacher of this course. As was noted in the *Teacher account creation* section, if you have teachers with similar names (for example, one name overlaps another), the Bulk Course Upload tool will generate an error and stop processing without creating courses. Also, use **teacher2_account**, **teacher3_account**, and so on to assign multiple teachers to a course.

- **teacher1_role**: Enter the role of the teacher being assigned to the course in this field. For a teacher with full editing permissions, use the role shortname, `editingteacher`. For a teacher who does not have permissions to edit content inside the course, use the shortname, `teacher`. These short names are the defaults that can be viewed by clicking on **Permissions** and then **Define roles** from the **Site Administration** block found on the front page of your site.

- **template**: This function allows you to specify a template course; a course that already exists on your Moodle site, from which some information will be copied as the new course is created. Some blocks and other basic formatting settings are copied from the template course but activities and other content from the template course are not. Please experiment with this feature to see if it is useful for your application.

- **theme**: If your site is set to allow courses to use their own individual themes from the themes installed in the site, you can specify a theme for the course using this field. Note however, that this could cause problems if you are using a theme such as the one that we have selected for this book. In other words, if you use a theme that provides easy access to various components of your site (courses and other information), it may not be a good idea to allow this to be overridden at the course level.

- **timecreated** and **timemodified**: These fields allow you to enter times for both when the course was created and when it was modified. These values can only be referenced by accessing the database directly and are thus not of primary concern for the purposes of setting up our system.

- ❑ **topic0, topic1, topic2**: The number of these specified should not exceed the number you specified in **numsections** plus one. The **topic0** is the 'plus one' as it is for the unnumbered main heading located in the top section of your course. The numbered topics coincide with the number of sections set in **numsections**.

- ❑ **visible**: This field allows you to make the course invisible, and thus only accessible by users with a teaching role or higher, by entering a 0, or visible to all users by entering a 1.

10. While the list of all the possible fields and explanation for each field seems long and complicated, formatting a CSV file and experimenting with bulk course creation will enable you to quickly understand how to format your file and if you are creating many courses, will very quickly demonstrate the power and efficiency of the tool.

11. As I mentioned earlier, we are going to create eighty courses with each of our twenty teachers assigned to teach four courses, one from each of our four levels. I have deleted the categories we created earlier in the *Manual creation of course categories* section, as I wanted to create the categories on the fly while I was creating the courses. Creating courses inside existing categories is however, equally as easy. Just remember to spell and capitalize the categories in your CSV file exactly as they appear on your site. To follow this tutorial, you should also delete all of the categories that you created earlier.

12. Once the file has been constructed and saved in CSV format, access the Bulk Course Upload tool by entering `http://localhost:8888/moodle19/admin/uploadcourse.php` in your browser address bar when logged into your site as admin. Click on **Browse** to locate your CSV file and then **Upload** to upload and initiate the course creation process. The following screenshot is of the results page that is displayed after the tool has finished executing the file.

```
Parsed 80 course(s) from CSV

Created 80 course(s) out of 80

20 new category(ies) were created

You may wish to manually Re-Sort the categories

Re-Sorted courses

ANALYZE Database Tables OK

OPTIMIZE Database Tables OK

Total Execution Time: 1.57 s
```

13. To download a copy of the course creation file being used for this example, visit www.packtpub.com/support.

What just happened?

That was fast, wasn't it? While the creation of the CSV file may take a little time and thought, once the file is prepared, execution and creation of the courses takes literally a matter of seconds. Our creation of eighty courses here took a whopping 1.57 seconds! Logging in to our site as admin now reveals all of the courses and categories we have just created in our **MyCourses** block, as shown in the following screenshot:

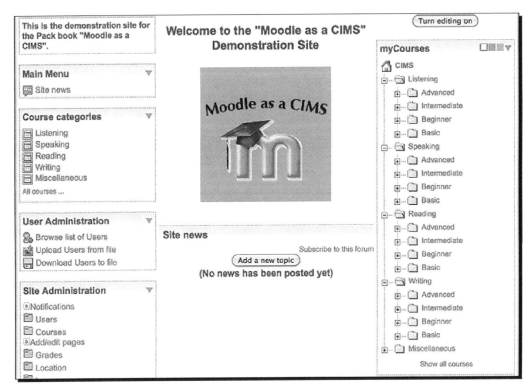

Further expanding each of the level categories by clicking on the plus sign, will reveal five courses in each level. Each course created has also been assigned a teacher. To demonstrate the ability to assign multiple teachers to courses, we have assigned two teachers to the first course listed in the CSV file.

Summary

In this chapter, you have learned how to set up and organize course categories manually via the editing screen of your Moodle site. You then walked through the process of creating accounts for teachers that were going to be assigned to courses through the use of the Bulk Course Upload tool. We then introduced the Bulk Course Upload tool and explained how to get it installed on your system. You walked through an explanation of the fields that can be specified in the CSV file used by the tool and then practiced creating courses and assigning them teachers in order to get a *seeing is believing* perspective on the usefulness of the tool. In the next chapter, we'll continue to build on the system we have created so far by adding students and registering them in courses.

3
Student Account Creation and Enrollment

We have now set up our site and begun building the foundation of our CIMS by creating accounts for our teachers and then creating courses, categories, and assigning teachers to those courses all at the same time, with the Bulk Course Upload tool. It's now time to learn how to create student accounts in bulk and experiment with different ways of enrolling those students in courses on our site.

In this chapter, we will cover the following:

- ◆ Auto-enrollment at the time of bulk account creation
- ◆ Basic bulk enrollment for existing user accounts
- ◆ Explore other enrollment options

Many educational programs place students in courses without requiring students to select and register for their own courses. This may be the case for all of the courses offered within an educational program or only for a portion of the curriculum. An elementary school, for example, will, in most cases, assign groups of students to teachers each year, thus forming the classes that we are all familiar with. Many junior and senior high schools, in addition to colleges, universities, and other educational programs, designate some courses for students while requiring them to register for others.

The following two explanations, auto-enrollment when creating accounts and bulk enrollment for existing users, assume that student enrollment in courses is either predetermined by the school or program, or that the enrollment information is obtained from a tool external to the Moodle system such as a proprietary registration system. Additionally, to position Moodle as a CIMS, it is important to create all of the courses that exist in an educational program and enroll all the students registered for those courses in the courses in the Moodle system even if the teacher of the course does not plan to use Moodle as an instructional tool in his or her course. This is, therefore, the approach taken in the following examples.

Course enrollment controlled via Moodle will be discussed briefly later in this chapter and in more detail later in this book in *Chapter 10, Advanced Enrollment Plugin*.

Bulk account creation and course enrollment

For educational programs that place students into courses upon their entrance into the institution, or that can utilize registration data from an external system in order to mirror that data in the Moodle enrollment, account creation and initial course enrollment can be accomplished at the same time via the use of the Upload users tool. This tool is included as a core feature independent of the enrollment plugin in a standard Moodle installation. This is a useful feature that makes the initial account creation process a bit more efficient by allowing users to be enrolled in courses as their accounts are created.

Time for action – enrolling students when creating their accounts

We are going to create accounts for 500 students and enroll each student in two of our eighty courses that we created in *Chapter 2, Building the Foundation—Creating Categories and Courses*. I've chosen these numbers for our example in order to end up with each of the listening and speaking courses having an enrollment of 25 students. Real-world situations will, of course, vary depending upon registration policies, placement procedures, proficiency level variations, and any number of other factors unique to each educational program. Additionally, as we are setting up Moodle to function as a CIMS, we are operating under the assumption that all new students will have accounts created for them in the Moodle system. The creation process could be accomplished through a variety of procedures available within Moodle but for this example, we will use the **Manual accounts** setting and use a pre-formatted CSV (Comma-separated values) file to perform the enrollment. To enroll students as their accounts are created, follow these steps:

1. Access the authentication plugins via the **Site Administration** block by clicking on **Users | Authentication | Manage authentication**. Modify the authentication plugins such that **Manual accounts** is the default and disable **Self registration** via the pulldown window found under the **Common Settings** heading. The following screenshot shows how your authentication plugin screen will appear with these settings:

Active authentication plugins			
Name	Enable	Up/Down	Settings
Manual accounts			Settings
No login			Settings
Email-based self-registration	👁		Settings
CAS server (SSO)	👁		Settings
External database	👁		Settings
FirstClass server	👁		Settings
IMAP server	👁		Settings
LDAP server	👁		Settings
Moodle Network authentication	👁		Settings
NNTP server	👁		Settings
No authentication	👁		Settings
PAM (Pluggable Authentication Modules)	👁		Settings
POP3 server	👁		Settings
RADIUS server	👁		Settings
Shibboleth	👁		Settings

Please choose the authentication plugins you wish to use and arrange them in order of fallthrough.
Changes in table above are saved automatically.

Common settings

Self registration [Disable ▼] Default: Disable
registerauth

If an authentication plugin, such as email-based self-registration, is selected, then it enables potential users to register themselves and create accounts. This results in the possibility of spammers creating accounts in order to use forum posts, blog entries etc. for spam. To avoid this risk, self-registration should be disabled or limited by *Allowed email domains* setting.

2. As we are going to enroll students at the same time that we create their new accounts, we can use the spreadsheet introduced in *Chapter 2, Building the Foundation—Creating Categories and Courses*, for creating our teacher accounts, as a model. The fields we should include in this file are:

- **username**: Use of a systematic user naming system is recommended. For schools and programs that use student numbering systems, using that number here may be an easy way to provide students with a username that is easily remembered and standardized within your institution. If you plan to use names, the first initial of the first name followed by the last name with all letters in lower case is one system that is easy to implement. In the event of duplications, the use of the middle initial, after the first name initial, will often be sufficient to produce unique user names.

- **password**: Again, if student passwords are already used for other systems on campus, those should be used here as well. It is important to note here that you should decide whether or not the password field is going to be locked or not. Locking the password field will prevent a user from changing his or her password. Clicking on the **Settings** link, found to the right of the **Manual accounts** plugin shown in the previous screenshot, will present you with a screen that allows you to lock specific user fields. Locking the password field is recommended if, for example, your program uses a standard password for several systems and students are able to retrieve that password via some procedure external to your Moodle site. This is also important if you will be creating accounts with a dummy e-mail address, as we will be doing, because doing so makes it impossible for students to reset their password via the **Lost password?** link that appears in the login block on the front page of your site.

- **firstname**: User's first name.

- **lastname**: User's last name.

- **email**: This is a required field, so if your program either does not provide e-mail addresses to all students or you do not have e-mail addresses for them, you will need to create dummy accounts. Use the domain name of your school and student user names, for example, to create the accounts (S101345@Moodle-As-A-CIMS.COM).

- **emailstop**: If you are using dummy e-mail accounts this should be set to 1 to avoid having a huge number of undeliverable error messages sent to the site admin e-mail account.

- **institution**: Enter the name of your school or program.

- **city**: Enter the city in which your school or program is located.

- **country**: Enter the country in which your school or program is located. Note, the standard two-letter country code should be used here. One reference site for country codes is `http://en.wikipedia.org/wiki/ISO_3166-1_alpha-2`.

- **maildisplay**: This controls how student e-mail addresses are displayed in their user profile. Enter a `0` to have their e-mail address hidden from everyone, a `1` to allow only members of courses they are enrolled in to see their address, and a `2` to allow their e-mail address to be seen by everyone. Using `0` as a default is a safe option that protects the student's personal information. Students can change the setting via their profile if they so desire.

- **autosubscribe**: A `0` prevents students from being automatically subscribed to forums when they post in them. Use a `1` to have students automatically subscribed. If you are using dummy e-mail accounts, students will not be able to receive e-mails from forums until they have changed and activated their e-mail address anyway, therefore, this setting will have no effect on users until then.

- **course1** and **course2**: Enter the shortname of the courses in which you want to enroll students. We are using one and two because we will be enrolling the students in two courses.

3. The following screenshot is of a portion of the spreadsheet that will be used to create and enroll our students. Notice that the user naming convention that has been used for these accounts, creates usernames that are of uniform length using both letters and numbers and will thus avoid the overlap issue that was introduced in *Chapter 2, Building the Foundation—Creating Categories and Courses*. Download the sample enrollment file available at `www.packtpub.com/support` to see in detail how I have formatted the file that will be used to create these 500 students.

	A	B	C	D	E	F	G	H	I	J	K	L	M
1	username	password	firstna	lastna	email	email	institu	city	count	maildi	autos	course1	course2
2	S400001	S4001	Stude	Advan	S4000	1	CIMS	Mishir	JP	0	0	AdvList1	AdvSpk1
3	S400002	S4002	Stude	Advan	S4000	1	CIMS	Mishir	JP	0	0	AdvList1	AdvSpk1
4	S400003	S4003	Stude	Advan	S4000	1	CIMS	Mishir	JP	0	0	AdvList1	AdvSpk1
5	S400004	S4004	Stude	Advan	S4000	1	CIMS	Mishir	JP	0	0	AdvList1	AdvSpk1
6	S400005	S4005	Stude	Advan	S4000	1	CIMS	Mishir	JP	0	0	AdvList1	AdvSpk1
7	S400006	S4006	Stude	Advan	S4000	1	CIMS	Mishir	JP	0	0	AdvList1	AdvSpk1
8	S400007	S4007	Stude	Advan	S4000	1	CIMS	Mishir	JP	0	0	AdvList1	AdvSpk1
9	S400008	S4008	Stude	Advan	S4000	1	CIMS	Mishir	JP	0	0	AdvList1	AdvSpk1
10	S400009	S4009	Stude	Advan	S4000	1	CIMS	Mishir	JP	0	0	AdvList1	AdvSpk1
11	S400010	S4010	Stude	Advan	S4000	1	CIMS	Mishir	JP	0	0	AdvList1	AdvSpk1
12	S400011	S4011	Stude	Advan	S4000	1	CIMS	Mishir	JP	0	0	AdvList1	AdvSpk1
13	S400012	S4012	Stude	Advan	S4000	1	CIMS	Mishir	JP	0	0	AdvList1	AdvSpk1

4. Once you have finished formatting your file, save the file in CSV format. Make sure there are no commas in the data you have entered as they will be interpreted as field separators and cause an error to be generated when you try to upload the file to the Upload users tool.

5. Navigate to the **Upload users** page via the **Site Administration** block by clicking on **Users | Accounts | Upload users**. The page is shown in the following screenshot:

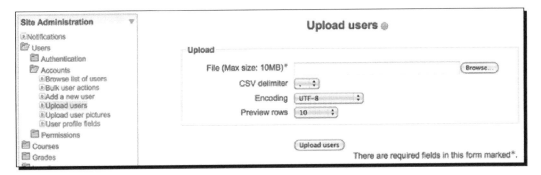

6. Click on **Browse...** to locate and select the CSV file on your computer.

7. After selecting the CSV file, click on **Upload users**. You will see a preview window with the first ten records from the CSV file and will be able to adjust some settings pertaining to the accounts being created. Leave the **Upload type** set to **Add new only, skip existing users** as we are only creating new accounts. All other defaults, as well, should be appropriate for the accounts we are creating. The screen, with the settings that have been described here, will look like the following screenshot:

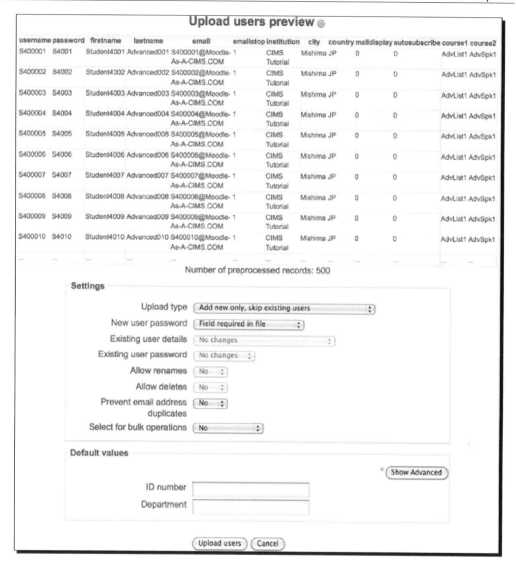

Upload users preview ⓘ

username	password	firstname	lastname	email	emailstop	institution	city	country	maildisplay	autosubscribe	course1	course2
S400001	S4001	Student4001	Advanced001	S400001@Moodle-As-A-CIMS.COM	1	CIMS Tutorial	Mishima	JP	0	0	AdvList1	AdvSpk1
S400002	S4002	Student4002	Advanced002	S400002@Moodle-As-A-CIMS.COM	1	CIMS Tutorial	Mishima	JP	0	0	AdvList1	AdvSpk1
S400003	S4003	Student4003	Advanced003	S400003@Moodle-As-A-CIMS.COM	1	CIMS Tutorial	Mishima	JP	0	0	AdvList1	AdvSpk1
S400004	S4004	Student4004	Advanced004	S400004@Moodle-As-A-CIMS.COM	1	CIMS Tutorial	Mishima	JP	0	0	AdvList1	AdvSpk1
S400005	S4005	Student4005	Advanced005	S400005@Moodle-As-A-CIMS.COM	1	CIMS Tutorial	Mishima	JP	0	0	AdvList1	AdvSpk1
S400006	S4006	Student4006	Advanced006	S400006@Moodle-As-A-CIMS.COM	1	CIMS Tutorial	Mishima	JP	0	0	AdvList1	AdvSpk1
S400007	S4007	Student4007	Advanced007	S400007@Moodle-As-A-CIMS.COM	1	CIMS Tutorial	Mishima	JP	0	0	AdvList1	AdvSpk1
S400008	S4008	Student4008	Advanced008	S400008@Moodle-As-A-CIMS.COM	1	CIMS Tutorial	Mishima	JP	0	0	AdvList1	AdvSpk1
S400009	S4009	Student4009	Advanced009	S400009@Moodle-As-A-CIMS.COM	1	CIMS Tutorial	Mishima	JP	0	0	AdvList1	AdvSpk1
S400010	S4010	Student4010	Advanced010	S400010@Moodle-As-A-CIMS.COM	1	CIMS Tutorial	Mishima	JP	0	0	AdvList1	AdvSpk1
...	...	...	...						...	...	...	...

Number of preprocessed records: 500

Settings

Upload type	Add new only, skip existing users
New user password	Field required in file
Existing user details	No changes
Existing user password	No changes
Allow renames	No
Allow deletes	No
Prevent email address duplicates	No
Select for bulk operations	No

Default values

* (Show Advanced)

ID number	
Department	

(Upload users) (Cancel)

8. Click on **Upload users** to create the accounts and, at the same time, enroll each user in the courses specified in the file.

9. As the accounts are created, you will see enrollment information on the right side of the screen. Scroll down to the bottom of the window when the process is finished, which should be in approximately 5 to 10 seconds depending on the speed of your computer, and check the creation report at the bottom of the screen just above the **Continue** button. If you downloaded and used the sample file, it will look like the following screenshot:

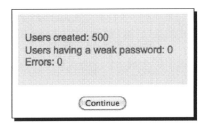

10. Click on **Continue** to go back to the **Upload users** page, and then on the front page breadcrumb (**CIMS** in our Moodle example site, as shown in the following screenshot) to navigate back to the front page of your site.

What just happened?

In a matter of a few seconds, new accounts for 500 users have been successfully created and each user has been enrolled in two courses. While it does take some time to format the CSV file that is used by the **Upload users** tool, the time is miniscule in comparison to the amount of time it would take to create and enroll each of these users individually. Additionally, the CSV file, or its spreadsheet template 'parent', can be used for future updates to these users' accounts. This process will be introduced and covered later in this chapter.

Time for action – checking the enrollment status from the course context

In order to verify the account creation and course enrollments, and to visualize how the courses are organized, we will now quickly walk through a quick process of checking to see that the users we just created have been enrolled in courses. Follow these steps to check a few courses and their enrollments:

1. Navigate to a course using the **My Courses** navigation tree. We'll check the **Advanced Listening 1** course (Short name **AdvList1**) first, as shown in the following screenshot:

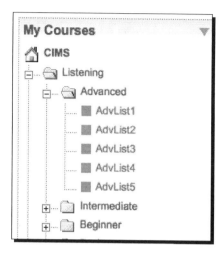

2. From inside the course, click on the **Participants** link found in the **People** block at the top-left of the course page, as shown in the following screenshot:

3. You will see 27 participants in this course. Why, you ask? Because, we have enrolled 25 students and remember, when we created the courses in *Chapter 2, Building the Foundation—Creating Categories and Courses*, we demonstrated how multiple teachers can be enrolled in courses by enrolling two teachers in this **Advanced Listening 1** course. The total number of participants therefore is 27.

4. To see the roles of users enrolled in the course, navigate back to the main page of the course and click on the **Assign roles** link found in the **Administration** block on the left side of the page, as shown in the following screenshot:

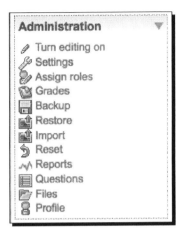

5. You will see that there are 25 students enrolled in the course and two teachers, as shown in the following screenshot:

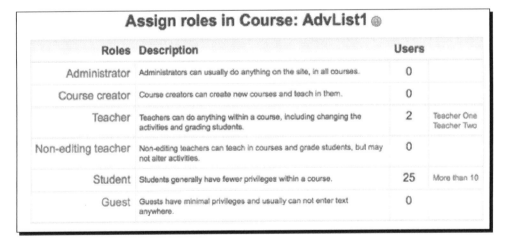

Roles	Description	Users	
Administrator	Administrators can usually do anything on the site, in all courses.	0	
Course creator	Course creators can create new courses and teach in them.	0	
Teacher	Teachers can do anything within a course, including changing the activities and grading students.	2	Teacher One Teacher Two
Non-editing teacher	Non-editing teachers can teach in courses and grade students, but may not alter activities.	0	
Student	Students generally have fewer privileges within a course.	25	More than 10
Guest	Guests have minimal privileges and usually can not enter text anywhere.	0	

Assign roles in Course: AdvList1

6. From the front page of the site, navigate to a few other courses to see that each course is now populated with users as a result of the file we just uploaded into the **Upload users** tool. Notice however, if you navigate to a reading or writing course, there are no students enrolled in those courses yet. We'll take care of that later in this chapter in the *Enroll existing users* section.

What just happened?

We have just confirmed that our users have been enrolled in courses as students. We did this by randomly selecting a course, navigating to the course, and clicking on the **Participants** link found inside the course. We also checked the roles of the users enrolled in our course via the use of the **Assign roles** link, also found from within each course. This allowed us to confirm that the users we bulk enrolled in the previous step, were all enrolled as desired.

Time for action – checking enrollment status from the user's profile page

Checking the enrollments from the course context allows us to confirm the enrollments and, at the same time, see how many students have been enrolled in a course. Another way to verify that a particular user was enrolled in the desired courses, from the perspective of individual users rather than that of the course, is to click on the **Browse list of users** link found in the **Site Administration** block. Viewing enrollments from this perspective allows us to see how many courses a user is enrolled in. To check the enrollment process using this method, follow these steps:

1. First, access a user's profile page by clicking on **Users | Accounts | Browse a list of users** from the **Site Administration** block found on the front page of your site, as shown in the following screenshot:

2. On the resulting page, shown in the following screenshot, you will see a total user count at the top of the page, followed by a filter that allows you to search for a specific user. In our sample site, there are 521 users registered because we have created 20 teachers, 500 students, and have one admin account. We are going to select an individual student and check the profile of that student to make sure that he or she has been enrolled in two courses. Select a student via one of the following methods:

- Use the filter to search for a specific student. Click on the **Show Advanced** button for various fine-tuning options for the filter.

- Select a student randomly from the list that appears on the screen.

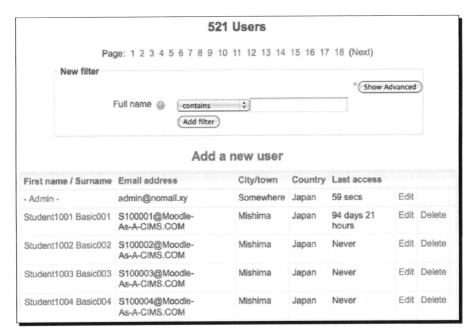

3. The following screenshot is of the filter that we used to find a specific student by typing `4110` in the default **Full name contains** filter. Click on the name link, **Student4110 Advanced110** in this case, to view the student's profile. Note here that filters are cumulative so if you attempt to search for another student or group of students, you will need to **remove** or delete, the first filter or it will interfere with subsequent filters.

4. The following screenshot is of the profile of **Student4110** that was found using the filter, shown previously. We can see that this student was correctly enrolled in the two courses that were specified in the CSV file.

What just happened?

We have just checked to see that one of the user accounts we created was enrolled in courses as specified in the CSV file. This also gave us the opportunity to use the user profile to check to see which courses a user is enrolled in. In *Chapter 5, Enabling your Moodle Site to Function as an Information Portal*, we will revisit user profiles when we make a small change to modify how many courses are displayed in each user's profile.

Bulk enrollment for existing users

The option to enroll users in courses at the time of account creation is useful when creating user accounts, but once accounts have been created, other options for bulk enrollment must be utilized. For programs that span a period of time that includes multiple courses delivered one after another, a need to enroll students, who already have accounts in their Moodle site, will exist. One basic method of performing this task is through the use of the **Upload users** tool that we just worked with.

In the previous example, we created accounts for 500 students and enrolled those students in two courses. We'll assume that they have completed those two courses and are now going to be placed into the next two courses that make up our program. In our example, those two remaining courses will be the reading and writing courses.

Time for action – preparing the CSV file

In order to enroll our students with existing accounts, we can use the spreadsheet that we used for the account creation. Follow these steps to prepare the CSV file that we'll use to bulk enroll our existing users:

1. Open the spreadsheet that we used for the bulk account creation and delete all of the columns except for those with the following three headings:

   - **username**
   - **course1**
   - **course2**

2. Simply delete the unneeded columns from the spreadsheet used earlier and add the information for the new course enrollments, as shown in the following screenshot. Note, the formatted file used for this example can be downloaded from www.packtpub.com/support.

	A	B	C
1	username	course1	course2
2	S400001	AdvRdg1	AdvWrt1
3	S400002	AdvRdg1	AdvWrt1
4	S400003	AdvRdg1	AdvWrt1
5	S400004	AdvRdg1	AdvWrt1
6	S400005	AdvRdg1	AdvWrt1
7	S400006	AdvRdg1	AdvWrt1
8	S400007	AdvRdg1	AdvWrt1
9	S400008	AdvRdg1	AdvWrt1
10	S400009	AdvRdg1	AdvWrt1
11	S400010	AdvRdg1	AdvWrt1
12	S400011	AdvRdg1	AdvWrt1
13	S400012	AdvRdg1	AdvWrt1
14	S400013	AdvRdg1	AdvWrt1

What just happened?

Using the spreadsheet file that we used to create accounts, we have quickly modified the information contained in the file in order that it may now be used as a CSV file to enroll existing users in courses. We will use the Upload users tool again to accomplish this enrollment task.

Time for action – enroll existing users

Once you have formatted the spreadsheet with the appropriate information and saved it in CSV format, the file may be used to enroll existing users via the use of the same **Upload users** page we used for account creation. Follow these steps to enroll existing users using the file we just formatted:

1. Access the **Upload users** page via the following path: Front page of your site, **Site Administration | Users | Accounts | Upload users**.

2. From the **Upload users page, to enroll existing users in courses, click on Browse** to locate and select your enrollment CSV file.

3. After selecting your CSV file, click on the **Upload users** button.

4. From the window displaying the first ten records from your file and the **Settings** and **Default values** settings areas, change the **Upload type** to **Update existing users only**.

5. The other default values in the **Settings** area can be left alone for our task.

6. Do not adjust any of the **Default values** settings as we have specified that no changes are to be made with **Existing user details.** If you wanted to change user details such as e-mail addresses, usernames, and so on, you would want to choose one of the other three options available in the **Existing user details** pull down menu. The preview screen, with the changes listed here, should look like the following screenshot:

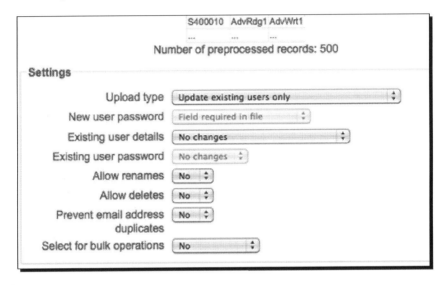

7. Click on **Upload users** to enroll the users listed in your CSV file.

8. Scroll to the bottom of the screen and note the status report screen, as shown in the following screenshot:

9. Because the only information that was added was course enrollment data, user accounts were not updated in terms of how Moodle groups the information for a user. For this reason, you will see the **Users updated: 0** message. Click on **Continue** and then on the front page bread crumb (**CIMS** for our example site) to return to the front page of your site.

What just happened?

The information from the CSV file that was formatted with only the username and the shortname of the courses to enroll users in was used to update the enrollment information for each of our 500 student accounts. The result is that all the students have now been enrolled in two new courses. This is a relatively easy and low-tech method of enrolling existing users in new courses.

Have a go hero

Now, practice what you learned earlier in this chapter and check the results of the new enrollment from either the course perspective or user perspective as outlined earlier. You'll see that all of the Reading and Writing courses now have 25 students enrolled in them and that each student has four courses listed in his or her profile.

Additionally, there are quite a few options available when using the **Upload users** feature built into Moodle. Experiment with them a little using either the file that we used to create user accounts earlier in this chapter, or the one that we just used to enroll existing users. Use **Update existing users only** again, but this time experiment with some of the options for changing user details using both information from the file and information that you enter in the **Default values** section. Modifying user details in such a manner can be useful, for example, when students change departments or majors, or when other user-related information that you store in user profiles, is changed.

Pop quiz

1. To quickly create new user accounts for 100 users and enroll each of those users in two courses at the time of account creation, which of the following would be the best process?

    a. Create each user one at a time via the **Add a new user** link, found in the **Site Administration** block under **Users and Accounts**, and then enroll each of them in courses from the **Assign roles** link found in the **Administration** block.

    b. Create a CSV file with the account and course information for all of the users and upload it to the site via the **Upload users** tool to create new accounts and enroll the subsequent users in courses at the same time.

    c. Use the **Update existing users only** feature built into the **Upload users** tool to enroll the students in courses after creating their accounts one at a time.

    d. Ask all of your students to create their own accounts and enroll in whatever course or courses they like.

Other enrollment options

As stated earlier in this chapter, both enrolling users when creating their accounts and enrolling them after their accounts exist, via the use of the **Upload users** tool, are only practical given one of the two following circumstances:

- The program places students into classes automatically based upon some predetermined criteria (for example, student performance on a placement test and has that placement information in a format that can be used in the **Upload users** tool).

- The program utilizes a registration system, automated or otherwise, external to Moodle and is able to obtain data from that system such that it can be formatted for use within the **Upload users** tool.

While these two conditions may appear to include any type of possible enrollment within a course, there are options within the Moodle framework that do not fall cleanly into either of these categories. For example, if the default enrollment plugin in Moodle, internal enrollment, is used without an enrollment key or an enrollment period, controlling course enrollment from the CIMS perspective is difficult, if not impossible.

Understanding the various enrollment plugins available in Moodle will better enable us to build our CIMS such that it is easily and efficiently maintained. These enrollment plugins can all be accessed from the **Site Administration** block found on the front page of your site by clicking on the **Courses** link and then on **Enrolments**. The list of enrollment options as you will see it in your site, is shown in the following screenshot. Click on the **Edit** link found under **Settings** to view the settings for each plugin.

Please choose the enrolment plugins you wish to use. Don't forget to configure the settings properly.

You have to indicate which plugins are enabled, and **one** plugin can be set as the default plugin for *interactive* enrolment. To disable interactive enrolment, set "enrollable" to "No" in required courses.

Name	Enable	Default	Settings
Authorize.net Payment Gateway	☐	○	Edit
External Database	☐		Edit
Flat file	☐		Edit
IMS Enterprise file	☐		Edit
Internal Enrolment	☑	⦿	Edit
LDAP	☐		Edit
Moodle Networking	☐		Edit
PayPal	☑	○	Edit

(Save changes)

Enrollment plugins

The following is a reordered list of these enrollment options in order of simplicity of setup and practicality from the CIMS perspective, followed by an explanation of how some of them may be used when positioning your Moodle site as a CIMS:

- Internal Enrollment
- Flat file
- External Database
- LDAP
- IMS Enterprise
- Moodle Networking
- Authorize.net Payment Gateway
- PayPal

The following is the explanation of enrollment options:

- **Internal Enrollment**: This is the default enrollment plugin in Moodle. It is one of several plugins that allows students to self-enroll in courses. The account creation and enrollment tasks performed in the previous section of this chapter were performed with the internal enrollment plugin set as the default plugin. The **Availability** settings, found in the **Settings** window of a course, control to some degree, the enrollment options as follows:

  - **Availability setting**: The course can be set to be available or unavailable to students.

  - **Enrollment key**: If set to be available, students can only enroll in the course if they enter the enrollment key as specified here. In our bulk enrollment examples, this key or password only serves to prevent students from entering courses that they are not enrolled in. Likewise, the teacher does not need to know the key as it simply functions as a lock to keep unenrolled students from entering the course.

  - The **Course enrollable**, **Start date**, **End date**, and **Enrolment duration** settings found under the **Enrolment** heading in the course **Settings** area also allow for some control of the internal enrollment plugin.

Using the **Upload users** feature in Moodle, with the internal enrollment plugin set as the default plugin, to manage enrollment is an easy and effective but fairly low-tech method of managing course enrollment. For programs that span a lengthy course of time and thus consist of multiple courses that are offered in chronological succession, this method of enrollment can get complicated and a little messy due to the need to maintain enrollment data in spreadsheets that can get cumbersome and that are external to the Moodle system. Programs in which multiple enrollment periods exist over the course of a short period of time may also find this method difficult to maintain. The need for very little technical skill however, makes it a feasible option for many programs that wish to begin experimenting with positioning their Moodle site as a CIMS.

◆ **Flat file**: This plugin allows you to format a text file, with the following fields, that is used by Moodle to process enrollments:

  ❑ **operation**: This is set to a value of either **add** or **del** and either enrolls a user or removes them from a course.

  ❑ **role**: This is the role for the user specified (student, teacher, editingteacher).

  ❑ **idnumber(user)**: This is the ID number associated with the user from the user table in the database.

  ❑ **idnumber(course)**: This is the ID number associated with the course from the course table in the database.

  ❑ **starttime**: This is an option field for specifying the start time of the course. It is formatted in seconds per the Unix time stamp system.

  ❑ **endtime**: This is an optional field for specifying the end time of the course. It is formatted in seconds per the Unix time stamp system. Note, one convenient website for converting traditional dates to Unix time stamps is www.onlineconversion.com.

When the flat file enrollment plugin is used, the file is deleted after being read. If an automated system for generating this file exists, it may be an attractive option, but if the file is being generated manually, there is little advantage to this method over the **Upload users** method presented earlier.

◆ **External Database**: This enrollment plugin allows you to configure Moodle to connect to an external database, or even to a table within the database used by Moodle, and retrieve enrollment information. In addition to settings that allow Moodle to connect to your database, you will need to specify course, user, and role field names for tables in both the local and remote database. Several other options allow for setting a default role, the auto-creation of courses, ignoring invisible courses, and turning off the unenroll feature for users previously enrolled with this plugin that no longer appear in the external database.

This is a powerful enrollment plugin that can be very useful to institutions that already maintain enrollment information in an external system, such as a course registration system. We will explore the use of this plugin further in *Chapter 8, Setting Up a Mini SIS*.

◆ **LDAP**: This acronym stands for **Lightweight Directory Access Protocol** and requires a server setup to function as the LDAP host. While very powerful if functional, this enrollment plugin is on the advanced side in terms of setup and maintenance and thus not recommended for institutions that do not already have an LDAP server in place. If you have an LDAP server that contains student information and can easily be modified to include course registration information, then you may want to consider using this option to enroll users in your courses on Moodle. For all other environments, I recommend first experimenting with the simple procedure outlined earlier in this chapter and then moving on to possibly using the external database enrollment option.

◆ **IMS Enterprise**: This plugin utilizes a text file formatted to conform with the IMS Enterprise specifications for the purpose of creating, modifying, and deleting accounts, enrolling users in courses, and for modification of some other course-related settings. Much like the LDAP plugin, this plugin is most useful to institutions that use applications capable of generating the IMS Enterprise formatted file automatically and is thus not recommended for programs that do not already have such a system in place.

◆ **Moodle Networking**: This plugin enables cross-site enrollment when you have Moodle networking turned on. This means that students with accounts on one Moodle site would be able to navigate to a networked Moodle site and enroll in courses offered on that site. Likewise, a teacher or administrator is able to enroll students from one Moodle site to courses on another networked site. Networking must first be turned on and various settings allowing for cross-site enrollment must be activated. This plugin introduces many options for separating Moodle instances within an institution based upon departments, for example, but does not in and of itself automate the enrollment process. Setting up a Moodle network is outside the scope of this book but you can access the Moodle Docs page at `http://docs.moodle.org/en/Moodle_Network` to learn more about this feature.

◆ **Authorize.net and PayPal**: I have grouped these two plugins together because they are both structured to allow you to offer courses that are enrolled in by the user through a payment system. Both Authorize.net and PayPal are web-based solutions for accepting payments via the web. Use of this type of enrollment system and course offering is not central to the CIMS structure that this book attempts to build so we will not go into a detailed discussion of these options. Later in *Chapter 8, Setting Up a Mini SIS* however, we will explore methods for aggregating all of the enrollment data that exists in your Moodle site and, will at that point, briefly revisit these plugins.

CIMS enrollment review

In order to position your Moodle site as a CIMS, that is, to create all of the courses offered in your educational program and enroll users in those courses such that every user registered for or assigned to a course in your program is also enrolled in the same course on your Moodle site, you need to decide upon a practical enrollment option. The easiest option, although arguably not the most advanced and efficient, is to use the **Upload users** tool included in the Moodle core installation. As you become more familiar and comfortable with your CIMS and start to expand upon its potential, you may choose to explore other more sophisticated enrollment options.

Summary

In the first half of this chapter, we learned how to create user accounts and enroll those users in courses at the same time as their accounts were being created. We then reviewed the easiest and most straightforward method of enrolling existing students in courses on the Moodle site via the **Update existing users only** option in the **Upload users** tool. In the second half of the chapter, the enrollment options in Moodle, which exist in the form of plugins, were introduced. These options were evaluated from the perspective of setting up Moodle to function as a CIMS. Using the **Upload users** tool within the **Internal enrolment** option was presented as being the easiest method and we learned that the external database plugin is one that holds the most possibility for expanding the efficiency and sophistication of the enrollment process in our CIMS. In the following chapter, we will explore methods of incorporating standards into the use of our Moodle CIMS.

4
Incorporating Educational Standards

Now that our Moodle site is taking shape as a CIMS with courses created, teachers assigned to courses, and students enrolled in their courses, we can begin to build standards into our site that reflect the standards, or policies, that are implemented in our educational program. We'll also streamline procedures, such as the submission of grades, and in the process, attempt to make the jobs of both teachers and educational administrators a little easier.

In this chapter, we will introduce and explain the following tasks that will enable you to start to incorporate educational standards in your Moodle CIMS site:

- ◆ Bulk setup of the attendance module
- ◆ Setting the Gradebook to reflect educational program standards
- ◆ Implementing a final grade submission process through your Moodle CIMS
- ◆ Setting up a procedure for implementing a program-wide assessment test

Implementing standard policies and procedures in your Moodle site

Almost every educational program, to varying degrees, has in place standards upon which it operates in order to ensure that every student is treated fairly and equitably. These standards may be in the form of rules that govern student evaluation methods, procedures for filing paperwork required of instructors, or policies that must be adhered to by students in a program such as attendance requirements. One aspect of expanding Moodle to function as a CIMS is through the implementation of many of these standards in the Moodle site. Doing so will not only introduce a heightened level of efficiency, it will also serve to make your program-wide standards more transparent and thus, more easily adopted and adhered to by everyone involved in your program. The following examples are just a few introductory ideas for how to implement standards through your Moodle site. Once you have experimented with these, I encourage you to think of other standards, policies, and procedures that can be implemented through your Moodle CIMS.

Attendance standards

Traditional educational programs in which students meet in a classroom for face-to-face interaction with a teacher, very often keep records of student attendance percentages. This data may be used for the purpose of enforcing attendance regulations or simply to allow educators and administrators to track attendance rates for purposes such as correlation with scholastic achievement. The attendance module in Moodle can be used in such programs to:

 ◆ Help a program implement a standardized attendance policy
 ◆ Enable a program to track attendance rates quickly and efficiently

Bulk setup of the attendance module

For the following example, we are going to use the attendance module, that we installed in our Moodle site in the first chapter of this book, to help our program implement a standardized attendance policy that we are asking all of our teachers and students to adhere to. The policy is outlined as follows:

 ◆ Students are required to attend 80 percent of the total class sessions per semester
 ◆ Being 15 or more minutes late to class is counted as a *Late*
 ◆ Four *Late* attendances equal one *absence*
 ◆ Excused absences will count for 75 percent of an attendance

This is, of course, simply an example attendance policy. Additional rules that are external to the Moodle attendance module tabulation system may be established and implemented to allow for more flexibility on the part of the educators. Virtually any mathematical calculation based upon attendance data however, can be implemented within the attendance module. The example outlined here consists of three stages:

 ◆ Creation of template courses
 ◆ Setting up of the attendance template within the template course
 ◆ Importing the attendance template into other courses

Time for action – creating a template course

We are going to set up a course to use as a 'template' course in which we will create the **Attendance** activity that we are going to use to import attendance settings into our courses. Follow these steps to get your template course ready:

1. Log in to your site as admin or as a user with administrative privileges and navigate to the **Course categories** page. One way to do this is to click on the **Show all courses** link found at the bottom of your **MyCourses** block, as shown in the following screenshot. The direct URL to this page will always be `http://www.yoursite. com/course/`.

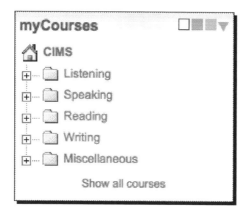

2. From the **Course categories** page, click on the **Turn editing on** button.

3. With editing turned on, click on the **Miscellaneous** link to enter the miscellaneous category and then click on the **Add a new course** button.

4. Create the new course with a **Full name** and **Short name** that will enable you to identify it easily. This course will hold attendance settings that are going to be used as a template for classes that meet on Monday and Thursday during the first period, so we are using `Attendance Template M-Th 1` as the **Full name** and `AT-M-Th-1` as the **Short name**, as shown in the following screenshot:

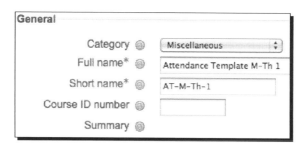

5. You might also want to enter a simple explanation of what the course is being used for, to help identify the course to site administrators. An example is provided in the following screenshot:

> This course will be used to create an attendance module to be used as a template for importing to other courses that have Monday/Thursday 1st period class sessions.

6. Make sure that the **Course start date** is set such that it falls before the first day that attendance will be taken in the course. For our example, we should use April 1 as that was the date used as the start date for our courses. Note, if you create attendance sessions for dates that occur prior to the start date of the course, they will not appear in the attendance sessions window and will be reported as invisible sessions. The only way to access these sessions is to change the course start date to a date that falls before the dates used for the invisible sessions.

7. Finally, before creating the course, change the **Availability** setting to **This course is not available to students**, as shown in the following screenshot. This will ensure that students do not accidentally enroll in this template course.

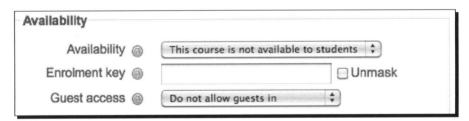

8. After you have entered all of your settings and clicked on **Save changes**, the course will be created and you will be prompted to assign roles, as shown in the following screenshot. If you plan to have users with other roles, such as non-editing teachers or users with other administrative roles that we will discuss in a future chapter, using this course, you may assign them here. Because the admin will always be able to access this course, for now we will skip this assignment process and click on **Click here to enter your course**, as shown in the following screenshot:

Assign roles in Course: AT-M-Th-1 ◉

Roles	Description	Users
Administrator	Administrators can usually do anything on the site, in all courses.	0
Course creator	Course creators can create new courses and teach in them.	0
Teacher	Teachers can do anything within a course, including changing the activities and grading students.	0
Non-editing teacher	Non-editing teachers can teach in courses and grade students, but may not alter activities.	0
Student	Students generally have fewer privileges within a course.	0
Guest	Guests have minimal privileges and usually can not enter text anywhere.	0

(Click here to enter your course)

What just happened?

We just set up a course that will function as a template course because we will use it as a place to set up an attendance activity with the sessions we want to be able to import into various courses. This is being done because it is not easily possible to create pre-populated attendance activities in multiple courses simultaneously via any other method. Use of this type of a template course is an easy way to allow you to set up attendance activities in multiple courses in a relatively short amount of time.

Time for action – setting up the attendance template

We are now ready to create an instance of the attendance module activity and pre-populate it with the settings we want to use for our classes that meet on Mondays and Thursdays during the first period. Follow these steps to set up the attendance module:

1. If editing is not already turned on, click on the **Turn editing on** button found at the top-right of the screen.

2. In the top section of the page, the one that includes the default **News forum**, click on the **Add an activity...** drop-down menu bar and select **Attendance**, as shown in the following screenshot:

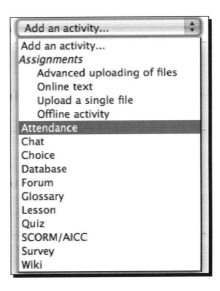

3. In the **Adding a new Attendance** screen, shown in the following screenshot, you can change the name of the attendance module you are inserting in this course. You can also change the grade here if you like. For our example, we will keep all of the default settings and simply click on **Save and display**.

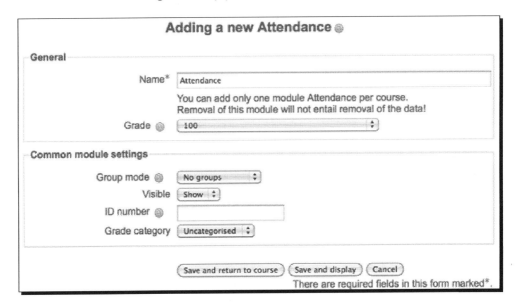

4. An instance of the attendance module activity has now been inserted into the course and, because we clicked on **Save and display**, we are presented with a screen that allows us to set up the module. From the setup screen, shown in the following screenshot, click on the **Add** tab.

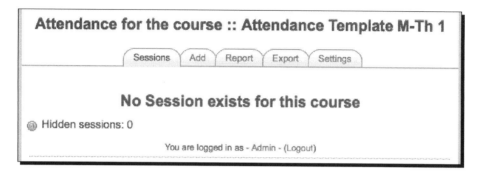

5. In the subsequent screen, first, click on the **Create multiple sessions** tickbox. We are going to create multiple class sessions for a class that begins on 4/1/2010 and runs until 7/15/2010. This class meets on Mondays and Thursdays during the first period, which in our sample institution is from 9 A.M. to 10:30 A.M., thus the duration setting of one hour and thirty minutes. The settings entered are shown in the following screenshot. Click on the **Add session** button to create the sessions.

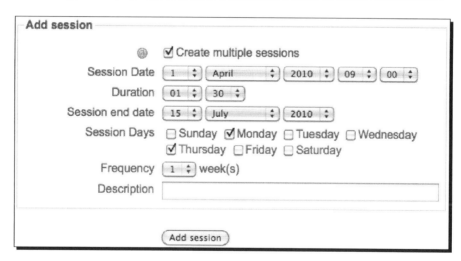

6. You will get a **Sessions successfully generated** message as shown in the following screenshot. From this screen, click on the **Sessions** tab to view the sessions you just created. Note, if you click on the **Continue** button, you will be taken back to the **Add session** screen. You can select the **Sessions** tab from this screen as well.

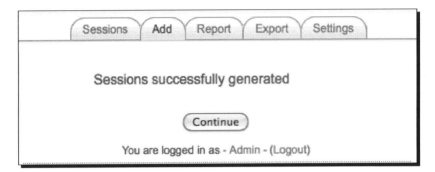

7. Notice that there are 31 sessions with each session titled **Regular class session**. Let's remove the 31st of May for *Memorial Day* and the 17th of June for a *School Founders Day* holiday. These sessions can be deleted one at a time by clicking on the red X or together by first clicking in the **Select** box found at the far right for both days and then using the **With selected** drop-down menu found at the bottom of the page. The following screenshot is of the confirmation window that appears after selecting both dates using the **Select** box and then using the drop-down menu to delete the sessions at the same time.

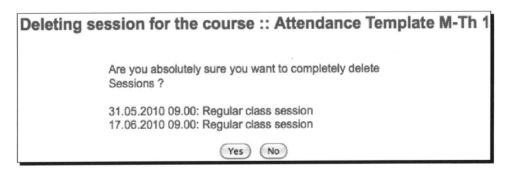

8. After we have deleted the two unneeded sessions, let's change the name of the 1st and last sessions to `First Day of Class` and `Last Day of Class`. Click on the small pencil icon to edit the individual session and enter the new title, as shown in the following screenshot. Click on **Update** to save the changes and then do the same for the last day of class, the 15th of July.

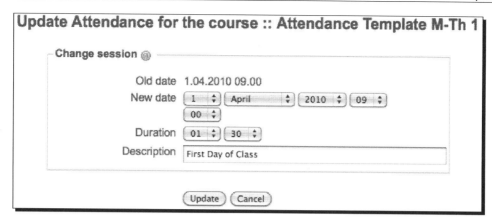

9. We should now have 29 sessions in our **Attendance** activity. Lastly, we want to enter the settings that will allow the conditions, described earlier, to be calculated by the module.

   - **Students must attend 80 percent or more of the class sessions**: This will be calculated for us because we set the module to calculate out of 100 points.

   - **Four Late attendances equal one absence**: To accomplish this we will set a regular attendance to be worth 4 points and a late attendance to be worth 3 points.

   - **An excused absence will count for 75 percent of an attendance**: This means that an excused absence will also be worth 3 points.

10. Click on the **Settings** tab to enter the settings that will look like the following screenshot. Click the **Update** button to save the new settings.

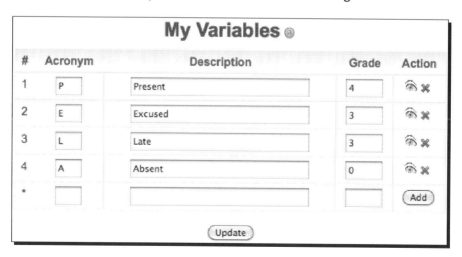

What just happened?

We have just created an attendance template using the attendance module. In our template, we have created 29 attendance sessions for classes that meet on Mondays and Thursdays from 9 A.M. to 10:30 A.M. between the 1st of April and the 15th of July. We also added settings that govern how many points a student gets for being present to class, late to class, absent from class, and for an excused absence. Next, we'll use this template to quickly add pre-formatted instances of the **Attendance** activity to other courses.

Time for action – importing the attendance template to other courses

For this example, we will import this attendance setup into all advanced listening and advanced speaking courses. This means we'll need to import the attendance settings into a total of ten courses. Carry out the following steps to import an instance of the pre-formatted attendance module activity that will include all of the dated sessions we created in the template, into these courses:

1. Navigate to the first course we are going to import the attendance module into. Using the **MyCourses** block, click on **AdvList1**, as shown in the following screenshot:

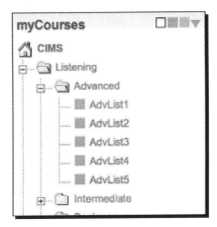

2. From inside this course, click on the **Import** link found in the **Administration** block on the left side of the screen, as shown in the following screenshot:

3. Enter the short name of the course that was used to create the attendance template (AT-M-Th-1) in the **Search courses** field and click on the **Search courses** button, as shown in the following screenshot:

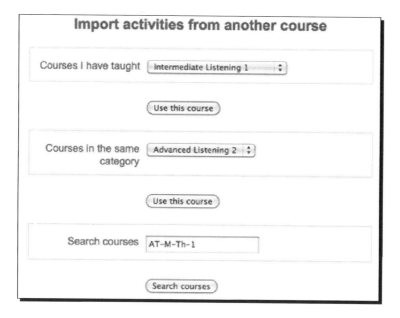

4. The result of the search will present the **Attendance Template** course we created earlier, as shown in the following screenshot. Click on the **Use this course** link.

5. The **Import course data** screen will present a list of activities that may be imported from the course you have selected. We only want to import the **Attendance** module so we will unselect the **Forums** items by clicking on the tickbox. Additionally, we will set the **Course files** and **Site files used in this course** drop-down menus to **No** as we don't want any files to be backed up. Finally, click on **Continue** to begin the import process. These settings are all shown in the following screenshot:

Import course data: Attendance Template M-Th 1 (AT-M-Th-1)

Include All/None

- ☐ Forums
  - ☐ News forum
- ☑ Attendances
  - ☑ Attendance

Course files   No ⏶⏷
Site files used in this course ◉   No ⏶⏷

(Continue) (Cancel)

6. The following screenshot will present a note in red text stating that there are no users in the course being used for the backup. This is ok as we are not attempting to backup user data. Click on **Continue** to proceed with the import.

Import course data: Attendance Template M-Th 1 (AT-M-Th-1)

Note: This backup contains no users and so all activities have been switched to "without user data" mode. Exercise and Workshop activities will not be included in the backup, since these modules are not compatible with this type of backup.

Include Attendances without user data

Attendance	
Sessions	29

(Continue) (Cancel)

7. The next screen will present a list of items that are being included in the backup that will be used for the import. Click on the **Continue** button shown at the bottom of the screen.

8. The next screen will consist of a simple **Import course data** message with a **Continue** button. Click on the **Continue** button to proceed.

9. The following **Import course data** screen will show the list of items that were presented in step 7. These are the items that have been unzipped from the backup file and were used for the import. Click on **Continue** to proceed to the course that we imported the attendance module into.

10. Click on the **Attendance** link in the target course, **Advanced Listening 1**, to confirm that all of the sessions have been imported just as they existed in the template course.

What just happened?

We have just imported the template attendance activity, complete with its settings, into our **Advanced Listening 1** course. This method allows for the relatively easy and efficient creation of a standardized attendance module activity within courses throughout an educational program. Cooperation from teachers in maintaining their attendance records on the Moodle site then enables administrators to quickly access attendance data throughout their program. Later in this book, we will explore methods of aggregating the attendance data without having to navigate to each individual course.

Have a go hero

Following the process described, practice the import process and import the attendance module into the remainder of the **Advanced Listening** courses and the **Advanced Speaking** courses. Copy the short name of the course that is used as a template and paste it into the **Search courses** field to speed up the process a little. Note, if you plan to set up a pre-formatted Gradebook for all of your teachers, jump forward to the next section before importing the attendance module into any more courses.

Grading standards

Educational programs utilize grading standards to varying degrees ranging from simply identifying a common grading scale to defining how much of a student's grade is determined by certain evaluation categories such as attendance, participation, standardized testing, and the like. Moodle can be set up to help make the grading and grade reporting process more standardized, transparent, and efficient. In the following section, we will discuss and demonstrate how to implement grading standards through our Moodle CIMS site via the following two methods:

- Creating a standard grading scale
- Creating a Gradebook template complete with standard graded items

Time for action – creating a standard grading scale

Let's start by first adjusting the site-wide settings for grades on our site to coincide with the scale used in our program. The scale we'll use is a simple 90, 80, 70, 60 scale used in many educational programs as shown:

A → >= 90%

B → >= 80% ~ <90%

C → >= 70% ~ <80%

D → >= 60% ~ <70%

F → < 60%

To change the site-wide grading scale to our scale, follow these steps:

1. From the front page of our site, logged in as admin or a user with administrative permissions, click on the **Grades** link found in the **Site Administration** block. Then click on **Letters** to reveal the default letter grade settings. The default grade letter settings uses pluses and minuses so we will need to change the settings to agree with the scale we are going to use. After entering the new settings, the **Grade letters** screen will look like the following screenshot. Click on **Save changes** when you have finished modifying the settings.

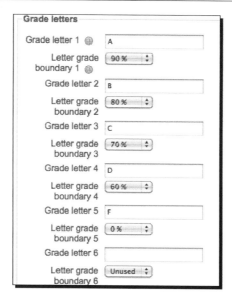

2. To confirm that the settings are working correctly, navigate to any course and click on the **Grades** link found in the **Administration** block. From the **Grader report** window click on the **Choose an action...** pull down menu and select **View** under **Letters**, as shown in the following screenshot:

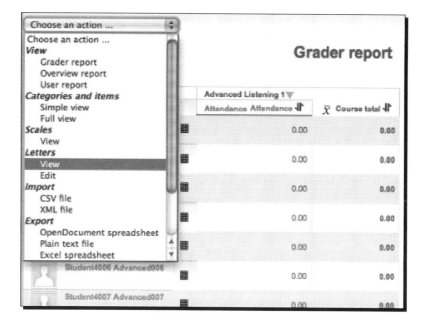

3. You will see the scale we just entered in the site-wide settings, as shown in the following screenshot. Note that in addition to viewing the **Letters** setting, teachers also have the ability to edit this setting. Later in this book, we will discuss how to modify user role permissions. This may be useful if you wish to remove the capability to change the grading scale from the teacher role.

Grade letters

Highest	Lowest	Letter
100.00 %	90.00 %	A
89.99 %	80.00 %	B
79.99 %	70.00 %	C
69.99 %	60.00 %	D
59.99 %	0.00 %	F

What just happened?

We have successfully modified the site-wide settings for the grading scale that is used by the Gradebook within Moodle. This allows us to dictate the default scale that will appear in all courses throughout our Moodle site and thus can help to implement a standardized grading system.

Time for action – creating a Gradebook template

Next, we will set up a Gradebook complete with standardized categories that are used by every teacher in our program. For our example, we will be using *Attendance* and *Final Exam* as categories that are used by every teacher. Grading for these two categories is standardized as follows:

Attendance = 20% of a student's final grade

Final Exam = 40% of a student's final grade

 In this example, the two categories only add up to 60 percent. The remaining 40 percent would be filled by individual teachers with other categories and items such as *Participation*, *Quizzes*, and so on.

1. We will start by first creating the Gradebook template in the template course we used to set up the attendance template. Navigate to the attendance template course (**AT-M-Th-1** in our example) and then click on the **Grades** link found in the **Administration** block. From the **Choose an action...** pull-down menu, select **Full view** found under **Categories and items**. From the subsequent **Edit categories and items: Full view** window, enter the following settings:

  ❑ Change the **Aggregation** method from the pull-down menu to **Weighted mean of grades**.

  ❑ Click on the **Add category** button and add the following two categories (Note, enter the category name and click on **Save changes**. You can ignore the other settings that will appear.):

    ❑ Attendance

    ❑ Final Exam

  ❑ After entering the two categories, make sure that the **Aggregation** method is set to **Weighted mean of grades**. Click on the **Save changes** button at the bottom of the screen, if you make any changes.

  ❑ Move the **Attendance** item inside of the **Attendance** category you just created by clicking on the arrows found on the right side of the screen under **Actions**. See the following double-imaged screenshot for reference:

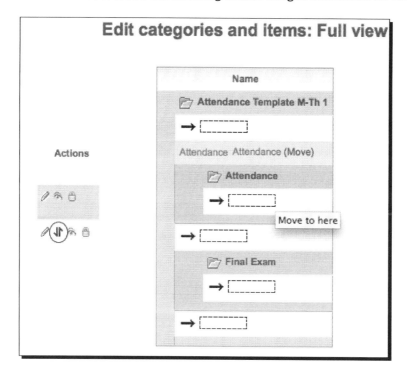

2. Next, we want to create an activity that will serve as a placeholder for our final exam scores. Go back to the front page of your course and, with editing turned on, click on the **Add an activity** drop-down menu and select **Offline activity**, as shown in the following screenshot:

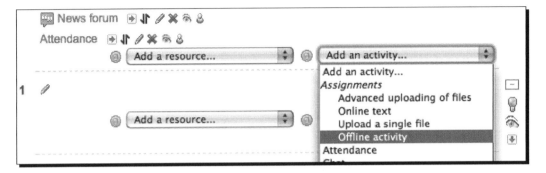

3. Title the activity **Final Exam**, enter a short description, and click on both of the **Disable** tickboxes to disable the availability period. Because this activity is only going to be used as a place to store final exam scores, it does not need to be set to be available to students for any specific time period. For other activities, the availability setting allows you to specify when students will have access to the assignment. Click on **Save and return to course** to create the activity and return to the main page of the course.

4. From the front page of the course, click on **Grades** again and then select **Full view** of **Categories and items** from the **Choose an action...** pull-down menu.

5. You will now see the **Final Exam offline activity** that we just created but it needs to be moved inside the **Final Exam** category. Move it the same way we previously moved the **Attendance** item into the **Attendance** category.

6. Make sure all of the **Aggregation** methods are set to **Weighted mean of grades**.

7. Finally, change the weight for the **Attendance** category to 20 and for **Final Exam** to 40. Note that the **Weight** for the actual items should be set to 100. The following screenshot shows these weighting settings as they should appear once you have finished moving the items to their categories and assigning them weights. Click on **Save changes** to make sure your settings are saved.

Edit categories and items: Full view

Name	Aggregation	Weight	Max grade	Aggregate including subcategories	Drop the lowest	Multiplicator	Offset	Actions	Select
Attendance Template M-Th 1	Weighted mean of grades	-		☐	0	-	-	🖉 ✎ 🗑	All None
Attendance	Weighted mean of grades	20.0000	-	☐	0	-	-	🖉 ✖ ⇅ ✎ 🗑	All None
Attendance Attendance	-	100.0000	100.00	-	-	1.0000	0.0000	🖉 ⇅ ✎ 🗑	☐
x̄ Category total	-		100.00	-	-			🗑 ✎ 🗑	
Final Exam	Weighted mean of grades	40.0000	-	☐	0	-	-	🖉 ✖ ⇅ ✎ 🗑	All None
Final Exam	-	100.0000	100.00	-	-	1.0000	0.0000	🖉 ⇅ ✎ 🗑	☐
x̄ Category total	-		100.00	-	-			🗑 ✎ 🗑	
x̄ Course total	-		100.00	-	-			🗑 ✎ 🗑	

(Save changes)

What just happened?

We have just created a Gradebook template complete with two categories that each contain one graded item. The template will be used to import a pre-formatted standardized Gradebook into other courses throughout our Moodle site.

Time for action – preparing the target course

We are going to be using the **Import** tool from within the target course the same way we did when we imported the attendance activity template. As we must import the attendance module from the template course together with the newly formatted Gradebook, in order to have the Gradebook categories imported correctly, we will need to first delete the **Attendance** activity we have created. Deletion of the **Attendance** activity should be done as follows to ensure that all of its components are removed from the course. Simply deleting the **Attendance** activity from the top of the course is not sufficient. Doing so will not delete the **Attendance Sessions** and **Settings Variables**, which will mean that they will be included in the **Attendance** activity that we are planning to import later. This will create a situation in which we have multiple instances of the same sessions and settings. To make sure this does not happen, follow these steps:

1. Go to the front page of the course we imported the attendance module into (**AdvList1**) and click on the **Attendance** link found at the top of the page.

2. From the **Sessions** tab view, scroll down to the bottom of the page and click on **Select all**. From the **With selected** drop-down menu select **Delete** and then click on the **OK** button to delete the sessions.

3. Next, click on the **Settings** tab and use the red X on the right side of the screen to delete all four of the **Variables**. These will have to be deleted one at a time.

4. Once the **Sessions** and **Settings Variables** have been deleted, go back to the front page of the course and, with editing turned on, click on the red X next to the **Attendance** activity link to delete the activity. (Note, future versions of the attendance module will likely be improved such that simply deleting the instance of the attendance module from the front page of the course will delete all of the attendance-related data from that course. As of October 2010 however, this is not the case, so please make sure to delete everything as outlined in this section.)

What just happened?

The **Attendance** activity has now been completely deleted from the course and we can use the **Import** function again, this time to import the pre-formatted **Attendance** activity, an Offline graded item for Final Exam scores, and a pre-formatted Gradebook.

Time for action – importing the Gradebook template

We are now ready to import the Gradebook template. Because the template now includes not only the Gradebook, but also two activities, the attendance activity and a final exam score placeholder, it is in reality more appropriate to think of this as the standardized component of a course and thus a template course. The import process is virtually the same as the one used for importing the **Attendance** activity.

1. First, click on the **Import** link found in the **Administration** block from the front page of the course.

2. Next, use the **Search courses** field to locate our template course (**AT-M-Th-1**). Select the **Use this course** link from the search results.

3. From the **Import course data** screen, untick the **Forums** box, as the default forum already exists in the target course and we don't want to create another.

4. Click **Continue** to start the import process and then on **Continue** again on the next screen that contains the backup **Note**.

5. Click **Continue** again on the **Import course data** details screen.

6. Click **Continue** on the empty **Import course data** screen.

7. Click **Continue** on the **Import course data** completion screen, which will take you to the course where you can confirm that the attendance module activity has been created and the Final Exam Offline graded item has been added.

8. To confirm that the Gradebook template has been imported to the course, click on the **Grades** link from the **Administration** block and then select **Full view** for **Categories and items** from the **Choose an action...** pull-down menu. The screen you see will be identical to the previous screenshot from the setup in our Gradebook template.

What just happened?

We have just imported the Gradebook, or course, template into another course in our Moodle site and then verified that the import resulted in the creation of two activities, the **Attendance** activity and a final exam placeholder assignment. The import process also set up our Gradebook with two weighted categories with each housing one of the graded items that were imported. This type of process can enable an educational program to set up a standardized evaluation system that is easily implemented, maintained, and monitored.

Have a go hero

Now that you have walked through the process for creating a course and grading template, try importing the template into other courses or be adventurous and design your own template in another new course and try importing it to a different course. Experimentation with this process will likely influence you to come up with additional ideas about template formatting that will best serve your institution.

Implementing a final grade submission process

Most educational institutions have grading policies and procedures that can be incorporated into your Moodle site relatively easily, as we have just observed. Additionally, most institutions require their teachers to submit grades when courses or terms are complete. In recent days, this submission process often includes an online or electronic component in addition to a paper-based component. In these 'dual-submission' systems, the paper-based component usually serves as a backup hard copy. The following is an explanation of one way that Moodle can be utilized in the grade submission process. This method assumes that we have set up Moodle to function as a CIMS, meaning that all courses in a program are created in the Moodle site and students and teachers are properly enrolled in those courses.

The policy

Regardless of whether instructors choose to use the Moodle GradeBook to calculate, and display grades to their students, it can be used to record final grades and provide educational administrators access to those grades. First, the details of the submission process should be determined and this information relayed to instructors. The following policy is an example of such a process:

- Teachers must submit their grades within two weeks of the final day of class.
- Final grades must be recorded in the Moodle Gradebook.
- A hard copy printout, with final grades clearly visible, must be provided in addition to the electronic submission copy. This can be in the form of a screen printout or of a printout of an exported Gradebook format, such as Excel.
- The hard copy format must include:
  - The instructor's printed name and signature
  - The official course name and course number
  - Clearly legible student names and numbers
  - Each student's final grade for the course in both percentage and letter format
- After the grade submission deadline has passed, Teachers will be locked out of their courses for a period of five days as grades are processed.

The process

The policy listed previously is, of course, simply an example of how a grading policy that utilizes Moodle might be presented. The following is an explanation and demonstration of how this policy could be implemented in Moodle.

The first four points from the policy simply require effective transmission of the policy details to teachers and possibly some hands-on training for teachers unfamiliar with Moodle and the Gradebook. The last point refers to locking teachers out of their courses, is the only portion of the policy that requires adjustments be made in Moodle.

The process of implementing this final point within Moodle could range from being very complicated and involved in terms of setup to being very simple and straightforward. The following is an explanation and demonstration of the simple and straightforward method followed by a brief discussion of its limitations and other possible options.

Time for action – locking courses for grade retrieval

The Gradebook cannot actually be locked in a clean, quick, and easy fashion, so we will instead remove the teacher's ability to access the course in order to give us time to extract the grades from the Gradebook, so that they can be transferred to whatever student records management system is in use on our campus. For our example, all Listening courses are offered in the same term and thus have the same ending date. To prevent access to these courses do the following:

1. On the day that falls two weeks beyond the last day of class, we will log in to our site as admin and access the main course page found at `http://oursite.com/course/`. From the course page, click on the **Turn editing on** button and then select the category containing the courses we want to prevent access to. In our example, this is the **Listening** category. Click on the small eye icon next to the **Listening** category to hide this category and all of its contents. The resulting screen will look like the following screenshot with the **Listening** category colored in grey:

    ### Course categories

Course categories	Courses	Edit	Move category to:
Listening	0	✏ ✖ 👁 ⬇	Top
Advanced	5	✏ ✖ 👁 ⬇	Listening
Intermediate	5	✏ ✖ 👁 ⬆ ⬇	Listening
Beginner	5	✏ ✖ 👁 ⬆ ⬇	Listening
Basic	5	✏ ✖ 👁 ⬆	Listening
Speaking	0	✏ ✖ 👁 ⬆ ⬇	Top

2. Click on the **Front Page** link and then the **Front Page settings** link found in the **Site Administration** block on the front page of the site. Scroll down to the bottom of the page and make sure that the **Allow visible courses in hidden categories** box is unticked.

3. Next, we need to modify the permission settings for the editing teacher role in order to prevent teachers from accessing courses that have been hidden. Access the role permissions via the **Site Administration** block by clicking on **Users | Permissions | Define roles**.

4. From the subsequent **Roles** screen, click on the **Teachers** role link and then on **Edit** to view the editing screen for the permissions associated with this role. Change the following two permissions to **Prevent**, as shown in the following screenshot:

   ❑ **Course categories**: **See hidden categories** (Prevent)

   ❑ **Course**: **View hidden courses** (Prevent)

5. Click on the **Save changes** button at the bottom of the screen to save the changes made to the role.

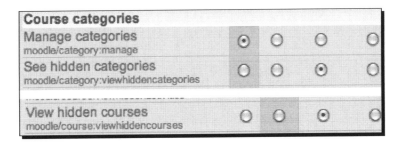

What just happened?

We have just made our Listening courses inaccessible to teachers by making the **Listening** category invisible and by modifying the permissions associated with the teacher role. If you now log in as a user that has the role of a teacher in any of the Listening courses, you will see that the entire **Listening** category and all of its contents have disappeared and both are inaccessible. The category and courses within are however, still intact and accessible to the site admin.

This method of 'locking' courses allows the educational program to suspend access to courses, thereby ensuring that grades will not be modified and thus enables administrators to retrieve grades for use in other systems. The weakness of this method however, is that it does not completely ensure that the grades retrieved from the Moodle system will be the same as those submitted by the teacher on the hard copy format. This is because of the time window allotted to teachers at the end of the course or term. If a teacher, for example, finalizes his or her grades the day after classes have finished and prints out the hard copy for submission at that time, there is still the possibility of a student entering the course and interacting with a graded item that may change his or her grade in the Gradebook. In this scenario, the grades retrieved from Moodle by program administrators could differ from those submitted in hard copy format by the teacher. Development of a **Grade Submission** block is currently being explored and will hopefully be available to the Moodle community soon. This block will allow for a one time electronic submission of grades by the instructor to a location that is not accessible by students. As long as the teacher prints out his or her grades at the same time as submitting them via the block, the possibility of inconsistencies will be eliminated.

Setting up a program-wide testing procedure

Another standard utilized by many educational programs is the test. Many programs administer a standardized test to students and include performance on the test in the student's overall grade for a class or classes within a program. As we set up Moodle to function as a CIMS, we can implement a testing procedure that greatly increases the efficiency of the test administration as well as the grading process.

For our example, all students in **Listening** classes are required to take a program-wide final exam. This final exam is the one that comprises 40 percent of the student's grade as set up in our Gradebook template, introduced earlier in this chapter. The following two examples will cover the two main methods of implementing a program-wide testing procedure of this nature. These are the administration of an exam outside of the Moodle system and the administration of an exam via the Moodle Quiz module.

Time for action – an exam administered outside of Moodle

The first step in setting up a system within Moodle for organizing an exam that is administered outside of Moodle is to create a new course.

1. Click on the **Show all courses** link found at the bottom of the **MyCourses** block and then scroll down to the bottom of the subsequent page and click on **Add a new course**.

2. We will put this example course in the **Miscellaneous** category but you can, of course, place the course wherever you like. Use a course name that clearly defines the course and enter a brief explanation in the **Summary** box. Select **Yes** for the **Is this a meta course?** question and enter an **Enrolment key** to keep users who are not supposed to have access to the course from accessing the course. We are using a meta course here because doing so will allow us to easily enroll students in the course by specifying the child courses that are to be linked to the meta course. For more information about meta courses, please visit the relevant Moodle docs page at `http://docs.moodle.org/en/Meta_course`. The following screenshot provides an example of possible settings for this meta course:

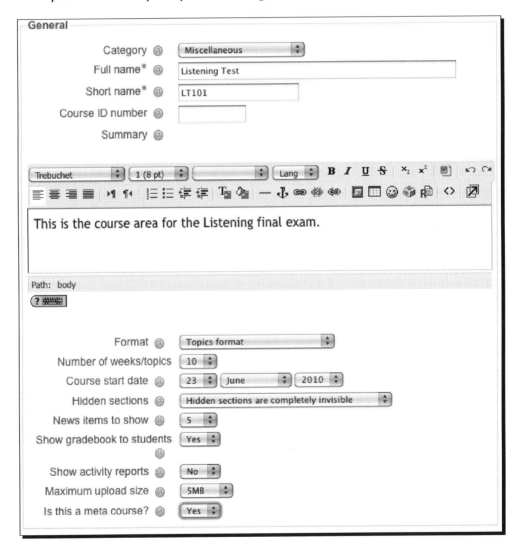

3. Click **Save changes** to create the course and from the following screen, select the courses that are to be specified as **Child courses**. In our example, all students in Listening classes are required to take the test so we have included all of the Listening classes as **Child courses**.

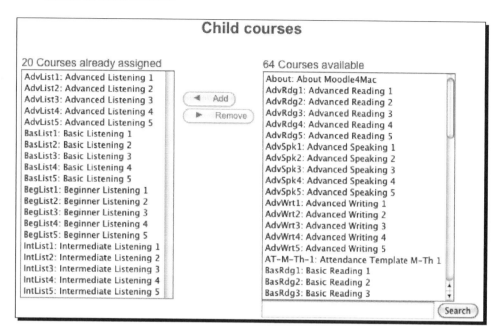

4. Once all of the child courses have been added, click on the course breadcrumb link found at the top-left of the screen. In our example, this is **LT101** as that is the **Short name** we designated for our course, as shown in the screenshot before step 3.

5. Clicking on the **Assign roles** link found in the **Administration** block will reveal that all 500 of our students and 20 teachers have been automatically enrolled in the course from the child courses.

6. Next, click on **Import** and search for our template course. Import all of the contents of the template course, except for the **News forum**, to the Listening test meta course.

7. Once the import is complete, click on the **Attendance** link and delete all but one of the attendance dates. Note, if you see **Hidden sessions**, you may need to change the start date of your meta course to the same date as the template course. You can access and change the start date of the course by clicking on the **Settings** link from inside the course.

8. Now, change the date of the remaining attendance session to the date the exam will be administered.

What just happened?

We now have a meta course that can be used to check in students on the exam day via the attendance module. Additionally, all students eligible to take the test are enrolled in the course and can be exported via the Gradebook. This export can be used to format a file that can then be used to reimport the results of the exam. Simply select the **Export Excel spreadsheet** option from the **Choose an action...** drop-down menu, as shown in the following screenshot:

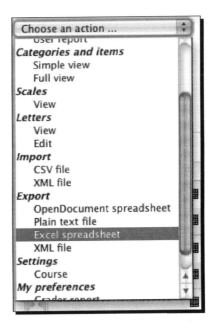

Then download the exported information by clicking on the **Download** button, as shown in the following screenshot:

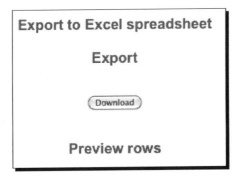

Scores can be merged from the spreadsheet containing the results of the test into the Final **Exam** column and then imported back into the Gradebook via the **Import CSV file** option found in the drop-down menu in the Gradebook. Alternatively, grades for each course could be uploaded directly into the courses for teachers. A more advanced technique would be to set up an automated script that searches for test scores in the meta course and automatically copies the scores into the appropriate location for each user in the child courses. Exploration of this technique will be discussed in *Chapter 7, Advanced Data Access and Display*.

An exam administered via the Moodle quiz module

For a final examination that is actually delivered through the Moodle system, the previous setup can also be used. The only difference will be that the exam will need to be created in or imported to the meta course that will serve as the administration site for the test. As all of the students from child courses are automatically enrolled in the meta course, they will be able to access the quiz module, that will contain the final examination, and take the test. The only difference in working with the test results data via this process is that the scores will already be stored in the Moodle Gradebook. In this case, the advanced option of automatically having scores copied over to the appropriate location in the child courses, that was mentioned in the previous paragraph, is likely one of the best choices for working with the grades.

Summary

In this chapter, you learned how to implement some basic program standards by setting up the attendance module as a standardized module for all courses in an educational program. We also explored standardization of grading through site-wide settings for the Gradebook as well as through the creation of a Gradebook template. This template was used to create a base Gradebook for teachers to build upon, which already contains categories and items that are standardized within the educational program. Towards the end of the chapter, we worked with implementation of a grade submission policy that allows Moodle to function as an electronic grade submission tool. Further development of this process, that will allow for a more precise grade submission system, was introduced and will hopefully be available shortly after this text has been published. Lastly, we discussed and demonstrated how Moodle can be used to organize a program-wide testing process. This chapter has thus taken an additional step in positioning our Moodle site as a CIMS. In the next chapter, we will continue to build upon this system by expanding Moodle's capability to serve as an information portal for an educational program.

5
Enabling your Moodle Site to Function as an Information Portal

Our Moodle site is truly starting to take shape as a CIMS now that we have created course categories, created and enrolled teachers in courses in each of our categories, created student accounts and enrolled students in courses, and finally, set up our site such that it will support and conform to standards adhered to by our institution. It is time now to take a step back from the educational administrator's or teacher's perspective and look at our site from the perspective of the students who will be interacting with it.

Most educational programs present students or, in the case of very young students, their parents or guardians with detailed information about the programs offered. Likewise, most educational programs that are made up of a series of courses almost always deliver those courses and their curriculum, in a somewhat regulated fashion. For example, a student is not allowed to take an advanced math class prior to completing an entry-level course or series of courses. Additionally, many programs that organize their curriculum such that students work toward obtaining certificates and degrees, also provide information to students about required classes they must take, and how many elective courses they may select freely as well as from which category or categories the electives may be chosen.

With minor modification, Moodle can serve as an information portal allowing an institution to efficiently deliver detailed information about its faculty, programs, and curricula to students and their families.

In this chapter, we will explore some of these possibilities through discussion of and experimentation with the following:

- Modifying display settings
- Removing course lists from the category page
- Increasing the detailed summary settings
- Increasing the number of courses displayed in a user's profile
- Expanding content display possibilities
- Installation and use of the Content Pages block
- Customization of third party themes

Modifying display settings

As we have learned so far, Moodle is a very powerful and flexible tool for setting up a Virtual Learning Environment (VLE). As we mold our Moodle site into a CIMS however, we might stumble into a few settings, written into Moodle's core, that we'd like to 'tweak' a little to better enable us to use Moodle to help us manage our curriculum and the information that surrounds it.

Time for action – removing course lists from the category page

The first of these such 'tweaks' is to change how the **Course category** page is displayed. It is important to note that this will involve making a small change to the core Moodle code. This will mean that when you upgrade your Moodle instance to a newer version, you will need to make this adjustment again in the new version. Ideally, you should keep adjustments like this, sometimes called hacks, to a minimum as they can complicate the upgrade process. Always keep a record of the changes you make so that you can easily transfer them to your new instance of Moodle when you upgrade. Additionally, if your adjustment involves a feature that you feel should really be a part of the Moodle core complete with an adjustable setting via the Moodle browser interface, please make the request via the Moodle Tracker found at `http://tracker.moodle.org/secure/Dashboard.jspa`.

To see the page display that we are going to modify, navigate to the following page of the site, that we have built up to this point, found at `http://yoursite.com/moodle19/course/index.php` and you will see a screen similar to the following screenshot:

Course categories

▣ **Listening**
    ▣ **Advanced**
        Advanced Listening 1   🔑 ⊕
        Advanced Listening 2   🔑 ⊕
        Advanced Listening 3   🔑 ⊕
        Advanced Listening 4   🔑 ⊕
        Advanced Listening 5   🔑 ⊕
    ▣ **Intermediate**
        Intermediate Listening 1   🔑 ⊕
        Intermediate Listening 2   🔑 ⊕
        Intermediate Listening 3   🔑 ⊕
        Intermediate Listening 4   🔑 ⊕
        Intermediate Listening 5   🔑 ⊕
    ▣ **Beginner**
        Beginner Listening 1   🔑 ⊕
        Beginner Listening 2   🔑 ⊕
        Beginner Listening 3   🔑 ⊕
        Beginner Listening 4   🔑 ⊕
        Beginner Listening 5   🔑 ⊕
    ▣ **Basic**
        Basic Listening 1   🔑 ⊕
        Basic Listening 2   🔑 ⊕
        Basic Listening 3   🔑 ⊕
        Basic Listening 4

You'll notice, as you scroll down the window, that this list is rather cumbersome due to the fact that all of the courses in each category are being displayed on this page. For our program, we want to display only the categories on this page so we will change the Moodle core settings to accomplish this task through a very simple edit in one Moodle file. Follow these steps to make the change:

1. If you don't already have a text editing program that you are comfortable with, download and install one from the internet. Here are a couple of open source recommendations:

   - Mac OS: TextWrangler (`http://www.barebones.com/products/`)

   - Windows: Notepad++ (`http://notepad-plus-plus.org/`)

2. Open your text editing program and with it then open the `lib.php` file located at the following path: `yourmoodledirectory/course/lib.php`.

3. On or around line 17, you will see the following PHP code:

```
if (!defined('FRONTPAGECOURSELIMIT')) {
define('FRONTPAGECOURSELIMIT',    200); // maximum number of
courses displayed on the frontpage
```

4. Change the 200 to a 1 and save the file.

5. Now refresh the page at `http://yoursite.com/moodle19/course/index.php` and you will see the course listings disappear, as shown in the following screenshot:

Course categories	
Listening	
Advanced	5
Intermediate	5
Beginner	5
Basic	5
Speaking	
Advanced	5
Intermediate	5
Beginner	5
Basic	5
Reading	
Advanced	5
Intermediate	5
Beginner	5
Basic	5
Writing	
Advanced	5
Intermediate	5
Beginner	5
Basic	5
Miscellaneous	4

What just happened?

By changing the 200 to a 1 in the `lib.php` file, we have modified Moodle to display categories only when there is more than one course on the site. In addition to keeping a record of this change somewhere outside of your Moodle site, you may also want to place a comment in the code file using two forward slashes (//), as you see on the line containing the setting we changed. For example, you could add a quick explanation behind the maximum number of courses line to explain that you changed the setting to 1 from the default value of 200. This comment might look like the following code:

```
CODE      // maximum number of courses *changed from 200 to 1
```

Note that the actual code has been replaced with the term CODE in order to keep the text on the same line.

Time for action – increasing the detailed summary setting

Now that we have modified the course category display setting, the categories, and the number of courses they contain, are the only things that can be seen from the **Course category** page. Clicking on a category will display the courses contained within, as shown in the following screenshot:

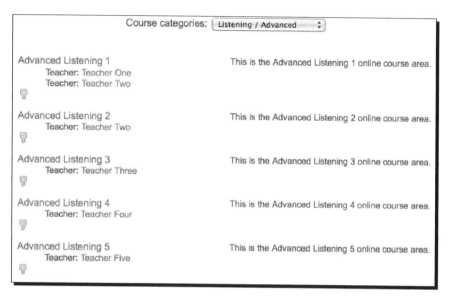

The example provided here is ideal as the listing for each course can contain detailed information about the course, such as the days and times it meets, the location, information about the syllabus, the name and even possibly a picture of the instructor if it is entered through the HTML editor portion of the description setting from within the course. However, a problem arises when we have more than ten courses in a category. In a default Moodle installation, Moodle is set to abbreviate the course descriptions when there are more than ten on a page. The following screenshot shows this abbreviation style with just five courses (this was accomplished by changing a core setting that we will edit shortly):

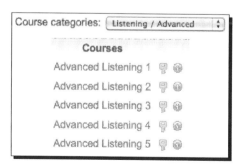

This style is much more efficient in terms of screen space but it does not provide students, who might be considering registering for a course, with enough information about the course, its requirements, the syllabus, the instructor, and so on. To obtain this information, the student must click on i for "information" and view the details in a pop-up window. The need to do so for multiple courses can be quite tedious from the perspective of the student who is browsing the curriculum and designing his or her schedule. We will therefore change the default setting of ten courses per category to a larger number to ensure that the detailed summaries are displayed for all courses when listed inside their categories. To do so, follow these steps:

1. Open your text editor and use it to open the same file that we edited for the previous task found at this path: `yourmoodledirectory/course/lib.php`.

2. On or around line 9, you will see the following code:

   ```
   define('COURSE_MAX_SUMMARIES_PER_PAGE', 10); // courses
   ```

3. Change the `10` to a number high enough to accommodate the maximum number of courses you have in a category. We'll make this `40`. This far exceeds the number of courses we have, or can conceive of, in categories and thus should be more than sufficient.

4. Refresh your screen and, if you had more than 10 courses in a category, you will see a change in how they were displayed. If you are following the tutorial outlined in this book, you will only have five courses per category. To see the abbreviated display style as shown in the previous screenshot, you can change the setting to `1`, save the file, and then refresh your screen. Just don't forget to change it back to a larger number once you have finished experimenting with the setting.

What just happened?

By changing one number in one line of code, we have modified how courses are displayed within categories in order to ensure that more detail is displayed with each course. For an institution that wishes to use Moodle as the primary course registration system, this allows students more comprehensive access to courses without having to view a pop-up window for each course.

Pop quiz

1. Why did we change the setting that controls how many course summaries are listed on a page?

   a. Because we want the list to be as brief as possible.

   b. Because we want the course list to include the instructor and summary information.

c. Because the abbreviated list shows more information than we really need.

d. Because we weren't sure how many courses we would have in each category that we create.

Time for action – increasing the number of courses displayed in a user's profile

The last setting that we will modify for now is the number of courses that are displayed in a user's profile. When you click on a user's name in Moodle, your browser is redirected to the profile page for that user where various details, including the courses the user is enrolled in, are displayed. As a default setting, Moodle will only display 20 courses for a user. If the number of courses a user is enrolled in has exceeded 20, the course list for that user will end with three dots, as shown in the following screenshot. Note, this screenshot shows only one course followed by the three dots. This is a result of the setting we are about to change being set to 1 for the purpose of demonstration.

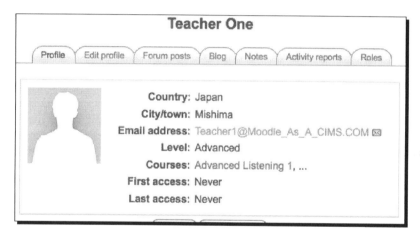

Change the setting from the default of 20 to a higher number by following these steps:

1. Open the following file with your text editor: `yourmoodledirectory/user/view.php`.

2. Look for the following line of code found on or around line 356:

```
if($shown==20) {
```

3. Change the 20 to a higher number such as 40.

4. Save the file and refresh the screen containing a user profile to see the results. If you are following the tutorial outlined in this book, each teacher will only be teaching four classes so the display will not be affected. To see the abbreviated list display style, as shown in the previous screenshot, you can change the setting to 1, save the file, and then refresh your screen. Just don't forget to change it back to a larger number once you have finished experimenting with the setting.

What just happened?

By again changing just one number in one line of code, we changed the setting that governs how many courses are displayed on a user's profile page. The default setting is 20 so we changed the setting to 40 to make sure that all courses will be displayed. This may seem a bit strange, as it is probably unlikely that a user would be teaching or taking more than 20 courses at a time. The reason for wanting to be able to see all courses a user is enrolled in that we will discuss in detail in a later chapter, is that we will be making courses invisible but keeping their enrollment intact and want to make sure that all of the enrollment information is displayed to the site admin via the user profile page.

Expanding content display possibilities

In addition to customizing how Moodle displays course and category information, we want to be able to display information that is not directly linked to any single course. Information about degree or certificate requirements, as mentioned earlier, for example, is something that is frequently provided to students and stakeholders by educational institutions. This information can be included in our Moodle site via the use of a contributed block called Content Pages.

Time for action – installation of Content Pages block

To install the Content Pages block, which will allow us to create web pages that can be accessed by any user viewing our site, whether they are registered users or not, follow these steps:

1. The Content Pages block is not currently a block that is maintained on the Moodle **Modules and Plugins** page although, it may soon be added. First check the **Modules and Plugins** page for the block to see if it is available.

2. If the Content Pages block can be found in the Modules and Plugins database, you should download the most recent package and follow the installation process from step 6 below.

3. If the block cannot be found on the **Modules and Plugins** page, you will need to navigate to the Moodle Tracker site, which can be found from the front page of `http://www.moodle.org` by moving your mouse over the **Development** drop-down menu and then clicking on **Moodle Tracker**, as shown in the following screenshot:

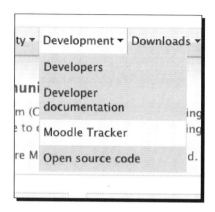

4. From the front page of the Moodle Tracker enter `CONTRIB-1303` in the **Quick Search** field, as shown in the next screenshot, and press enter/return to initiate the search:

5. The result will be a Tracker record for the Content Pages block. The package to download will be the zipped file. As this book goes to press, the newest version is `moodle195-pages-SENT_TRACK-CONTRIB-1303-26Jan2010.zip`. Click on the newest package to download it to your computer.

6. Decompress the zipped package and note that the contents include a folder for each of the following directories:

- admin
- blocks
- lib

7. The admin folder will contain two subdirectories or folders (**roles** and **settings**), each containing PHP files. Locate the target directory/folder in your Moodle directory and first move the file already in your Moodle directory with the same name to a backup location such as your desktop. Then move the contents of each subdirectory from the unzipped package to the appropriate location in your Moodle directory.

8. For the **blocks** folder, there will not be a **page** folder in your **block** directory, so you will only need to copy the contents to the **block** directory in your Moodle directory.

9. Repeat step 8 for the **lib** folder making sure to first copy the existing files to a backup location.

10. Once you have moved all of the Content Pages block components into their appropriate locations, navigate to the front page of your Moodle site logged in as a user with administrative privileges and click on the **Notifications** link. This will initiate the installation process, which entails the creation and set up of the database table that will be used by this block, as shown in the following screenshot:

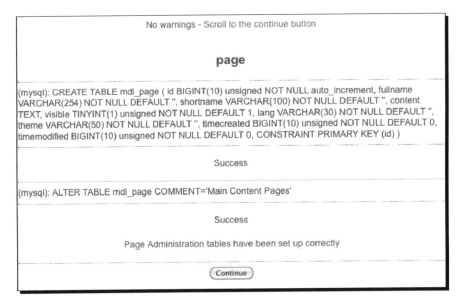

11. Click on the **Continue** button to finish the process and then on the top-left breadcrumb to return to the front page of your site. You will notice a new link in the **Site Administration** block between the **Courses** and **Grades** folders titled **Add/edit pages**, as shown in the following screenshot:

12. Click on the **Add/edit pages** link to view the Content Pages block interface. As we have not yet created any pages with the block, the list will be empty and only a page title and an **Add a new page** button will appear, as shown in the following screenshot:

13. Click on the **Add a new page** button to create a new page. For this example, we will create a page that summarizes our program and its focus. The **Full name** will appear at the top of the page you are creating, so make it something that is suitable as a title. The **Short name** is what will be used in the breadcrumb path so use something that is short but explanatory. Our example is shown in the following screenshot:

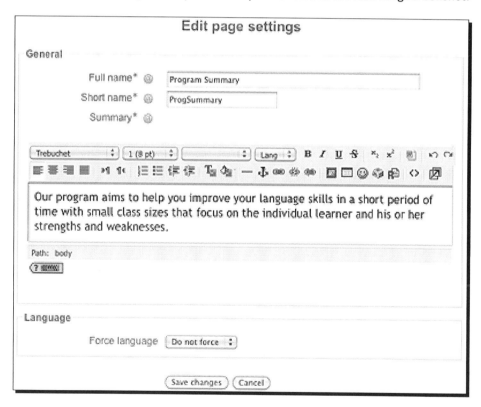

14. Click on the **Save changes** button to create and view the page. Your page will look similar to the following screenshot:

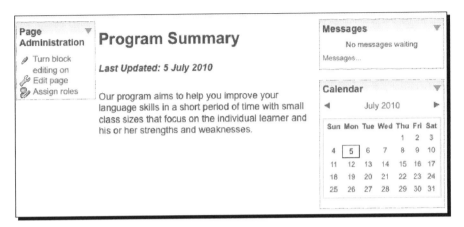

15. If you copy the address that appears in your browser window, log out of your site, and point your browser to that address, you will see that the **Page Administration** block is no longer visible but everything else appears the same.

What just happened?

We have just installed the Content Pages block, which included adding or, in the case of some files, overwriting some files to the Moodle directory. Next we finished the installation process by clicking on the **Notifications** link found in the **Site Administration** block from the front page of our site, which triggered Moodle to install a new table in the database that is used to store page information. Finally, we created a simple test page using the newly installed Content Pages block. The Content Pages block will allow us to create various web pages that can be accessed from the menu bar of the theme that we installed in Chapter 1, *Welcome to Moodle as a Curriculum and Information Management System (CIMS)!* Additionally, web pages can, of course, be added and nested within pages that are linked from the menu bar via the use of links. As mentioned earlier in this chapter, this enables our Moodle site to organize and display information about our educational program to students and other stakeholders such as parents and guardians.

Time for action – customizing the Content Pages block

Although it is not necessary, for the purpose of esthetics, and to again demonstrate how easy it is to customize your site, we are now going to remove the last updated line, center the title, and remove the blocks displayed on the right side of the page. Follow these steps to make these additional changes:

1. With your text editor, open the file found at the following path:
   `yourmoodledirectory/blocks/page/view.php` and comment out the line found on or around line 116. The line is:

   ```
   print_heading("<i>Last Updated: ".userdate($page->timemodified,
   get_string('strftimedate'))."</i>", 'left', 4);
   ```

2. It can be "commented out" by placing two forward slashes at the beginning of the line. After you have added the slashes, save the file and refresh your browser window. You will see that the **Last Updated** message has disappeared.

3. Next, in the same file, on the line just above the line we just commented out, which should be on or around line 115, change the alignment of the heading from left to center, as shown in the following code:

   ```
   print_heading($page->fullname, 'center', 1);
   ```

4. Save the file and refresh your browser window and you will see the heading move to the center of the page.

5. Finally, to remove the blocks shown on the right side of the page, we will need to comment out a small portion of the code found in this same file. Add double forward slashes to the portion used to format the right column of the page found from around lines 124 to 132. The commented out code will look like this:

   ```
   // The right column
   //if (blocks_have_content($pageblocks, BLOCK_POS_RIGHT) ||
   $editing || $PAGE->user_allowed_editing()) {
   //    echo '<td id="right-column">';
   //    print_container_start();
   //    blocks_print_group($PAGE, $pageblocks, BLOCK_POS_RIGHT);
   //    print_container_end();
   //    echo '</td>';
   //}
   //    break;
   ```

6. Save the file again and refresh your browser window and you will see the message and calendar blocks on the right side of the page disappear. The page we just created should now look like the following screenshot:

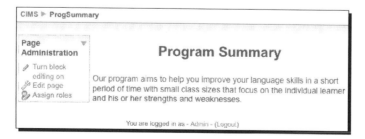

7. Note again here that if you copy the address from your browser address bar, log out of your site, and view the page, the **Page Administration** block does not appear. The administration block is only viewable by the site administrator and will not clutter the window for students and other users.

What just happened?

In order to modify the display settings for the pages we create with the Content Pages block, we opened and edited the `view.php` file found in the `page` directory located in the `blocks` directory that is found inside the `Moodle` directory. The simple modifications we made were to remove a line that provides information about when the page was last edited, as well as to prevent blocks from being displayed on the right side of the screen by commenting out the portion of the code that performs this function. Additionally, we changed a formatting setting to center the page heading instead of having it aligned on the left side of the page. These changes are all very simple and require no detailed knowledge of PHP.

Have a go hero

In the next section of this chapter, we are going to walk through the process of customizing our third-party theme and part of this customization process will require some web pages to link to. So before you move on, take a minute to create seven more pages using the Content Pages block. These pages will be linked to the submenu links that appear when you move your mouse over the **Menu One** title in the menu bar of our Aardvark theme. Get a little creative and add some pictures or graphics to experiment with the types of pages you might create with this block.

Customization of third party themes

In chapter one, we installed a third party theme called Aardvark. One of the reasons for using this theme, as opposed to the default Moodle theme, will now become more apparent as we link some pages to links provided by the drop-down menus that appear on the front page of our site. We will start by customizing the five menu items that appear at the top of the page, as shown in the following screenshot:

Time for action – customizing the menu bar

To change the titles of the menu items shown in the menu bar, follow these steps:

1. With your text editor, open the file found at the following path:

   `yourmoodledirectory/theme/aardvark_pro/aardvark_menu.php`.

2. On or around line 43, change the text **Menu One** to **Listening**, as shown in the following code:

   ```
   <li><div><a href="<?php echo $CFG->wwwroot.'/' ?>">Listening</a>
   ```

3. Save the file and refresh your browser window. You will see **Listening** take the place of the **Menu One** title, just as it appears in the following screenshot:

Using foreign language fonts in the menu bar

If you want to use foreign language menus that contain letters or characters outside of the Latin alphabet, you will need to save the `aardvark_pro.php` file using the UTF-8 character encoding method. Additionally, you'll want to choose the option **No BOM** when you save the file. You may need to experiment with the **BOM (Bit Order Mark)** setting to obtain the result you desire. In the case of Japanese language fonts, for example, saving the file without **No BOM** selected may result in the text for the menus moving down and outside of the black background, as shown in the following screenshot. With TextWrangler, this can be accomplished by clicking on **Options** from within the **Save As** window and selecting the **No BOM** option.

4. Repeat this process for all of the menu titles. Each menu title appears in a line of code that looks like the one provided in step 2. The locations are on or around the following lines in the file:

   - **Menu Two**: Line 64
   - **Menu Three**: Line 85
   - **Menu Four**: Line 106
   - **Menu Five**: Line 126

5. Once you have changed all of the menu titles, save the file and refresh your browser window to see the changes take effect. Our example looks like the following screenshot (note that, I decided to move the **Listening** menu title to the right to make room for a **Program** link):

What just happened?

We just modified the `aardvark_menu.php` file in order to add more descriptive menu titles to the menu bar of our theme. This simple process allows us to categorize each list of links that appear when visitors to the site move their mouse over each menu item.

Time for action – customizing the submenus

Now that we have customized the menu titles, we need to continue by customizing the titles that appear in each box that shows up when we move our mouse over the title. We also need to make sure that each link, the menu title as well as the items that appear in the boxes, points to a page with relevant information. For our example, we will work with the **Program** menu item and its submenu. In its current state, it looks like the following screenshot:

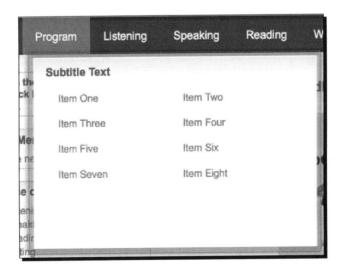

To change the title that appears at the top of the window, as well as the text for the eight items, follow these steps:

1. With your text editor, open the `yourmoodledirectory/theme/aardvark_pro/aardvark_menu.php` file to change the menu bar titles.

2. The text we need to edit can be found between lines 46 and 57. I will change the titles for our example as follows (note that, the line numbers listed are approximate and may vary depending on the version of the file):

   ❑ Line 46: **Subtitle Text: Program Overview**

   ❑ Line 50: **Item One: Curriculum**

   ❑ Line 51: **Item Two: Teachers**

   ❑ Line 52: **Item Three: Textbooks**

   ❑ Line 53: **Item Four: Evaluation**

   ❑ Line 54: **Item Five: Resources**

   ❑ Line 55: **Item Six: Academic Calendar**

   ❑ Line 56: **Item Seven: Tuition**

   ❑ Line 57: **Item Eight: Rules & Regulations**

3. The following is a copy of the lines of code from the `aardvark_menu.php` file after being edited for our example:

```
<h4>Program Overview</h4>
<?php
  $text ='<li><a href="">Curriculum</a></li>';
  $text .='<li><a href="">Teachers</a></li>';
  $text .='<li><a href="">Textbooks</a></li>';
  $text .='<li><a href="">Evaluation</a></li>';
  $text .='<li><a href="">Resources</a></li>';
  $text .='<li><a href="">Academic Calendar</a></li>';
  $text .='<li><a href="">Tuition</a></li>';
  $text .='<li><a href="">Rules & Regulations</a></li>';
```

4. After changing the titles, save the file and refresh your browser window. Move your mouse over the **Program** menu item to activate the submenu window and observe the changes that have been made. The following is a screenshot of our example:

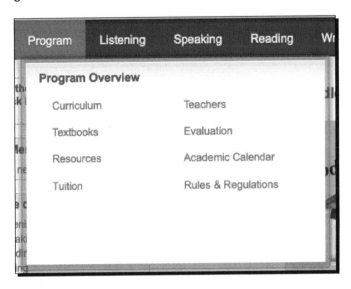

What just happened?

We have just changed the titles of the submenu items that appear when you move your mouse over the **Program** heading, which we changed earlier. For our example program, these submenu links will lead us to pages that we created with the Content Pages block. This will allow us to provide access to various types of information about our educational program from the front page of our Moodle site.

Time for action – adding links to the submenu items

The final step in this process is to add link destinations for all of the menu items that appear as links. This includes the eight items that appear in the submenu window as well as the **Program** and other menu items in the menu bar. Links to pages we have created with the Content Pages block as well as to any other location in your Moodle site or to an external site are possible. To insert the links, follow these steps:

1. With your text editor, again open the file we just edited found at
   `yourmoodledirectory/theme/aardvark_pro/aardvark_menu.php`.

2. Add links to the code from approximately lines 43 to 57 as shown in the following code snippet. For the submenu items, adding a link is as simple as copying and pasting a link between the quotation marks that appear after the `href=` code. One simple way to copy a link is by navigating to the desired page with your browser and copying the link from the address bar. To add a link to the menu item, remove all of the code found between the quotation marks and enter your link. Here is the code after adding all of our links. (Note, I have used only links to pages created via the Content Pages block but you can add any link here. Also note that the address contains `//localhost:8888/moodle19...` This is specific to the Mac OS MAMP package. If you are using XAMPP on Mac or Windows, the address will not contain 8888.)

```
<li><div><a href="http://localhost:8888/moodle19/blocks/page/view.
php?id=1">Program</a>
   <ul>
   <h4>Program Overview</h4>
   <?php
$text ='<li><a href="http://localhost:8888/moodle19/blocks/page/
view.php?id=2">Curriculum</a></li>';
$text .='<li><a href="http://localhost:8888/moodle19/blocks/page/
view.php?id=6">Teachers</a></li>';
$text .='<li><a href="http://localhost:8888/moodle19/blocks/page/
view.php?id=3">Textbooks</a></li>';
$text .='<li><a href="http://localhost:8888/moodle19/blocks/page/
view.php?id=7">Evaluation</a></li>';
$text .='<li><a href="http://localhost:8888/moodle19/blocks/page/
view.php?id=4">Resources</a></li>';
$text .='<li><a href="http://localhost:8888/moodle19/blocks/page/
view.php?id=8">Academic Calendar</a></li>';
$text .='<li><a href="http://localhost:8888/moodle19/blocks/page/
view.php?id=5">Tuition</a></li>';
$text .='<li><a href="http://localhost:8888/moodle19/blocks/page/
view.php?id=9">Rules & Regulations</a></li>';
```

3. Once you have entered all of the links, save the file and refresh your browser window. Move your mouse over the first menu item and click on one of the links to verify that the links are functioning as desired.

4. Note, the links entered in the previous code are from a series of pages created via the Content Pages block. Viewing the pages from the Content Pages administration page, which is accessible via the **Add/edit pages** link found in the **Site Administration** block, will provide you with a quick and easy way to access each page and copy its link from your browser address bar so you can then paste it into the `aardvark_menu.php` file. Our page list appears, as shown in the following screenshot:

What just happened?

We have just added link destinations to all of the submenu items that appear under the **Program** heading in the menu bar of our Aardvark theme. For our example, we used pages that were created by the Content Pages block but you could, of course, use any web page address desired.

Time for action – adjusting the display style of the Content Pages admin block

It is necessary to make note here of one additional small adjustment that should be made to correct a minor block formatting issue that appeared when we removed the blocks from the right side of the page by editing a file in the Content Pages block package. Under the following conditions, you will notice that when viewing a page created by the Content Pages block, the **Page Administration** block is being resized to take up half of the width in your page:

1. You are logged in as admin.

2. The information you have entered in the page does not take up much horizontal space.

3. You are using the Aardvark theme (note, depending on how they are styled, other themes may have the same display issue).

4. The following screenshot demonstrates this formatting issue and, while it is only visible when logged in as admin, it is nice to fix it as, in some cases, it will better enable you to see what your page is going to look like to other users without having to logout of your site and view the page:

5. To correct this display issue, follow these simple steps:

   ❑ With your text editor, open the file located at the following path: /yourmoodledirectory/theme/aardvark_pro/aardvark.css.

   ❑ On or around lines 62 to 65, you will see settings that control how the left column is formatted. Add a line containing width:150px; after the following lines:

```
#layout-table #left-column{
vertical-align:top;
padding-left:4px;
padding-right:0px;
```

6. Save the file and refresh your browser window while viewing a page created with the Content Pages block. If you were experiencing the issue shown in the previous screenshot, you will see the **Page Administration** block being resized to roughly the width of the longest item it contains, as shown in the following screenshot. If you prefer to have the **Page Administration** title on one line, increase the width pixel setting until you achieve the desired result.

What just happened?

In order to make sure that the width of the **Page Administration** block is constant and does not expand to take up a large portion of the window, we also made a small adjustment to the CSS (Cascading Style Sheet) file in our theme in order to control the size of the **Page Administration** block. This fixed a minor cosmetic issue that was apparent when we logged into our site as a user with administrative permissions and viewed a page that we created with the Content Pages block that did not have a large amount of text.

Have a go hero

Now it's your turn! Plan out a scheme for the types of information that you'd like to have accessible from the front page of your Moodle site. Make pages with the Content Pages block and link them to the menu items available in the menu bar. Provide links to courses in your Moodle site or to other websites hosted by your institution or to other websites relevant to your program. As you implement this plan using the menu bar and Content Pages block, your Moodle site will begin to stand even more strongly as a CIMS.

Time for action – customizing the logo

One last thing that we should customize before finishing up this chapter is the logo that appears at the top of the front page. In *Chapter 1, Welcome to Moodle as a Curriculum and Information Management System (CIMS)!*, we added a graphic to the topic section that appears at the top of the front page, but we may want to use that area for other purposes and as there is already space at the top of the page allocated for a logo, it only makes sense to add our school or program logo there. To change the Aardvark logo, follow these steps:

1. Navigate to the following location: `yourmoodledirectory/theme/aardvark_pro/images/header`.

2. In the header directory, you will see an image file entitled `logo.png`.

3. Replace this file with the image that you want to appear at the top of your page. Make sure that you use the same, or similar, dimensions as the default image to ensure that your image is formatted correctly in the header area of the theme. Opening and editing the `logo.png` image is one way to accomplish this or, if you already have an image or logo that you wish to use, you may need to reduce its size to a height of not more than 100 pixels.

4. The following screenshot is of a simple image created for this demonstration as it appears on the front page after being placed inside the header directory:

What just happened?

Through the very simple process of simply replacing one image with another that is given the same name, we modified the Aardvark theme header image. You can replace this image with another at any time using this process and only need to remember to make sure that the dimensions are appropriate to allow the image to be displayed properly.

Summary

In this chapter, we have moved our Moodle site forward as a CIMS by first making small changes to three core file settings in order to modify the way categories are displayed, the way courses are displayed within categories, and to modify how many courses are displayed in a user's profile. These simple modifications enable us to better present a curriculum in a fashion that makes it easy to navigate and understand. We then installed the Content Pages block and set up several web pages inside our Moodle site with the block. Finally, we edited our third-party theme, Aardvark, in order to make the web pages we created easily accessible from the front page of our site. All of these tasks were performed with the purpose of adding an information 'skin' to our Moodle site that allows it to not only function as a VLE but also as an information portal for our educational program. In the next chapter, we will move inside the Moodle system and explore various methods for monitoring student access to the site and reporting on various activities for the purposes of communication, evaluation, and research.

6
Customized Roles

Educational programs usually track students' progress on a macro level via the use of evaluative tools such as tests, individual course grades, and more frequently, cumulative grade averages through the use of Grade Point Averaging systems. In addition to being able to record, and thus track this type of information in your Moodle site, it is also possible to monitor student access and activity at a micro level. We can, for example, determine how often a student logs into the site, what time of day he or she most frequently logs into the site, and what he or she does while logged in.

We will explore various methods for monitoring and reporting on student access and performance in the Moodle site.

While there are numerous methods for accessing the wealth of information that is stored within the Moodle database, in this chapter, we will focus on methods that are easy to set up and use but that do however, provide detailed information. In this chapter, we will be:

- Creating and demonstrating the use of a censored student role
- Creating and explaining how to use an assistant administrator role
- Creating and explaining the use of an administrative monitor role
- Creating and discussing the use of a mentor, advisor, or parental monitoring role

Permissions and roles

We referenced system roles earlier when we talked about enrolling users in courses as **students**, or when other users were enrolled in courses as **teachers**, and also each time you are directed to log in to your site as **admin**. These roles (student, teacher, and admin) are three of the seven default roles that exist in a default installation of Moodle. From the front page of your site, click on the **Define roles** link found in the **Site Administration** block inside the **Users** and then **Permissions** directories, as shown in the following screenshot:

The seven default roles, as shown in the following screenshot, are **Administrator**, **Course creator**, **Teacher**, **Non-editing teacher**, **Student**, **Guest**, and **Authenticated user**. Each of these roles has an extended set of permission settings, also known as capabilities, that control what each user assigned with each specific role is allowed to do within different areas of the site, also known as contexts.

Roles

Name	Description	Short name	Edit
Administrator	Administrators can usually do anything on the site, in all courses.	admin	✎ ✖ ⬆
Course creator	Course creators can create new courses and teach in them.	coursecreator	✎ ✖ ⬆ ⬇
Teacher	Teachers can do anything within a course, including changing the activities and grading students.	editingteacher	✎ ✖ ⬆ ⬇
Non-editing teacher	Non-editing teachers can teach in courses and grade students, but may not alter activities.	teacher	✎ ✖ ⬆ ⬇
Student	Students generally have fewer privileges within a course.	student	✎ ⬆ ⬇
Guest	Guests have minimal privileges and usually can not enter text anywhere.	guest	✎ ⬆ ⬇
Authenticated user	All logged in users.	user	✎ ⬆

(Add a new role)

Click on one of the role names to view the permission settings for the role. For example, clicking on the **Teacher** role will reveal a long list of permission settings, which define the capabilities associated with that particular role, the top of which looks like the following screenshot:

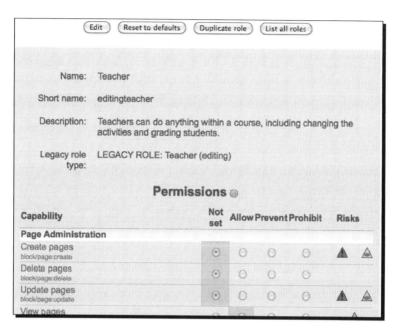

Each permission can be assigned one of the four settings, which include **Not set**, **Allow**, **Prevent**, and **Prohibit**. **Allow** and **Prevent** are self-explanatory and will result in either allowing the user to perform the action listed or preventing him or her access to it. **Not set** is a little more vague however, and simply means that the capability is prevented for that role but if the user has multiple roles and is allowed access to that capability with a different role in the same context, then he or she will be able to perform that action. For example, if a user is assigned the role of both student and teacher in a course and an action is set to **Not set** for the student role but to **Allow** for the teacher role, the user will be able to perform the action in that specific course because the capability is an Allowed capability for the teacher role. If the same user is enrolled in a different course as a student only, however, he or she will not be able to perform the action in that course because the only role the user has in that course context is the student role. **Prohibit** is a setting that is similar to **Not set**, but that allows you to restrict access to an action that cannot be overridden by other roles, except for the Admin role. Outside of possibly using this to prevent specific users from actively participating in forums and other activities, it will probably rarely be used with existing roles.

Creating a censored student role

We are going to start with a role that prohibits a student, or any user assigned the role, from posting new information of any type in a course or the entire site, depending upon how the role is assigned. This role could be used to temporarily silence a student who has posted inappropriate material, information, or the like, to the site.

Time for action – creating and using a censored student role

To set up a role that will prevent users to whom it is assigned from posting content to courses and possibly the front page of the site, and then assign the role, follow these steps:

1. Log in to your site as admin and click on the **Define roles** link found by clicking on **Users** and then **Permissions** from inside the **Site Administration** block, as explained earlier in this chapter.

2. From the **Roles** screen, click on the **Student** role.

3. From the **View role details** screen, click on the **Duplicate role** button (shown in the following screenshot):

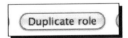

4. Click the **Yes** button on the confirmation message that will appear (shown in the following screenshot) to duplicate the role:

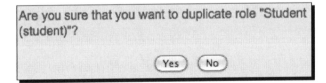

5. After clicking **Yes** to duplicate the role, you will be returned to the **Roles** screen and will see the new role, titled **Student copy 1**, at the bottom of the list of roles. Click on the **Student copy 1** link to view the details of the role.

6. From this **View role details** screen, click on the **Edit** button (shown in the following screenshot) to access the role editing screen:

7. From the **Edit role** screen, enter a **Name**, **Short name**, and **Description** for the new role. An example is provided in the following screenshot:

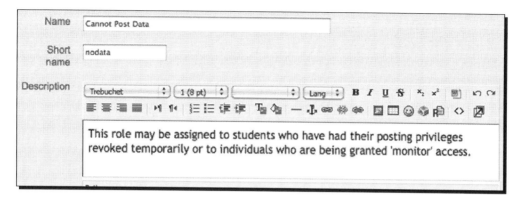

8. Scroll down through the **Permissions**. Change the settings from **Allow** to **Prohibit** for every setting that involves posting information on the site. The following is a list that will need to be changed for a default instance of Moodle. If you have installed third-party blocks or modules that allow students to post data to the site, you will need to change the settings for those as well.

- **Chat—Access a chat room**: Prohibit
- **Database—Write comments**: Prohibit
- **Database—Write entries**: Prohibit
- **Forum—Create attachments**: Prohibit
- **Forum—Reply to posts**: Prohibit
- **Forum—Start new discussions**: Prohibit
- **Glossary—Create comments**: Prohibit
- **Glossary—Create new entries**: Prohibit
- **Wiki—Edit wiki pages**: Prohibit

9. Note that many **Allow** settings have been left untouched. The majority of these are settings that allow a student to view content and activities. Some however, are settings that allow students to post content to the site. Most of these, such as the **Assignment—Submit assignment** setting, allow the student to post information that is only viewable by users with the role of teacher or higher. For this reason, we will keep these permissions set to **Allow** even for censored students.

10. When all of the settings have been adjusted, scroll to the bottom of the screen and click on the **Save changes** button.

11. The newly edited role, with its new name, description, and short name, will appear at the bottom of the list.

12. Now, navigate to a course to put the role to use. We'll use the **Advanced Listening 1** course from the site we have built up to now for this example. As shown in the following screenshot, from your **MyCourses** block, click on the plus sign to expand the **Listening** folder, then on the plus again to expand the **Advanced** folder, and then on the **AdvList1** short name link to navigate to the course.

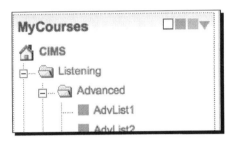

13. Before we assign the role to a student, that we want to prohibit from posting any public information to the course, we should create an activity that allows students to post to in order to be able to better demonstrate how the role functions. Click on the **Turn editing on** button found at the top-right of the page and then from the **Add an activity** drop-down menu, select **Forum**, as shown in the following screenshot:

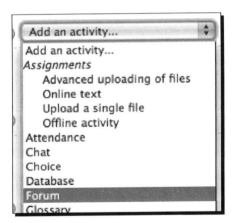

14. Give the forum a simple **Name** such as Test Forum and a simple **Forum introduction** such as Post a comment if you are able. Use the default values for all of the other settings and scroll to the bottom of the page and click on the **Save and return to course** button to create the forum.

15. There are several methods of confirming that the role functions as intended. The fastest and easiest method is to simply use the **Switch role to...** drop-down menu found at the top of the window on the right side next to the **Turn editing on** button, as shown in the following screenshot:

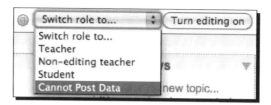

16. Change your role to **Student** and view the forum that was just created by clicking on the activity link, **Test Forum** for our example, to confirm that a student is allowed to **Add a new discussion topic**. Now click on the **Return to my normal role** button found at the top-right of the screen as shown in the next screenshot:

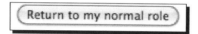

17. Next, change your role to the new role we created, **Cannot Post Data** in our example, as shown in the following screenshot, and then view the **Test Forum** by clicking on the activity link.

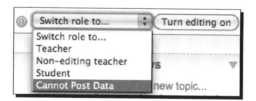

18. You will now see that the **Cannot Post Data** role is not allowed to **Add a new discussion topic** as the button does not appear at all in the forum area.

What just happened?

We have just created a new role copied from the student role and limited the permissions allocated to that role using the **Prohibit** permission setting. This allowed us to create a role that can be assigned to students who, for whatever reason, we want to prevent from posting any information in the form of text or uploaded files to all public areas within a course. We left the capability to post information to some modules in which the posts are only viewable by the teacher but we could opt to prohibit those as well if desired. After creating the role, we checked to see that it is functioning via the **Switch role to...** pull-down menu.

Have a go hero

We did a quick check of this role when logged into our site as admin, but to really get a feel for how it's going to work, try the following on your own. Add a forum to a selected course that students can post to. Pick two students that are enrolled in a course and log in as each student and post a short message in the forum. Then log back in as admin and assign the **Cannot Post Data** role to one of the students. Now, log in as that student and observe the permission changes. Note here that, because we used the **Prohibit** permission setting, you didn't have to remove the student's student role and only had to add the new role.

Assistant administrator role

Another role that can be very useful is an administrator role with limited permissions. This type of role can be used to assign specific capabilities to a user who will be performing administrative tasks via the site. As has been the case throughout this book, the term administrator is being used to describe an individual who works in a clerical function within an educational program. Such educational administrators might be, for example, checking attendance records or aggregating grade data for a series of classes during a given period.

Time for action – creating and using an assistant administrator role

For the example here, we will create a role that is allowed to do the following:

- Post and edit news items on the front page of the site
- Edit and add new pages via the **Content Pages** block

This role might be assigned to a program secretary or any other individual responsible for disseminating information relevant to a program to teachers and students within the program. To set up and assign the role, follow these steps:

1. Log in to your site as admin and click on the **Define roles** link found by clicking on **Users** and then **Permissions** from inside the **Site Administration** block, as explained earlier in this chapter.

2. From the **Roles** page, click on the **Add a new role** button, as shown in the following screenshot:

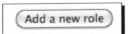

3. Enter a **Name**, **Short name**, and **Description** for the role and change all of the capability settings for **Page Administration** to **Allow**, as shown in the following screenshot:

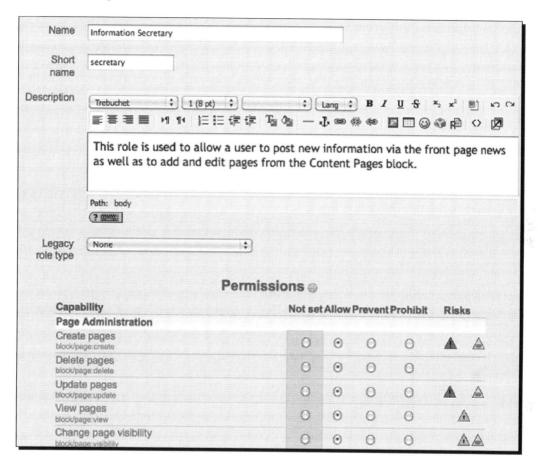

4. Scroll down the **Permissions** page to the **Forum** heading and also change the following permissions to **Allow**, as shown in the following screenshot:

    ❑   **Add news**

    ❑   **Create attachments**

    ❑   **Delete any posts (anytime)**

    ❑   **Edit any post**

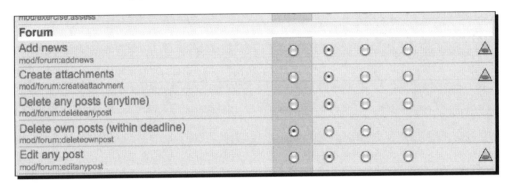

5. Scroll to the bottom of the page and click on the **Add a new role** button, as shown in the following screenshot:

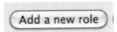

What just happened?

We have just created a new role and enabled the capabilities within the role that will allow users who are assigned the role to post information to the news forum on the front page of the site as well as to add and edit content pages created with the content pages block we installed in *Chapter 5, Enabling your Moodle Site to Function as an Information Portal.*

Time for action – testing the role

We should now test the role to confirm that it functions as desired. Once we have confirmed that the role allows users, who it has been assigned to, to post new news information and add and edit pages via the **Content Pages** block, we will be ready to assign it to users in our system. To test the role, follow these steps:

1. Choose a user that is to function as the **Information Secretary**. For our example, we will use teacher1.

2. First, log out as admin and log back in as teacher1 to verify that the user is not allowed to post news items or to modify or add content pages. You can log in as teacher1 by using `teacher1` as the username and `1234` as the password, if you have followed all of the examples for creating our sample site to this point. The following screenshot shows the front page, as Teacher One would see it.

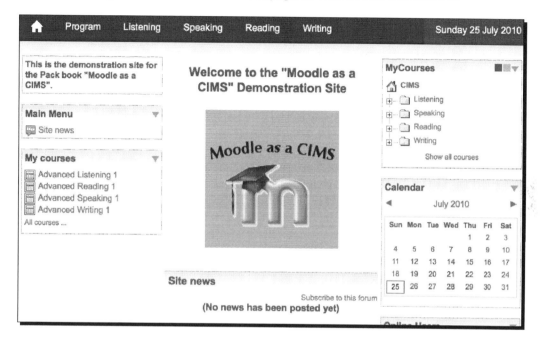

3. Notice that this user has no access to the site news or to any of the pages created by the **Content Pages** block.

4. Now we will add the role and assign it to Teacher One. Log out of the site and back in as admin.

5. Click on **Assign system roles** from the **Site Administration** block, as shown in the following screenshot:

6. From the **Assign roles in System** screen, click on the **Information Secretary** role, as shown in the following screenshot:

Assign roles in System ⊚

WARNING! Any roles you assign from this page will apply to the assigned users throughout the entire system, including the front page and all the courses.

Roles	Description	Users	
Administrator	Administrators can usually do anything on the site, in all courses.	1	- Admin -
Course creator	Course creators can create new courses and teach in them.	0	
Teacher	Teachers can do anything within a course, including changing the activities and grading students.	0	
Non-editing teacher	Non-editing teachers can teach in courses and grade students, but may not alter activities.	0	
Student	Students generally have fewer privileges within a course.	0	
Guest	Guests have minimal privileges and usually can not enter text anywhere.	0	
Cannot Post Data	This role may be assigned to students who have had their posting privileges revoked temporarily or to individuals who are being granted 'monitor' access.	0	
Information Secretary	This role is used to allow a user to post new information via the front page news as well as to add and edit pages from the Content Pages block.	0	

7. From the next **Assign roles in System** screen that will look like the following screenshot, enter **teacher1** in the search field, search for the user and enroll the user by clicking once on the appropriate name from the search results in the box on the right side of the window and then clicking on the **Add** button to add the user to the box on the left of the screen. The following screenshot shows that **Teacher One** has been selected to be assigned the role of **Information Secretary**.

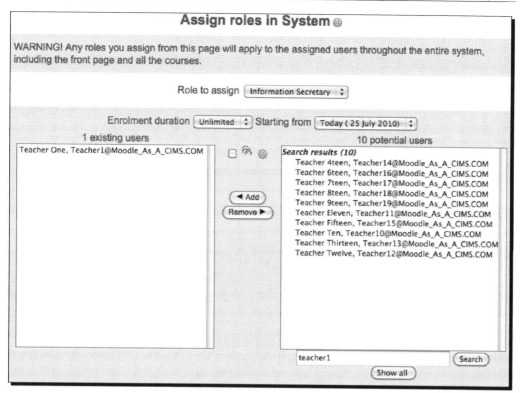

8. Finally, click on the **Assign roles in System** button found at the bottom of the page. You will now see that one user has been assigned the **Information Secretary** role.

9. To verify the role permissions, log out of the site and then back in as teacher1. You will now see that this user is allowed to add news items by clicking on the **Add a new topic** button and is also able to manage pages via the **Add/edit pages** link found in the **Site Administration** block that now appears, as shown in the following screenshot:

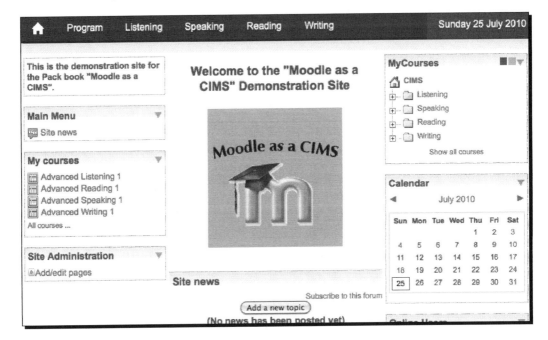

What just happened?

We just successfully created a new role that was designed to allow a user to post and edit news posts on the front page of the site and to also edit and create new pages via the **Content Pages** block. This role was then assigned to one of the teacher accounts in our test site in order to demonstrate its functionality. This would be an ideal role to assign to someone who is responsible for relaying information to anyone who views the site.

Administrative monitor role

In many educational programs, there is a need to be able to monitor, from time to time, the activities taking place in classrooms throughout the program. This task may be accomplished via classroom observation or through the administration of survey questionnaires. In a program that has a strong online component, this task can also be accomplished through the creation and use of a monitor or surveyor role.

Time for action – creating and using an administrative monitor role

This is a very easy role to create and provides the user with extensive monitoring capabilities. We will outline two different methods of assigning this role. One will grant view-only access to all courses on the site and the other will grant the same access to all courses within one category. To set up and assign the role, follow these steps:

1. Log in to your site as admin and click on the **Define roles** link found by clicking on **Users** and then **Permissions** from inside the **Site Administration** block, as explained earlier in this chapter.

2. Click on the **Add a new role** button to start the creation process and enter a **Name**, **Short name**, and **Description**, as shown in the following screenshot:

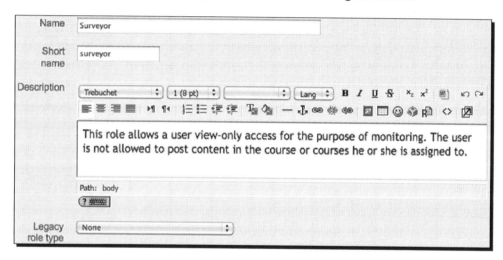

3. Scroll down the **Permissions** list to the **Course** heading and change the **View courses** setting (shown in the following screenshot) to **Allow**.

4. Scroll down to the bottom of the page and click on the **Add a new role** button to finish the role creation process.

What just happened?

We have just created a new role and given it the capability to view courses by changing the **Permission** setting to **Allow**. This will enable users with this role to view courses in our Moodle system.

Time for action – assigning and testing the role

Now, to assign the Surveyor role to a user, we will follow the same process as outlined earlier. Follow these steps:

1. From the front page of your site, click on the **Users** link found in the **Site Administration** block, then on **Permissions**, and finally on **Assign system roles**.

2. Click on the **Surveyor** role to open the **Assign roles in system** window. For this example, we will assign the **Surveyor** role to teacher2 so enter teacher2 in the search window and click on the **Search** button. From the **Search results** window, click once on **Teacher Two** and then select the hidden assignment tickbox found next to the eye icon. This will prevent the user from appearing in the **Participants** list that is viewable from within each course.

3. Click on the **Assign roles in System** button to finish the role assignment process. The following screenshot is of the hidden assignment explained here:

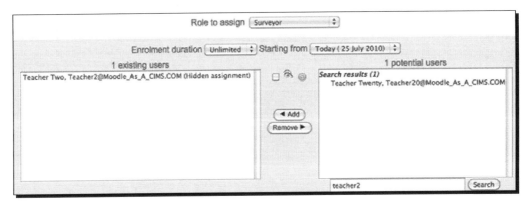

4. You will see now, from the **Assign roles in System** screen, that you have assigned one user, **Teacher Two**, to the **Surveyor** role, as shown in the following partial screenshot:

Information Secretary	This role is used to allow a user to post new information via the front page news as well as to add and edit pages from the Content Pages block.	1	Teacher One
Surveyor	This role allows a user view-only access for the purpose of monitoring. The user is not allowed to post content in the course or courses he or she is assigned to.	1	Teacher Two

5. Log out of your site and then back in as Teacher Two. Use `teacher2` as the username and `1234` as the password if you have followed the site setup to this point. You will see that Teacher Two is now able to access all courses on the site. Note that Teacher Two retains teacher permissions for courses that were already assigned to Teacher Two. For all other courses, this teacher, functioning as **Surveyor**, can only view content.

6. Next, let's explore one other option for assigning the **Surveyor** role. Log in to your site as admin (log out as Teacher Two first if necessary) and navigate to the **Assign system roles** page, as explained at the beginning of this *Time for action* section.

7. Click on the **Surveyor** role link and remove the role assignment for Teacher Two by clicking once on the assignment and then clicking on the **Remove** button.

8. Now navigate back to the front page of your site and click on the **Listening** category link from the **MyCourses** block. You will be presented with the **Course categories** screen for the **Listening** category, which displays the **Sub-categories**, as shown in the following screenshot:

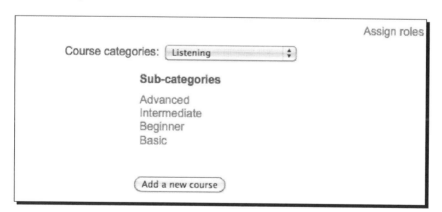

9. Click on the **Assign roles** link found in the upper-right area of the window. As a result, you will see the **Assign roles in Category: Listening** window. Scroll down and click on the **Surveyor** role to open the next **Assign roles in Category: Listening** window, as shown in the following screenshot. Enter `teacher2` in the search window and click the **Search** button to find Teacher Two. Click once on **Teacher Two** and once again click the hidden assignment tickbox and then the **Add** button to assign the role, as a hidden assignment, to this teacher.

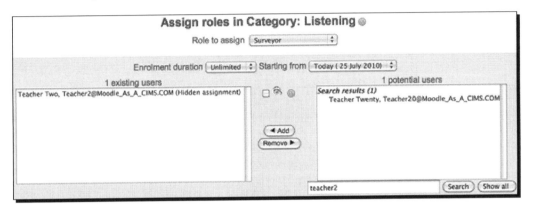

10. Finally, to check this assignment, log out of the site as admin and then back in as **Teacher Two**. Notice now that **Teacher Two** is able to view content for all courses in the **Listening** category only.

What just happened?

In this section, we created an administrative monitoring role, that we titled **Surveyor**. This role enables a user, who is assigned the role, to view all content in a course but not to post or interact in the course in any way. We then experimented with two different methods of assigning the role. First we assigned the role system-wide, thereby allowing the user to view all courses and then deleted the assignment and assigned the role to a specific category, which limited the surveyor's access to courses within that category.

Have a go hero

As you have most likely already realized, there are a variety of different methods for assigning roles. Try experimenting with several different role assignment methods, such as assignment to a single course and to one or more categories to get a feel for how you might use role assignments for some of the special roles you create.

The Mentor, Advisor, and Parental Monitor role

The final customized role that we will cover in this chapter is that of the Mentor, Advisor, or Parental Monitor. The permissions for the role will be identical, but you may choose to change the name depending on how the role is used. If, for example, you wish to set up a role that enables parents to monitor their child's activities within the site, the Parental Monitor role title is appropriate. You may wish to set up the same role for a mentoring or advisee system and thus use a different title.

Time for action – creating and using the Parental Monitor role

For this example, we are going to use the Parental Monitor role title. To set up and use this role, which will allow parents to monitor their child's activity, follow these steps:

1. Log in to your site as admin and click on the **Define roles** link found by clicking on **Users** and then **Permissions** from inside the **Site Administration** block, as explained earlier in this chapter.

2. Click on the **Add a new role** button to open the **Add a new role** window and enter a **Name**, **Short name**, and **Description**, as shown in the following screenshot:

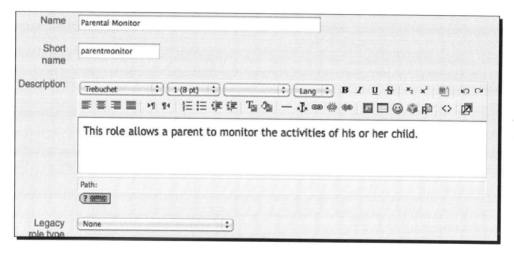

3. Set the following **Permissions** to **Allow**:

    ❑ **System**: Edit own user profile

    ❑ **Users**: Edit user profile

    ❑ **Users**: See all user blogs

    ❑ **Users**: See all user posts

    ❑ **Users**: See user activity reports

4. After changing the permission settings, scroll to the bottom of the page and click on the **Add a new role** button.

What just happened?

We have just created a role that will be assigned to a parent allowing the parent to view some of the activities his or her child is participating in on the Moodle site. In the next section, we'll demonstrate the role to show what it is capable of and where it is limited in terms of allowing a parent to monitor his or her child.

Time for action – creating a new account and assigning the role to it

Now that we have created the role, we are going to assign it to a parent user through the parent's child's profile page. First, however, let's quickly create a new user account for the parent so we have a user account that is not already assigned as a teacher or student in other courses. Follow these steps:

1. From the front page of your course, click on the **Users** link found in the **Site Administration** block. Then click on the **Accounts** link and finally the **Add a new user** link. Fill in information for the fields labeled with red text and an asterisk, scroll to the bottom of the page and click on the **Update profile** button to create the new user. We are going to assign the Parental Role to student 5 and thus opted to name the parent `Parent5`. An example of our parent account is shown in the following screenshot.

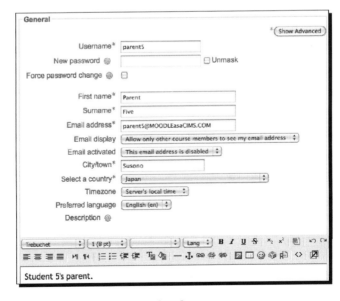

2. Once the new parent account has been created, navigate to the front page of your site and click on the **Users** link found inside the **Site Administration** block. Next, click on **Accounts** and then on **Browse a list of users**. Enter **Student1005** in the search filter field and click on **Add filter** to find the student. Click on the **Student1005 Basic005** name link to access the student's profile. From the student's profile page, shown in the following screenshot, click on the **Roles** tab:

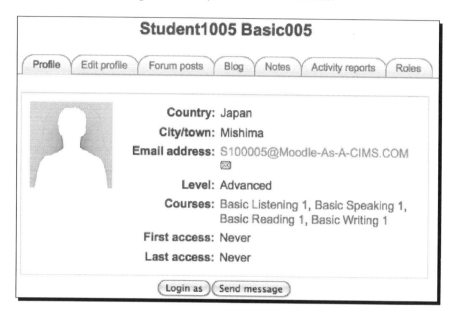

3. The window that appears will be the **Assign roles in User: Student1005 Basic005** window with a list of all the roles that exist in the system, as shown in the following screenshot. Click on the **Parental Monitor** role link to access the **Assign roles in user** screen.

Assign roles in User: Student1005 Basic005 ◉

Roles	Description	Users	
Administrator	Administrators can usually do anything on the site, in all courses.	0	
Course creator	Course creators can create new courses and teach in them.	0	
Teacher	Teachers can do anything within a course, including changing the activities and grading students.	0	
Non-editing teacher	Non-editing teachers can teach in courses and grade students, but may not alter activities.	0	
Student	Students generally have fewer privileges within a course.	1	Parent Five
Guest	Guests have minimal privileges and usually can not enter text anywhere.	0	
Cannot Post Data	This role may be assigned to students who have had their posting privileges revoked temporarily or to individuals who are being granted 'monitor' access.	0	
Information Secretary	This role is used to allow a user to post new information via the front page news as well as to add and edit pages from the Content Pages block.	0	
Surveyor	This role allows a user view-only access for the purpose of monitoring. The user is not allowed to post content in the course or courses he or she is assigned to.	0	
Parental Monitor	This role allows a parent to monitor the activities of his or her child.	0	

4. Enter **parent5** in the search field and click on the **Search** button to locate the parent's account. Select the parent's account by single clicking and then click on the **Add** button to add the account to the list on the left side of the screen.

5. Finally, click on the **Assign roles in user** button at the bottom of the screen to assign the role. The following screenshot is of the **Assign roles** screen prior to clicking on the **Assign roles in User** button.

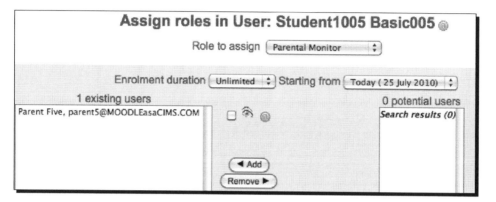

What just happened?

We just created a new user account in our system for a parent and then created a special role to be assigned to that parent. We then assigned the role to the parent from within the context of their child. Assigning the role in this fashion allows the parent to view activity from the perspective, or context, of their child. Additionally, by assigning the parental role, we created limits to what the parent is able to view and do when logged into the site.

Time for action – installing the Mentees block

In order for a logged-in parent to be able to easily access his or her child's information, you will need to install an instance of the Mentees block on the front page of your site. Follow these simple steps to set up the block on your site:

1. From the front page of your site, logged in as admin, click on the **Turn editing on** button located in the top-right of your browser window.

2. From the **Blocks** pull-down menu, select the **Mentees** block, as shown in the following screenshot:

3. Click on the pencil icon, shown in the following screenshot, on the newly installed Mentees block to change the title:

4. Change the name to something like My Child, as shown in the following screenshot, and click on the **Save changes** button to save the new title:

What just happened?

We have just inserted an instance of the **Mentees** block on the front page of our site. When a parent logs into the site, this block will provide them with easy access to their child's profile, where they can monitor some of his or her activity.

Time for action – checking the role functionality

Now that we have created a parental role, assigned it from within a user that is to serve as the child, and inserted an instance of the **Mentees** block on the front page, let's check to see what the parental role allows the parent to do and see. Follow these steps to check the role:

1. Log out of the site and log back in as the parent. Log in using the parental account we made earlier with username `parent5` and the password you set, `1234` in our case.

2. From the front page of the site, you will see the **My Child** block that contains a link to the child's profile page we assigned the **Parental Monitor** role to, as shown in the following screenshot:

3. Click on the **Student1005** link to access the student's profile page. The parent can now toggle through the tabs at the top of the profile to edit the student's profile, view forum posts and blog, and view activity reports. The following screenshot shows the first view the parent is presented with after clicking on their child's name in the **My Child** block.

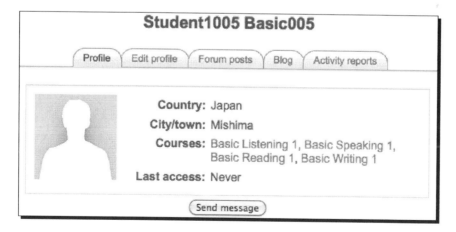

4. Notice here that if you click on the **Activity reports** tab, you can view two different types of report, two different types of logs, and the student's grade, as shown in the following screenshot:

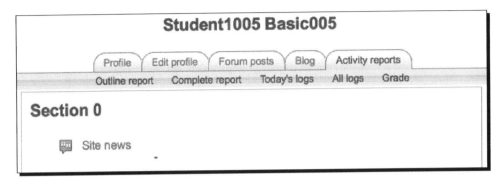

What just happened?

We created a Parental Role and assigned it to the parent in the student's profile in order that the parent may then log in to the site and monitor some of his or her child's activity. This required that we also create an account on the site for the parent and that we install the Mentees block on the front page of the site. This role enables a parent or mentor to track some basic information about their child or mentee. It is of note here however, that there are significant limitations to what a parent can view even after being assigned the parental role. Parents will be able to view and edit profile information, and will be able to view some of the report information and log information, however, concrete information such as the content of forum posts in courses will not be viewable to the parent who is not actually enrolled in the course. The role does nevertheless, allow for some basic monitoring of students on the site and can provide a parent or mentor valuable information about a student's interaction with the site.

Pop quiz

1. How do you, as a site admin, access the Roles screen in order to add or modify a role?

   a. From the **Site Administration** block, click on **Security** and then on **Site Policies**.

   b. From the **Site Administration** block, click on **Users**, **Permissions**, and then **Define roles**.

   c. Navigate to the course you wish to work with and click on the **Settings** link found in the **Administration** block.

   d. Navigate to the course you wish to work with and click on the **Assign Roles** link found in the **Administration** block.

2. Which permission setting would you use to keep a user from being able to access a specific action that cannot be overridden by assigning other roles, except for the Admin role?

   a. Not set

   b. Allow

   c. Prevent

   d. Prohibit

3. What is the name of the block that must be installed on the front page of your site in order to allow a parent to easily access their child's profile information?

   a. My Courses block

   b. Course Categories block

   c. Site Administration block

   d. Mentees block

Have a go hero

We have explored, in brief, the roles and permissions feature built into Moodle. Now try and see if you can come up with new roles that you can use in your educational program. Work with some roles that have very limited permissions that you might use to enroll mentors or parents in a course giving them even more access to the content that students are interacting with and creating. Keep in mind however, that when you create a role that allows a parent, mentor, or advisee to view content in a course or courses that you need to think very clearly about privacy issues to make sure that you are not exposing information to individuals who should not or are not approved to have access to it.

Summary

In this chapter, we introduced and set up four different roles that allow for various types of access and permissions to your Moodle site and the courses within. The first role was one that could be used to effectively silence a user or student who has demonstrated inappropriate behavior in the forums or other areas of the site. The second role was one that can be assigned to a secretary or possibly a marketing staff member such that they can update information on the site housed in either the pages created by the Content Pages block or via the news forum on the front page of the site. The third role was one that could be used to allow supervisors or directors to have access to all, or a group of, courses on the site. This role could provide for an online observation system that resembles a more traditional classroom observation system. The final role introduced was that of the parental monitor or mentor. This role allows a parent or mentor to log in to the site and access information about their child or mentee. The information available is somewhat limited but provides an overview of what the child or mentee is engaged in on the Moodle site. In the following chapter, we will explore more advanced methods of data access and retrieval from the Moodle site.

7
Advanced Data Access and Display

Information about how users are interacting with an educational program can provide insight into how well the program is serving the needs of its students. Monitoring things such as, but not limited to, student interaction, attendance, and assessed performance will help educators and educational administrators to make decisions about the curriculum and its execution. The ability, for example, to determine how many times a student interacts with the Moodle site, may provide insight into the student's level of motivation and interest. Additionally, the ability to monitor a student's performance as determined by assessment systems, automated or teacher-generated, may enable educational administrators to better assist students in need of guidance and to adjust the curriculum to meet the needs of those who would benefit from more academic challenges.

In this chapter, we will explore the installation and use of several tools that allow for more advanced methods of accessing data generated and used by your Moodle site. We will cover the following in this chapter:

- ◆ Installation and use of the Enhanced User Administration block
- ◆ Installation and use of the PHPMyAdmin database admin plugin
- ◆ Installation and basic use of the Custom SQL query tool
- ◆ Installation and basic setup of the embedded Xataface database application

The Enhanced User Administration block

The Enhanced User Administration block was designed to be used by users who have been granted admin level access to a Moodle site. This tool allows a user to perform various actions including filtering, enrolling, deleting, and others, on his or her accounts on the site. It was originally contributed to the Moodle community to fill a gap that existed in the Moodle standard package. The most recent versions of Moodle 1.9 have however, added a very similar capability, called **Bulk user actions**, that is accessible via the **Site Administration block** by clicking on **Users**, **Accounts**, and then **Bulk user actions**. While very similar in design, the **Enhanced User Administration** block and **Bulk user actions** tools are not identical in design or function and it is thus beneficial to have access to both.

Time for action – installation and use of the Enhanced User Admin block

Installing the Enhanced User Admin block is a process very similar to the installation of other packages, such as themes and modules, that has been previously explained in this book. To install the block follow these steps:

1. Download the block from `Moodle.org` from the Modules and Plugins page, as shown in the following screenshot. Note that there is one other user administration block available from `Moodle.org` titled simply **User Administration**. Use the **Enhanced User Administration (block)** to obtain the functionality that will be presented here.

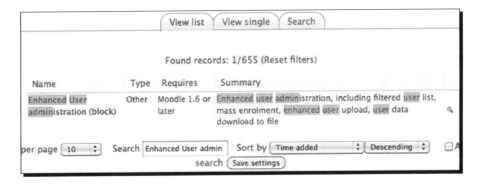

2. Download the block package by first clicking on the **Name** link and then on the **Download latest version** link found in the bottom-right corner of the explanation window, as shown in the following screenshot:

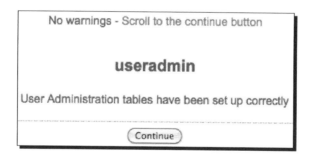

```
                    Discussion
           Download latest version
           Download for Moodle 1.9
           Download for Moodle 1.8
           Download for Moodle 1.6
```

3. Unzip the package that was downloaded to your computer.

4. If the name of the unzipped directory is `useradmin19`, change it to simply `useradmin`.

5. Copy the `useradmin` folder to the `blocks` directory in your Moodle root. This can be found at `/yourmoodleroot/blocks`.

6. Log in to your site as admin and click on the **Notifications** link found in the **Site Administration** block to finish the installation.

7. Click on the **Continue** button, shown in the following screenshot, after confirming the block setup:

```
No warnings - Scroll to the continue button


                    useradmin

User Administration tables have been set up correctly

                   ( Continue )
```

8. Go to the front page of your site, turn on editing, and add the **User Administration** block via the **Blocks** pull down menu.

9. Position the block, using the arrows shown with editing turned on, to a location that will be easily accessible. Just above the **Site Administration** block should be a convenient location.

10. Turn editing off and then click on the **Browse list of Users link** to access the block's features.

11. You will see the various filter settings at the top of the screen followed by a list of the users in your system, as shown in the following screenshot. Click once on the triangle shown at the top of the user list to display or hide the associated column.

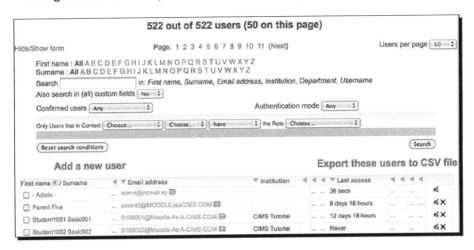

12. The following screenshot was taken from the window that is viewed via the **Bulk user actions** link, introduced earlier:

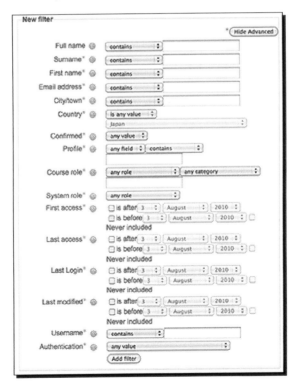

13. As mentioned earlier, the two tools are very similar in function. There are however, some key differences that make having access to both tools beneficial. The following are the two key differences in these tools provided in order to demonstrate the functionality offered by the Enhanced User Admin block, hereafter referred to as the UserAdmin block:

- ❑ The UserAdmin block allows for display and sorting (ascending/descending order) of columns from the filter results window. This sorting ability could allow for easy access to users who have accessed the site within the past day, for example. This cannot be performed via the **Bulk user actions** tool. Access information can be displayed via the **Browse a list of users** function found by clicking on **Users**, then **Accounts**, and then **Browse a list of users** from within the **Site Administration** block. Actions cannot however, be performed on the users displayed via the **Browse a list of users** window. Note also that customized user profile fields can also be added to the display window via the block settings that are accessible by clicking on **Modules**, then **Blocks**, and finally **User Administration** from the **Site Administration** block.

- ❑ From the **UserAdmin** search result display window, e-mail addresses can be activated or deactivated by simply clicking on the user's address. The same task can be performed from the **Bulk user actions** tool but must be performed on users returned from a search without knowing the current status of their e-mail. The display window of the **UserAdmin** tool however, displays whether a user's e-mail address is activated or deactivated. If, for example, I need to search for users whose e-mail is deactivated in a course or other specific context, the **UserAdmin** tool would be more appropriate than the **Bulk user actions** tool. If I simply wanted to activate the e-mail address of all users in a given context, the **Bulk user actions** tool would enable me to perform this task more quickly.

What just happened?

We have just downloaded and installed the Enhanced User Administration (UserAdmin for short) block. A basic comparison of the block with the **Bulk user actions** tool was then made in order to demonstrate the differences in functionality. While these two tools are very similar in function, two explanations of differences supporting the use of the **UserAdmin** block were provided.

Pop quiz

1. If you want to search for and download a list of users who accessed your Moodle site in the past six hours, which of the tools, just introduced, would you use?

    a. The **UserAdmin** block

    b. The **Bulk user actions** tool

2. If you want to check to see which students in a specific course may not have received communication mailed via the news forum in the course, which of the following would be the most time-efficient method?

    a. Navigate to the course in question, click on the **Participants** link and then check the e-mail status of each participant in the course by clicking each participant and viewing their profile.

    b. Click on **Browse a list of users** from the **User Administration** block, filter for the course in question and check to see which students have e-mail addresses that are not activated from the results display window.

    c. Use the **Bulk user actions** tool to filter for the participants in a course and then send them all a message to check to see if they are receiving e-mails.

3. If you want to activate the e-mail addresses of all the students in a course, which of the following would you use?

    a. The **UserAdmin** block

    b. The **Bulk user actions** tool

    c. The **Participants** display from the course main page

Have a go hero

While there are arguably more similarities than differences in the UserAdmin block and the Bulk user actions tool, the differences do allow for additional functionality in your Moodle site. Work with both tools and see if you can design a filter or find a search result that is better in one tool than in the other. This activity will help to familiarize you with both tools and better enable you to select the one appropriate to the task you wish to perform.

Installation and use of PHPMyAdmin

If your Moodle site runs on the MySQL database, as does the site we set up for this book, you may use the PHPMyAdmin plugin to access and administer the database directly. This plugin is a very powerful tool that allows you to access data stored in the Moodle database directly. With power however, also comes the ability to corrupt or completely destroy the Moodle database and all of its contents. It is thus important to use this tool with caution. Many, but not all, of the actions performed via the PHPMyAdmin tool will prompt you for confirmation before being executed and thus give you a last chance before execution. If you aren't sure of yourself, don't do it! Changes made via the PHPMyAdmin tool are often not reversible without considerable effort. Used with caution however, the PHPMyAdmin tool can enable you to very efficiently add to and retrieve information from the Moodle database.

Time for action – installing and using PHPMyAdmin

To download, install, and start using the PHPMyAdmin tool to give you direct access to the Moodle database, follow these steps:

1. Download the latest version of the PHPMyAdmin tool from the **Modules and Plugins** page on Moodle.org.

2. Search for **PHPMyAdmin**, click on the **Name** link and then on the **Download latest version** link found at the bottom-right of the plugin explanation page. (Note, the plugin title on Moodle.org is **MySQL Admin**)

3. Unzip the downloaded package and place the directory, titled mysql, in the admin directory of your Moodle site located at /yourmoodleroot/admin.

4. Log in to your site as admin and click on the **Server** link found in the **Site Administration** block.

5. A **Database** link should appear at the bottom of the list of items under the **Server** category. Click on the **Database** link to access the PHPMyAdmin tool, as shown in the following screenshot (Note, if you were already logged in as admin when you installed the package, you may need to refresh your browser window to get the **Database** link to appear).

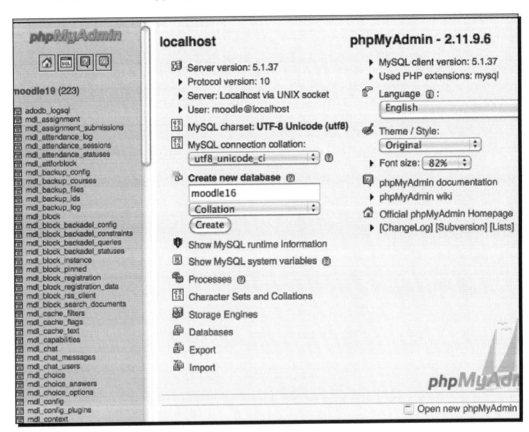

6. Each of the lines shown on the left side of the window represents a table in the Moodle database. The database that our example Moodle installation is running on contains 223 tables, as shown in parentheses at the top-left of the screen next to the database name in the previous screenshot. Click on one of the tables, `mdl_block`, for example, to view the **Structure** window for that table, as shown in the following screenshot:

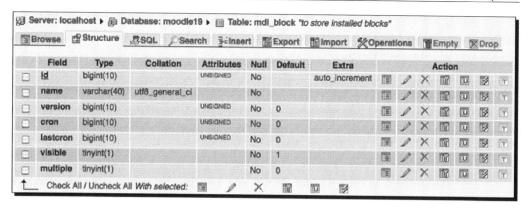

7. Now click on the **Browse** link, found at the top-left of the screen, to view a window that displays the contents of the table, as shown in the following screenshot:

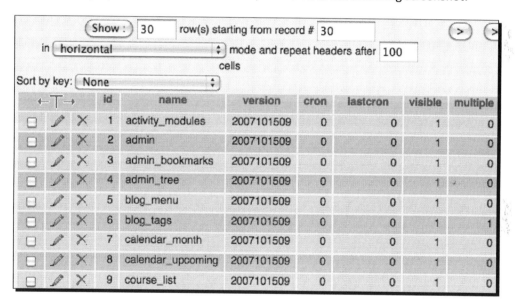

What just happened?

We have just downloaded and installed a database access and administration tool called PHPMyAdmin. We looked at the database via the PHPMyAdmin tool and viewed the contents of one table in our Moodle database. Interaction between the user (student, teacher, or administrator), and the database is normally facilitated by Moodle. For some specific administrative tasks however, using a tool that allows for access to the database directly, can enable an administrator to perform tasks in bulk much more efficiently than they could be performed through the Moodle site.

Until you become familiar with the structure of the Moodle database and are comfortable navigating through it using PHPMyAdmin, this tool may appear to be less than useful. In the next chapter of this book however, we will introduce a method for inserting test scores and other educational program-related data into the database that utilizes the PHPMyAdmin tool. While these tasks are possible via other methods, the use of PHPMyAdmin makes inserting data into the database in bulk a very fast, straightforward and relatively simple process. You will certainly begin to appreciate all that can be done with PHPMyAdmin as you start to use it for these types of tasks.

Have a go hero

You may be thinking that PHPMyAdmin looks like a very daunting tool that you'd rather not work with. Try the following so you don't have to wait until *Chapter 8, Setting Up a Mini SIS* to start to see how useful PHPMyAdmin can be. Scroll down the list of tables and find the table titled `mdl_user`. Browse the contents of this table and then browse through some other tables such as `mdl_attendance_log` and know that many of the tables are related to each other via one or more ID numbers. Think about how an educational administrator might be able to use data stored in the Moodle database if he or she could access and view it in an easy-to-understand format.

Installation and basic use of the Custom SQL query tool

The ability to create ad hoc queries that retrieve specific data from the Moodle database can enable you, as an educational administrator, to create monitoring tools that inform you and others on things such as the results of a test, attendance figures, and any other plethora of scenarios that you may dream up. Use of this tool will require basic SQL knowledge at the least and more advanced skills for sophisticated queries. There are many resources on the web that will help to get you started with SQL. A good place to start is `www.sql.org`.

Time for action – install and experiment with the Custom SQL query tool

Installation of the Custom SQL query tool is a straightforward process that resembles the process for installing blocks, modules, and other plugins. To install the tool follow these steps:

1. From the `Moodle.org`, **Modules and Plugins** page, search for **Custom SQL queries**.

2. Click on the **Custom SQL queries** name link found in the search results and then on the **Download for 1.9** link found at the bottom-right corner of the explanation window.

3. Unzip the `customsql.zip` package and place the resulting `customsql` directory in the admin reports directory found in your Moodle directory at `/yourmoodledirectory/admin/reports`.

4. Click on the **Notifications** link found in the **Site Administration** block to finish the installation process. You will see a screen that confirms that the customsql plugin has been set up correctly, as shown in the following screenshot:

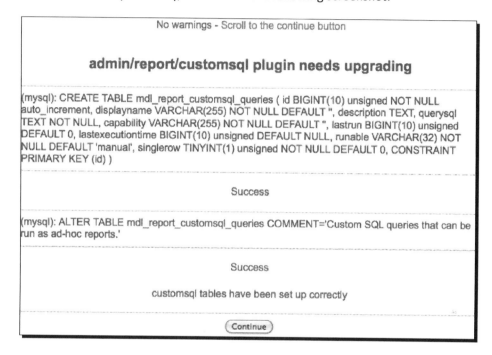

5. Click on the **Continue** button to finish the installation and then navigate to the front page of your Moodle site.

6. Click on the **Reports** link found in the **Site Administration** block and then on the **Ad-hoc database** queries link to access the Custom SQL queries tool.

What just happened?

We have just downloaded and installed the Custom SQL queries administrator tool. This tool will allow us to construct ad hoc queries to meet the various data gathering needs that exist in our educational institution.

SQL queries

As was mentioned earlier, writing SQL queries requires some basic knowledge of SQL and understanding of its logic. We will walk through the creation of one fairly simple query to demonstrate the power that is presented by this block.

Time for action – creating a sample query

The first time you access the Custom SQL queries tool via the **Ad-hoc database queries** link, you will see a screen that indicates there are **No queries available**, as shown in the following screenshot:

Once you create one or more SQL queries, the queries will appear in this window. To demonstrate the usefulness of this tool, we will set up a simple sample query. Our query is going to be designed to pull final grades from courses, so we will first need to navigate to one of our courses and enter several grades to ensure that we have data to pull from the database. Follow these steps:

1. Navigate to the **Advanced Listening 1** course on our test site by clicking on the **AdvList1** link in the **MyCourses** block, as shown in the following screenshot:

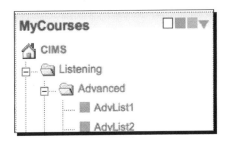

2. There are two graded items here, **Attendance** and **Final Exam**, from our course template imported from *Chapter 4, Incorporating Educational Standards*, so we already have some items that can be graded. You could enter attendance data and final exam scores by clicking on the item link (**Attendance** and **Final Exam**) found in the course and entering scores but we will take an easier approach for this activity. Click on the **Grades** link found in the **Administration** block on the left side of the screen.

3. You will now see the **Grader report** screen. Use the drop-down menu found in the top left-hand side of the window if you are in a different view.

4. Push the **Turn editing on** button found at the top-right of the screen.

5. Enter some scores for a few students, as shown in the following screenshot. (Note, the **Course total** figures are calculated by the weighting scheme setup in *Chapter 4, Incorporating Educational Standards.*)

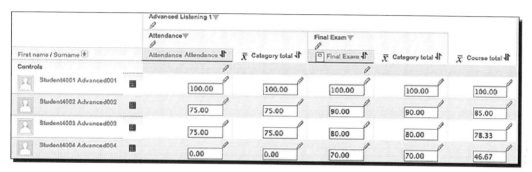

6. Click on the **Update** button found at the bottom of the screen.

7. Navigate back to the front page of your site.

8. Now that we have entered some grades into the system, we are ready to build and use an SQL query via the Ad-hoc database query tool. First, click on the **Ad-hoc database queries** link found by clicking on the **Reports** link located in the **Site Administration** block.

9. Click on the **Add a new query** button.

10. The **Editing an ad-hoc database query** screen will appear. Enter a **Query name** and **description** such as **Course Grades** and **Final scores from courses**.

11. In the Query SQL window, enter the following SQL code:

```
SELECT
prefix_course.fullname AS «Course»,
ROUND(prefix_grade_grades.finalgrade, 2) AS «Final Grade»,
prefix_user.firstname AS «First Name»,
prefix_user.lastname AS «Last Name»,
prefix_user.username AS «Username»
FROM
prefix_grade_grades
INNER JOIN prefix_user ON prefix_grade_grades.userid = prefix_
user.id
```

```
INNER JOIN prefix_grade_items ON prefix_grade_grades.itemid =
prefix_grade_items.id
INNER JOIN prefix_course ON prefix_grade_items.courseid = prefix_
course.id
WHERE prefix_grade_items.id = prefix_grade_grades.itemid
AND (prefix_grade_items.courseid = prefix_course.id)
AND (prefix_grade_grades.finalgrade > 0)
AND (prefix_user.deleted = 0)
AND prefix_grade_items.itemtype = <course>
ORDER BY prefix_course.id, prefix_user.id
```

12. Leave the **Who can access this query**, **Run**, and **Type of result** settings at their default values and click on the **Save changes** button located at the bottom of the page. The query will be executed and the results will be displayed, as shown in the following screenshot:

Course	Final Grade	First Name	Last Name	Username
Advanced Listening 1	100.00	Student4001	Advanced001	s400001
Advanced Listening 1	85.00	Student4002	Advanced002	s400002
Advanced Listening 1	78.33	Student4003	Advanced003	s400003
Advanced Listening 1	46.67	Student4004	Advanced004	s400004

What just happened?

We just successfully downloaded and installed the Custom SQL query tool and set up one SQL query designed to pull final grades directly from the table used by Moodle to store grades. This tool can be used to extract virtually any data from the Moodle database that you wish to access. If you have a systems engineer or technical support personnel on staff, you will likely be able to get help in designing advanced queries to access your Moodle database. If access to such personnel is limited you may need to search the web for helpful resources, purchase some introductory SQL manuals, or hire an outside contractor to help you get your system set up. Prior to doing so however, you should spend some time getting yourself familiarized with the Moodle database via browsing the tables and their fields with a tool such as the PHPMyAdmin plugin we installed earlier in this chapter. An additional place to start when experimenting with SQL queries is the Custom SQL query tool documentation page on Moodle.org found at `http://docs.moodle.org/en/Custom_SQL_queries_report`.

Have a go hero

We have demonstrated just one possible type of query that can be constructed with the Custom SQL query tool. Try and see if you can think of other queries that would provide valuable information to you and your institution as you position your Moodle site as a CIMS. Visit the Custom SQL queries report page at the Moodle Docs site (`http://docs.moodle.org`) for ideas and, once you've designed that perfect query, post it in the Docs for others to use!

Also, as this book goes to press, a new database report generating tool, in the form of a block, has been contributed to the Moodle community. The tool can be found and downloaded from the Modules and Plugins database on the `Moodle.org` website. Search for it using the string "`Block: Configurable Reports`". This tool is evolving quickly and promises to be a tool that will allow for customized reports that can be generated via a browser interface with little to no knowledge of SQL. It has been contributed and is being maintained by *Juan Leyva* from Madrid, Spain. Download it and give it a try and compliment Juan on his fabulous contribution!

Installation and basic setup of the embedded Xataface database application

In the previous two sections, we've seen that there is an enormous amount of data stored in the Moodle database and that some of it can be of value to educational program administrators. The limitation of both of the tools previously introduced is that both require some technical skill to use and can introduce serious vulnerabilities in terms of the types of access that they grant to the database. This is where a tool that allows educational administrators access to the Moodle database on limited terms can be very useful. The tool that we will introduce here and expand upon in *Chapter 8, Setting Up a Mini SIS*, is a database access tool called Xataface. Xataface is open source, just like Moodle, and has a relatively smooth learning curve.

Time for action – installation and basic setup of Xataface

Xataface does introduce a method for users to access the Moodle database directly, so we'll want to be very careful in how we install and set it up. It is highly recommended that you first set up Xataface in a test environment such as the MAMP server we have set up for this book. Follow these steps to get your Xataface tool downloaded, installed, and set up:

1. Navigate to the Xataface website found at: `http://xataface.com`.

2. Click on the **Download the latest version** link found on the front page of the site, as shown in the following screenshot:

3. The link will redirect you to a SourceForge page from which the latest version can be downloaded. The latest version will be at the top of the list and packaged both as `tar.gz` and `zip` packages. Download either of the compressed packages.

4. Expand the contents of the package and rename it to `Xataface`.

5. Create a new directory in your Moodle root directory called `CIMS` and place the `Xataface` directory and all of its contents inside the `CIMS` directory.

6. With your browser, navigate to the file titled `dataface_info.php` found in the directory that was just placed in the Moodle directory. Using the name we provided in step 4 earlier would result in `yourmoodlesite/cims/xataface/ dataface_info.php`. You should see the following screen, which will mean that your installation is functioning properly:

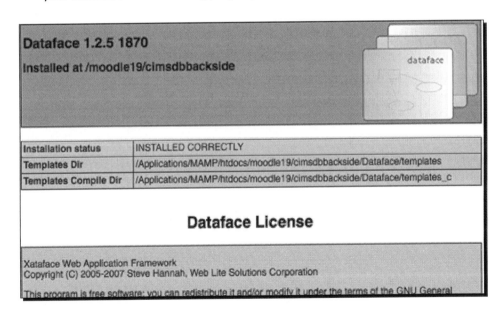

7. Once you have confirmed that the application is installed correctly, direct your browser to the following address: `yourmoodlesite/cims/xataface/installer.php`.

8. You will be prompted to enter the username and password for your database. If you have set up your development site as you worked through this book, both your username and password will be `moodle`. To confirm this information, look for the `config.php` file found in your `Moodle` directory and open it with your text editor. The user name and password are listed as: **dbuser** and **dbpass**.

9. Once you have entered the username and password and clicked enter, you will see a screen that presents you with two options, as shown in the following screenshot. Choose the first option, **Create application for existing database**, as we want to use the Moodle database.

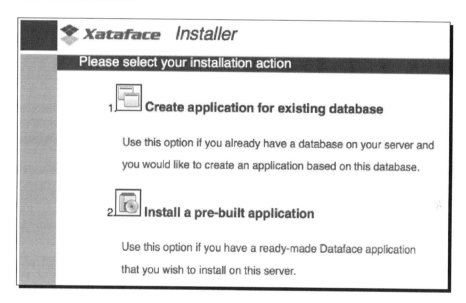

10. The next screen, as shown in the following screenshot, will prompt you to select a database using a drop-down menu. Pick the item that contains the word Moodle, which should be **moodle19**.

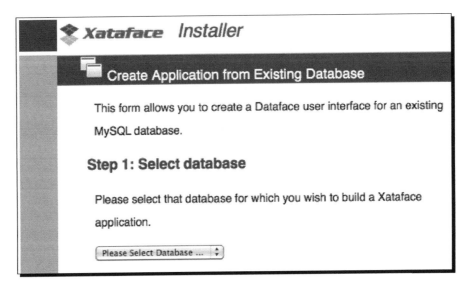

11. After selecting the database, you will be prompted to enter connection information, which consists of the username and password. These fields will already be populated with the username and password that you used to access the installer, so you should only need to click on the **Test DB Connection** button that will result in a **Connected to database successfully** message, on this screen before clicking on **proceed to next step**. The following screenshot is of the step 2 portion of the installation:

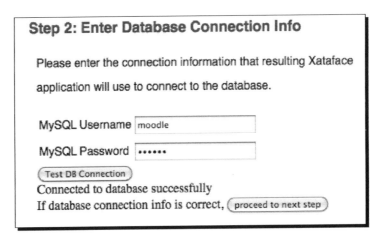

12. Clicking on **proceed to next step** will present Step 3, as shown in the following screenshot. Use the pull-down menu to select **Download Tarball** as we will be installing this in our local instance of Moodle. Click on the **Submit** button to initiate the download.

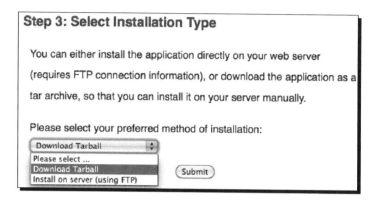

13. Expand the package that was downloaded and you will find a file titled `conf.ini` and one titled `index.php`. Place these two files inside the `CIMS` directory but not inside the `Xataface` directory.

14. Now, point your browser to `yourmoodlesite/cims/index.php` to access your Xataface application.

15. You will see a screen that resembles the following screenshot with access to all of the tables in your Moodle database. This would, of course, be unacceptable in a production environment, first because there is no authentication required for accessing the Xataface program at this point, and second because access is being granted to all tables in the Moodle database, which is unnecessary and unwanted. We'll work on basic setup next and will walk through further customization in the next chapter.

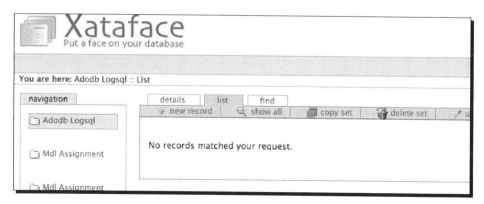

16. To get an idea of how Xataface displays table information, click on the **Mdl Assignment Submissions** link, shown on the left side of the page in the **navigation** menu, to view the contents of the table. The following screenshot is what you will see if you entered the grades for the SQL Query tool, explained earlier in this chapter.

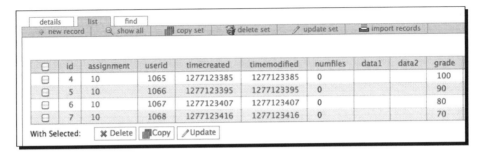

What just happened?

We have just successfully downloaded and installed the Xataface database access application. We then walked through the setup process in order to create an application that uses the Moodle database. We tested Xataface's functionality by clicking on a table link from the **navigation** menu found on the left side of the screen, to view the contents of the table. This application can provide an ideal backside access portal to the Moodle database that will enable educational administrators to field data from and enter information into the Moodle database.

Time for action – setup of our Xataface application

As we mentioned earlier, the default installation of Xataface is not appropriate as a backside portal for Moodle due to the fact that it grants universal and unlimited access to all of the tables in the Moodle database. There are a wealth of tutorials to help assist you customize your Xataface instance on the web in the Wiki area of the Xataface website at www.xataface.com. We will walk through a few of those that are considered to be crucial when using this package together with Moodle. We will start by setting up the authentication feature in Xataface in order to limit access to users who have been granted usernames and passwords. The types of access that can be granted to users will also be listed. To enable the authentication function, follow these steps:

1. Before we set up authentication in the Xataface application, we need to create a table in the database to store user information. This is a perfect chance for us to use the PHPMyAdmin tool, we installed earlier in this chapter. Navigate to the front page of your site, click on the **Server** link located in the **Site Administration** block and then on **Database** to access the database with PHPMyAdmin.

2. Click on the database name link found at the top-left of the screen, as shown in the following screenshot. In our test site case, this will be **moodle19**.

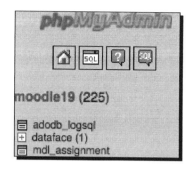

3. Scroll to the bottom of the main screen (not the table list on the left) and enter the following name in the **Name** field window under the **Create new table on database moodle19** heading: dataface__users. (Note, use two underbars here to include this table in **dataface** table heading in the table list, as seen in the previous screenshot. Adding this table will result in the number 2 in parenthesis after the **dataface** table title.)

4. Enter a 4 for the **Number of fields** and then click on the **Go** button. The following screenshot is an example of what you should see prior to clicking on the **Go** button:

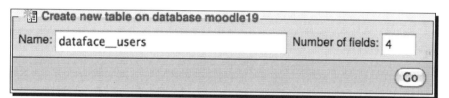

5. The next window will be a very wide window that will require you to scroll to the right to enter all of the required information. Use the following for the **Field** names, **Type**, and **Length/Values**:

Field	Type	Length/Values
UserID	INT	11
UserName	VARCHAR	32
Password	VARCHAR	32
Role	ENUM	'READ ONLY', 'NO ACCESS', 'ADMIN', 'REVIEWER'

6. Set the **Collation** to **utf8_general_ci** for all fields except the **UserID**.

7. Set the **Role** field to **NULL** but leave the other three **NOT NULL**.

8. The **Default** value for the **Role** field should be **READ ONLY**.

9. Set the **UserID** to **auto_increment** using the **Extra** pull-down menu.

10. Set the **UserID** as the **Primary key** by clicking on the radio button under the key. The **UserName** should be set to unique and the other two fields can be left untouched. The following screenshot is of these radio button settings:

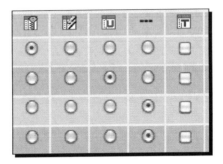

11. After having entered and selected all of the desired settings for the table, click on the **Save** button found on the far right of the screen.

12. The table will be created and from here you will need to enter one record to be used by the site admin. Click on **Insert** found at the top of the screen and enter a **UserName**, **Password**, and select the **ADMIN** role from the pull-down menu. The **UserID** field can be left blank as it will be automatically generated by the database. The following screenshot is an example of how you should fill in the information to create a new record in this table. Click on the **Go** button to enter the new record into the table.

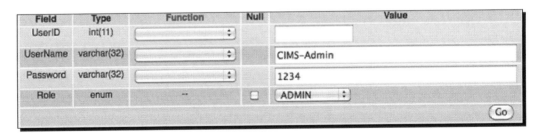

Field	Type	Function	Null	Value
UserID	int(11)			
UserName	varchar(32)			CIMS-Admin
Password	varchar(32)			1234
Role	enum	--	☐	ADMIN

13. From the next screen, click on the **Browse** link found at the top of the window, as shown in the following screenshot, to verify the new record in the table:

14. The record will appear in the table, as shown in the following screenshot. Next we will go to the Xataface application and activate the authentication feature and point it to this table in the database.

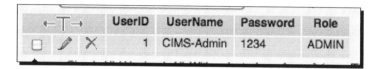

15. Now let's go to the Xataface application and enable the authentication feature and tell Xataface where to find the user information. Open the `conf.ini` file found in your Xataface application directory with your text editor. The directory containing the `conf.ini` file will be `CIMS`, if you have followed the instructions thus far.

16. In the `conf.ini` file, below the `[_database]` information, enter the following lines and then save the file:

```
[_auth]
users_table = dataface__users
username_column = UserName
password_column = Password

[allowed_tables]
Users = dataface__users
```

17. This code activates the authentication plugin and tells Xataface what table the user account information is stored in. Additionally, the `Users = dataface__Users` record was added under the `[allowed_tables]` heading because, by default, Xataface disallows all tables that begin with `dataface__`.

18. In your `CIMS` directory, create a new directory titled `conf`. Using your text editor, create a file inside the `conf` directory and type in the following code:

```php
<?php class conf_ApplicationDelegate {       function
getPermissions(&$record){// $record is a Dataface_Record object
$auth =& Dataface_AuthenticationTool::getInstance();
$user =& $auth->getLoggedInUser();
if ( $user ) return Dataface_PermissionsTool::ALL();
else return Dataface_PermissionsTool::NO_ACCESS();       } }
```

19. Save the file as `ApplicationDelegate.php` inside the `conf` directory. This code tells Xataface to require a login of anyone who navigates to the application.

20. Now access your Xataface application by navigating to `/yourmoodlesite/cims/` with your web browser. You will see a login window, as shown in the following screenshot, and notice that while the tables are all still listed, you cannot view the contents of any of them. To log in to the application, use the username and password we entered into the users table earlier: `CIMS-Admin` and `1234`.

Please Login to access this section of the site

```
┌─ Login Form ──────────────────────────────┐
│          Username:  [                     ] │
│          Password:  [                     ] │
│   [ Submit ]                                 │
└──────────────────────────────────────────────┘
```

What just happened?

We just created a new table in our Moodle database to house the user information for our Xataface application. We then populated the table with one user account, our admin account, and then changed the Xataface settings to require a login in all users and told Xataface where to look for user account information. Finally, we logged in to the application with the admin account we created to make sure everything functions as desired. Next, we'll continue to refine the appearance of our application by limiting the tables that are displayed from the database.

Time for action – limiting database table access

In order to clean up the appearance and to heighten security, we will remove the table navigation display from the left side of the screen and change settings that control access to the tables in the Moodle database. Follow these steps:

1. Once again, open the `conf.ini` file found in the `CIMS` directory located inside your Moodle directory. The [_tables] list, that you will see inside this file, is what controls the tables being displayed in the **navigation** column. This [_tables] heading only controls the display however, and even if a table is removed from this list, the table can still be accessed by typing the table name into the browser window. We will use the following two directives to either display a table or prevent access to it: [_tables] and [_disallowed_tables].

2. The [_tables] directive formatting requires the table be identified first and then given a title as in mdl_user = "Users". Add the tables that you wish to allow to this section. For our example, we will only add Mdl_user for now so we will add the line, mdl_user = "Users" to our [_tables] list.

3. The [_disallowed_tables] directive requires a name be specified first followed by an equals sign and then the table name as in Mdl_user_info_category=mdl_user_info_category. The [_tables] list however, is formatted with the table name first followed by an equals sign and title enclosed in quotation marks, including spaces between words. Inverting the order of these and removing the quotation marks and spaces is the easiest method of creating the [_disallowed_tables] list. The following calculation is one way to invert the table title and name after copying and pasting the table list to a spreadsheet: =SUBSTITUTE(CONCATENATE((MID(A1,(FIND("=",A1,1)+3),(LEN(A1)-(FIND("=",A1,1)+3)))),"=",LEFT(A1,(FIND("=",A1,1)-2)))," ","") Download the sample conf.ini file from the Packt website for reference if you have difficulties or would like to view a completed sample. A sample Excel spreadsheet with this conversion calculation is also available.

4. Once you have completed the process of adding your table to be listed under the [_tables] heading and including all of the tables you want to deny access to under the [_disallowed_tables] heading, you can save the file and navigate to yourmoodlesite.com/cims to view your Xataface application. The first screen you will see should look virtually identical to the following screenshot:

5. Note the **Users** tab at the top of the window in the previous screenshot. This is the only table that we have chosen to display via the [_tables] heading in the conf.ini file and is thus the only table that is accessible. And, of course, it is only accessible after logging in to the application. Log in with the admin **Username** and **Password** we created earlier: CIMS-Admin and 1234.

6. After logging in you will see a list view of the table that includes all of the columns in the table. We will clean this up as we customize our Xataface Moodle database backside in the next chapter. Be careful as you use the Xataface application to navigate through the table as the delete and update links found in the application will allow you to modify or delete information from the table. This data is used by Moodle and could be corrupted or lost permanently if you are not careful.

What just happened?

We have just limited the tables that are displayed in our Xataface application by using the [_tables] directive and also prevented access to all tables that we don't want users to have access to using the [_disallowed_tables] directive. These settings, or directives, allow us to fine tune the display and access capabilities of our Xataface application.

Time for action – another Xataface security measure

Before we finish this chapter, there is one additional security measure that should be introduced in order to ensure that your Xataface application is safe. We earlier created our admin account in the dataface__users table in the database and entered a simple password. We should, of course, use a more complex password and certainly recommend doing so on a live production website. It is also recommended that passwords be stored in an encrypted format in the database to prevent them from being viewed by anyone who has access to the database, legitimate or otherwise. Moodle encrypts passwords prior to inserting them into the database and Xataface can do so as well. Setup password encryption for your Xataface users table by following these steps:

1. Navigate to your Xataface application at yourmoodlesite/cims and log in using your admin account information: CIMS-Admin and 1234. Make sure you log in as admin before moving on to the next step. If you do not log in prior to completing the following steps, you will be unable to log in to your application.

2. In your CIMS directory, where you now have the following files and directories:
   - conf (directory)
   - conf.ini (file)
   - index.php (file)
   - Xataface (directory)

Create a directory titled `tables`.

3. Inside the `tables` directory you just created, create a directory titled `dataface__users`. The directory name should be the same as the title you used for the table that houses the Xataface user information.

4. Now, inside the `dataface__users` directory create a file with your text editor and enter the following code:

```
[Password]
    encryption=md5
```

5. Save the file with the following file name: `fields.ini`.

6. In your Xataface application, that you logged into before completing the previous steps, click on the **My Profile** link found on the right side of the screen just below the **Logout** link, as shown in the following screenshot:

7. Your profile, which consists of the information entered in the users table in the database will appear, as shown in the following screenshot. Click on the **edit** tab, enter a new password from the **edit** window and click on the **Save** button. (Note that clicking on the **new record** link here will allow you to create new user accounts.)

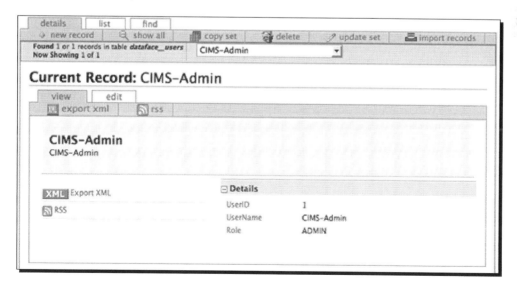

8. You can check to confirm that your password was encrypted by using PHPMyAdmin. Go to the front page of your Moodle site and click on the **Server** link and then on the **Database** link all found in the **Site Administration** block.

9. Click on the plus sign next to the **dataface** table from the table list on the left side of the page to expand the list of tables, as shown in the following screenshot:

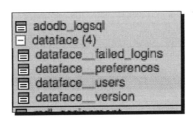

10. Click on the **dataface__users** table and then on the **Browse** link from the display window to the right of the table list. There should be only one entry in the table as we have only created the admin user. Notice that the password is now a long string of numbers and characters, as shown in the following screenshot. This confirms that Xataface is now encrypting the passwords stored in the user's table.

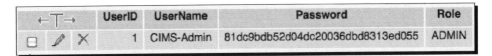

	UserID	UserName	Password	Role
1	CIMS-Admin	81dc9bdb52d04dc20036dbd8313ed055	ADMIN

What just happened?

We have now performed some basic setup tasks for our Xataface application by activating the authentication plugin included in Xataface, specifying which tables, from the Moodle database, we want to be able to access via Xataface, and then by applying a setting to the **dataface__users** table that tells Xataface to encrypt all passwords inserted into the **Password** field in the users table. This very basic setup process only scratches the surface in terms of the customization Xataface is capable of. We will explore Xataface more in the next chapter.

1. How can new user accounts with encrypted passwords, for people who are to be given access to the Xataface application, be easily created?

    a. By adding the username and password information to the `conf.ini` file.

    b. By logging into the application as admin, clicking on profile and then on the new record link.

    c. By using PHPMyAdmin to insert a username, password, and role into the table.

    d. By clicking on the **Users**, **Accounts**, and then **Add a new user** link from inside the **Site Administration** block found on your Moodle front page.

Summary

In this chapter, we installed four very useful tools that will help us to position our Moodle site solidly as a CIMS. The tools and the functions we have covered in this chapter are:

◆ **The Enhanced User Administration block**: This block allows you to sort and filter user accounts and perform various actions, bulk and single user, on the accounts. It can be a very handy tool for quickly retrieving simple user-related information from your Moodle site.

◆ **PHPMyAdmin**: We installed this very powerful database administration tool that is accessible via the Server link found in the Site Administration block of your site. We briefly demonstrated how this tool allows you to access and view all of the contents of the tables stored in the Moodle database.

◆ **Custom SQL Query tool**: This is a tool that is installed as a report and is accessible via the Reports link found in the Site Administration block on the front page of your Moodle site. We constructed one sample query that returns final grades from all courses on your site and thus demonstrated the usefulness of this tool to educational administrators.

◆ **Xataface**: We walked through the installation and a very basic setup process for this tool that allows for controlled and customizable backside access to the Moodle database.

We will continue to work with these tools, especially PHPMyAdmin and Xataface, in the next chapter, as we move into further enabling our Moodle site to function as a central portal for curriculum and information management.

8
Setting Up a Mini SIS

It is important for an educational program to maintain a wide variety of data related to each of the students matriculating through the program. This data can range from personal contact information to information about a student's performance in classes. The data, in the case of many schools, might include a student's grade point average, his or her test scores, as well as contact information for parents or guardians and may even include things such as a student's blood type and information about allergies. A Student Information System (SIS) is a computer-based system that organizes all of this data, and more, and makes it easy to access for administrators and teachers. Moodle is not designed specifically to function as an SIS but as much of the data that is often included in an SIS already exists in the Moodle database, it's not that difficult to bend Moodle to meet our needs.

In this chapter, we will explore two different methods of setting up Moodle to function as an SIS. The two methods we will explore are:

◆ Use of the custom user profile fields

◆ Use of the Xataface database 'backside' application

Custom user profile fields

The ability to create custom user profile fields has existed since Moodle 1.8. This feature allows a site administrator to add fields that, when populated with information or data, can be assigned to chosen users in your system. For example, if you administer an assessment test in your program, you can upload students' test scores to profile fields. You can choose to allow students to see the field in their profile or can make it invisible so that only the site administrators will have access to the data. As you increase the amount of information that is incorporated into user profile fields, you will slowly be turning your Moodle site into a mini SIS. In the following explanation, we'll show you how to set up and utilize user profile fields and will also walk you through a couple of different methods of accessing the data from the perspective of an educational program administrator.

Time for action – setting up a user profile field for assessment test scores

We will start by setting up three user profile fields, two will be used to house achievement scores from an assessment test given in our program twice a year, and the other will be used to record which of three programs a student is enrolled in. After setting up the fields, we will populate them with data and then demonstrate several methods of accessing aggregated data. To set up the profile fields, follow these steps:

1. Log in to your Moodle site as admin and click on the **User profile fields** link found by clicking on **Users** and then **Accounts** from within the **Site Administration** block, as shown in the following screenshot:

2. When you visit the **User profile fields** link, you will see a screen like the following screenshot. Use the drop-down menu to select **Text input**, as shown in the screenshot.

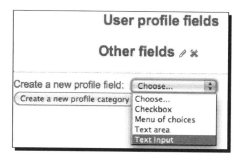

3. You will now see a window titled **Creating a new "Text input" profile field**. Enter a **Short name** and, although it is not stated in the window, use only lower case letters. Give the field a title using the **Name** text entry area. This is the name that will be displayed for this field. Enter a brief description for the field in the **Description** area. Change the **Is this field locked?** setting to **Yes** to prohibit users from changing the values and the **Who is this field visible to?** setting to **Visible to user** using the drop-down menus. At the bottom of the page, change the **Display size** and **Maximum length** settings to 15, leave the **Default value** blank, and the **Is this a password field?** setting set to **No**. The following screenshot is of this screen with all settings, except the **Display size** and **Maximum length** settings. Click on **Save changes** to create the field.

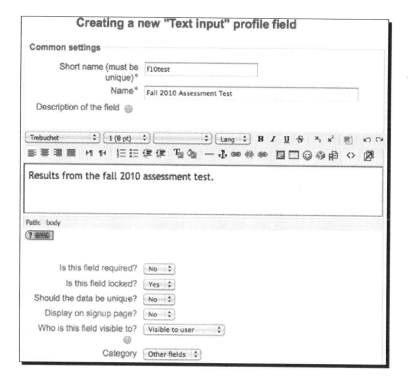

4. You will now see the field you just created, as shown in the following screenshot:

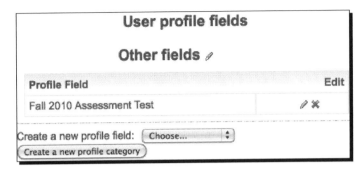

What just happened?

We have just created a field that will be used to house test scores associated with students in our program. We limited the length of the value stored in this field to 15 spaces, which, for a test score, is certainly more than sufficient. We have also locked the field so that it cannot be edited by the user and have set it so that only the user and site administrators can view the contents of the field.

Have a go hero

Now, set up the next assessment test score field in the same fashion as we did for the first. Change the name to **Spring 2011 Assessment Test**. Once you have completed the creation process for the second field and have navigated back to the **User profile fields** window, you should see something like the following screenshot with both of the fields listed:

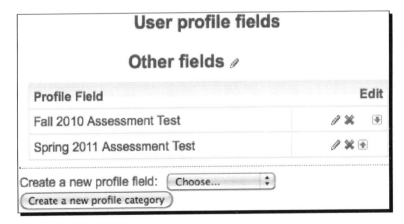

Time for action – a profile field for program enrollment information

For this example, we'll set up one more profile field to house information about educational programs a student is enrolled in. Notice that in the example site we have constructed thus far, this field will contain information that is related to programs of study that students are enrolled in that is peripheral in terms of the language program focus our site has taken thus far. This illustrates how our SIS is going to start taking shape by enabling us to house information that is at a level beyond our immediate educational program. In this case, the example could be from a college or university. Let's use the following three programs for this example:

♦ Teacher training program

♦ Pre-law program

♦ Business management program

To set up the user profile field that will hold this information, follow these steps:

1. Navigate to the **User profile fields** screen found in the **Site Administration** block under **Users|Accounts|User profile fields** from the front page of your site.

2. Use the **Create a new profile field** drop-down menu to select **Text input**, the same way you did for the previous two fields.

3. Give the field a short name such as **program** (remember to use all lowercase letters) and a **Name** such as **Program of Study**. Enter a short description and set the field as follows:

   ❑ Not required

   ❑ Locked

   ❑ Not unique

   ❑ Not displayed on the sign up page

   ❑ Visible to everyone

4. Change the **Display size** and **Maximum length** to **20** and click on **Save changes** to create the field. Your **User profile fields** screen should now look like the following screenshot:

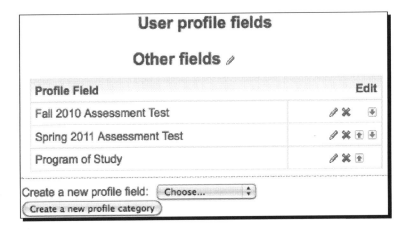

What just happened?

We have now created three user profile fields. Two will house assessment test scores and the third will contain information about programs that students are enrolled in. The first two fields have been set to be locked and invisible to everyone aside from each individual user and to the site administrators. The third program information field was also set to be locked but visible to everyone who can view user profiles on the site.

Time for action – populating the fields

The data that will be stored in these fields will, in the case of most programs, exist in spreadsheets or other storage systems external to Moodle, so we will need to migrate the scores and program enrollment information into Moodle. This can be easily accomplished by using the **Upload users** function we visited earlier in *Chapter 3, Student Account Creation and Enrollment*. Follow these steps to prepare a CSV file and use it to populate the user profile fields:

1. Obtain a list of the users in your Moodle site in a spreadsheet format. While this can be accomplished in many different ways, the easiest for this example will be to use the CSV file we used in *Chapter 3, Student Account Creation and Enrollment*, to create new student accounts. The file is available from the Packt website at www.packtpub.com/support. In a production site environment, you could use the Bulk user actions function in Moodle found from the front page of your site in the **Site Administration** block under **Users|Accounts|Bulk user actions**, to download a list of students.

2. Retain the **username** column in your file and delete all other columns.

3. Create three new columns using the short name for the profile fields we created as column headings. The profile field short names must be preceded by `profile_field`. The columns for the fields from our example will have the following headers:

- `profile_field_f10test`
- `profile_field_s11test`
- `profile_field_program`

4. Once you have added the column headings, add information for all of the desired users. For this example, you will have a file with four columns, as shown in the following screenshot. (Note, in a real world setting you will most likely have data associated with users via a name and possibly some type of ID number that will need to be matched to the username used in Moodle. For this reason, as was mentioned in a previous chapter, the use of student ID numbers as usernames can ease this process of matching data. For our example, the data shown next was simply generated randomly.)

◇	A	B	C	D
1	username	profile_field_f10test	profile_field_s11test	profile_field_program
2	S400001	98	94	Teacher Training
3	S400002	88	94	Pre Law
4	S400003	80	93	Business Management
5	S400004	100	97	Teacher Training
6	S400005	82	98	Pre Law
7	S400006	84	96	Business Management
8	S400007	82	93	Teacher Training

5. Save the file using the CSV format and navigate to the **Upload users** page found from the **Site Administration** block under **Users|Accounts|Upload users**.

6. Use the **Browse** button to find and select your CSV file. Leave the **Preview rows** setting on **10** and, once you have selected your file, click on the **Upload users** button. You will see something like the following screenshot:

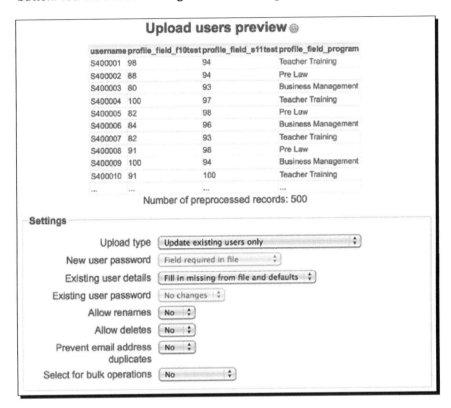

7. Change the **Upload type** to **Update existing users only** and **Existing user details** to **Fill in missing from file and defaults** using the drop-down menus, as shown in the preceding screenshot. Leave all of the other settings on their defaults and click the **Upload users** button found at the bottom of the page. The **Upload users results** window, shown in the following screenshot, indicates a successful update but does not display the profile field information that was added. Click the **Continue** button found at the bottom of the screen.

Upload users results

Status	CSV line	ID	Username	First name	Surname	Email address	Password	Authentication	Enrolments	Delete
User updated	2	1065	S400001							
User updated	3	1066	S400002							
User updated	4	1067	S400003							
User updated	5	1068	S400004							
User updated	6	1069	S400005							

8. Check to make sure the fields have been added, select any user by using the **User Administration** or **Browse a list of users** tools. You will see that all users have had the three fields added to their profiles, as shown in the following screenshot:

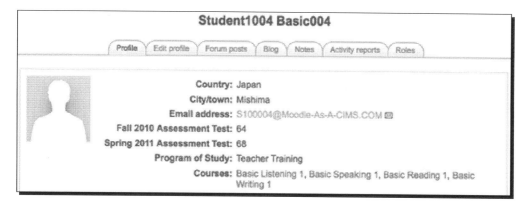

What just happened?

We have just populated all of the user profile fields, created earlier, with data using the **Upload users** tool and then checked a user's profile to see how the information is displayed. Adding various types of information and data to customized user profile fields will allow you to begin to construct an SIS in which you can maintain information about the students in your educational program.

Pop quiz

1. Which of the following two settings should be used when using a CSV file and the Upload users tool to populate user profile fields?

   a. Add new users only, skip existing users, and Fill in missing from file and defaults.

   b. Add new and update existing users and No changes.

   c. Add all, append counter to usernames if needed, and Create password if needed.

   d. Update existing users only and Fill in missing from file and defaults.

Have a go hero

We used the **Upload users** function in Moodle to insert information into the user profile fields we created. This task can also be accomplished via the PHPMyAdmin tool. It is a slightly more involved process but just as quick and efficient if you know what you are doing. You will need to use a series of SQL statements using INSERT INTO and WHERE. This method is handy if you created a short name for your profile field that includes capital letters and, for whatever reason, you do not want to change the name to lowercase because Moodle will generate an error if you use capital letters in the profile field column headings when attempting to update user information. Add a new profile field using the process outlined earlier in this chapter and then see if you can populate it using PHPMyAdmin and some basic SQL statements. You'll need to know the ID number used by the profile field you create, which can be determined by viewing the table with PHPMyAdmin. If we create a new field called Counselor, one SQL statement, designed to insert the counselor's name, might look like the following:

```
INSERT INTO mdl_user_info_data (data, fieldid, userid) VALUES
('Smith',8,49);
```

In this case, we are inserting the value Smith into the counselor field, which has an ID number of 8, for the user with the ID number of 49. The ID numbers used in the database can be found by browsing the following two tables with PhpMyAdmin:

- mdl_user (for the user's ID number)
- mdl_user_info_field (for the profile field ID number)

Using the user profile fields as the search criteria

Now that we have created and populated our customized user profile fields, how can we use the information as criteria for searching for groups of students? There are various methods for viewing the information entered into the user profile fields. One very simple method is to search for a student and view his or her profile to see the information stored in the fields. If however, we would like to produce a list of all students who are enrolled in the Pre-law program, for example, this method is not useful. The following are two methods of accessing lists of users based upon information or values stored in the user profile fields.

Time for action – searching using the Bulk user actions tool

To use the **Bulk user actions** tool to search for a group of students using the criteria based on values or information stored in the user profile fields, follow these steps:

1. Navigate to the **Bulk user actions** page by clicking on the **Bulk user actions** link found under **Users** and then **Accounts** from within the **Site Administration** block.

2. Click on the **Show Advanced** button under the **New filter** heading, shown in the following screenshot, to display the advanced settings for the filter:

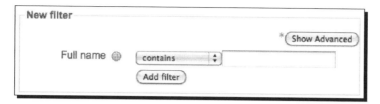

3. With the advanced options displayed, you will see sixteen different criteria that you can use to search for users in your system. For this example, we are going to be using the **Profile** fields so use the pull-down menu to change **any field** to **program** and then the search criteria to **is equal to** and type `Pre Law` into the text entry box. The filter settings should look like the following screenshot:

4. Scroll to the bottom of the **Filter** heading and click on the **Add filter** button.

5. On the resulting screen, you will see a new heading, with the title **Active filters**, below the **New filter** heading. Below the **Active filters** heading, you will see a heading titled **Users in list** that will display the results of the filter that was just applied. In our example, there were 167 users with Pre-law in their **program** profile field, as shown in the following screenshot:

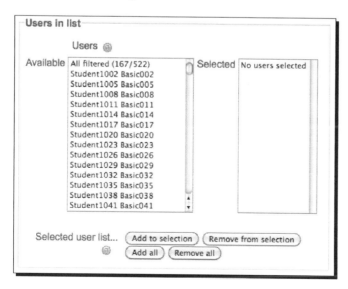

6. Click on the **Add all** button found at the bottom of the **Users in list** heading to move the users from the **Available** display window to the **Selected** window.

7. For this example, we are going to download this list of users. Use the pull-down menu next to the **With selected users** heading to select **Download** and then click the **Go** button, as shown in the following screenshot:

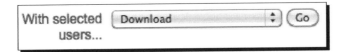

8. From the subsequent **Download** window, shown in the following screenshot, select the format you wish to download the information in, by clicking on the desired link. We will use Excel for this example. This will initiate the download, which, depending on your computer system and settings, may also present a popup that allows you to approve the download and select its location.

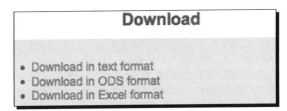

9. Once you have downloaded the file, click on the **Continue** button found at the bottom of the screen to return to the **Bulk user actions** screen.

10. Open the file that was downloaded to view the users. Notice that all of the profile fields are included in the information downloaded.

What just happened?

Using the `Bulk user actions` function built into Moodle, we searched for, and downloaded, a list of all the students enrolled in the Pre-law program. As mentioned earlier, the more information that is entered into user profile fields, the more possibilities exist in terms of sorting, or filtering, for groups of students within your educational program.

Have a go hero

If you want to use the **Bulk user actions** tool to filter users based upon numeric values, such as test scores, that have been entered into custom user profile fields, you will notice that the conditions upon which you can filter are somewhat limited. I have added several mathematical operators to the list of conditions for user profile fields that can be downloaded and added to your Moodle instance by downloading the modified files or the patch file from `http://tracker.moodle.org/browse/MDL-21979`. Either apply the patch or use the two modified files to find the lines that were added and add them to your core Moodle files. You can use the search string "added" to find the lines of PHP code that were added in each of the two files. Four lines were added to the `filters.php` language file and 12 lines were added to the `profilefield.php` file located at `/moodleroot/user/filters`. Once you have added the mathematical operators, try searching for all users with a **Fall 2010 Assessment Test Score**, using the **f10test** profile field short name, of 80 or higher.

Time for action – searching using PHPMyAdmin

In most cases, the filters that can be applied via the **Bulk user actions** tool are sufficient to allow you to obtain the students you are searching for in your system. In some cases however, it is much more efficient to search for the information directly using the PHPMyAdmin tool. One such case is when you have a large number of users in your system (several thousand or more) and wish to search using a numeric condition, such as greater than or equal to, using the profile fields. The Moodle core, as of 1.9.9+, does not perform this operation as efficiently as it should and executing such a command via the **Bulk user actions** tool can put a heavy enough load on your MySQL to cause it to freeze up. The Moodle development team is aware of this issue and it is scheduled to be fixed but it may take some time for it to be remedied as it is a minor issue compared to many of the other development projects they are working on. PHPMyAdmin can be used to perform such tasks, usually without over burdening the MySQL server. To search for a list of students who, for example, all scored over an 80 on the fall assessment test, follow these steps:

1. Log in to your site as admin and, from the front page of your site, access the PHPMyAdmin tool by clicking on **Server** and then **Database** from within the **Site Administration** block.

2. Scroll down the table list on the left side of the screen to the table titled `mdl_user_info_field` and click once on this table link. The table link is shown in the following screenshot:

3. The default display for the table, which you will see to the right of the table list in the main portion of your browser window is the **Structure** display. Click on the **Browse** tab found at the top-left of the main window frame, as shown in the following screenshot:

4. Scroll down to view the details of the three user fields that we have created so far. Note that the **Id** for the field that we are using to store fall assessment test scores is **4**, as shown in the following partial screenshot:

			id	shortname	name	datatype	description	categ
☐	🖊	✕	4	f10test	Fall 2010 Assessment Test	text	Results from the fall 2010 assessment test.	
☐	🖊	✕	5	s11test	Spring 2011 Assessment Test	text	Results from the spring 2011	

5. Scroll to the top of the screen and click on the **SQL** tab found two tabs to the right of the **Browse** tab.

6. Delete the default **SELECT** statement found in the **Run SQL query** window and enter the following SQL query:

```
SELECT mdl_user.username AS "Username", mdl_user.firstname AS
"First Name", mdl_user.lastname AS "Last Name", mdl_user_info_
data.data AS "Fall 2010 Assessment Test"
FROM mdl_user
INNER JOIN mdl_user_info_data ON mdl_user.id = mdl_user_info_data.
userid
WHERE mdl_user_info_data.data >=80
AND mdl_user_info_data.fieldid =4;
```

7. This query will return a list of all students who scored 80 or higher on the fall assessment test, as shown in the following partial screenshot:

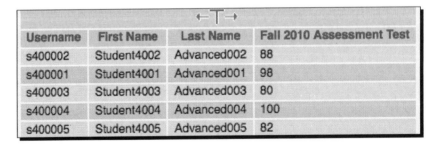

Username	First Name	Last Name	Fall 2010 Assessment Test
s400002	Student4002	Advanced002	88
s400001	Student4001	Advanced001	98
s400003	Student4003	Advanced003	80
s400004	Student4004	Advanced004	100
s400005	Student4005	Advanced005	82

8. Scroll down to the **Query results operations** heading, shown in the following screenshot, and click on **Export**.

9. Select the download format desired and make sure to tick the **Save as file** box, shown in the following screenshot. The default filename will be __TABLE__, so change it to an appropriate self-explanatory name and click on the **Go** button to export the results:

What just happened?

We just ran a very simple SQL query that allowed us to retrieve users from the Moodle database who scored an 80 or higher on the fall assessment test. This SQL query returns basically the same information that we filtered for with the **Bulk user actions** tool but can be, in the case of large sites with many users, much more time-efficient. The downside to the query is that it is difficult to retrieve information stored in other profile fields when using a condition based upon a test score such as this one.

The Xataface database 'backside' application

For many tasks related to maintaining student information, working through the Moodle interface is sufficient. If you wish to maintain data that is not used directly by Moodle however, and you also want to provide varying levels of access to that data to selected personnel in your educational program, you may wish to use the Xataface application that we set up in the previous chapter. Use of this application can enable you to set up a student information system that is both tightly integrated with Moodle and at the same time a system that operates in parallel with but independent of Moodle. Because Xataface is in simple terms a browser-based user interface for a database, its possibilities in conjunction with Moodle are virtually limitless. We will explore a few of those possibilities and continue to customize the application we have already set up in the remainder of this chapter. We'll introduce and explain the following:

♦ Customizing the Xataface table display

♦ Setting up relationships in Xataface

♦ Using Xataface to modify core Moodle data

♦ Xataface as an enrollment table maintenance tool

Time for action – customizing the Xataface table display

Xataface is designed to be extremely customizable from its appearance to how it functions. A thorough exploration of Xataface is beyond the scope of this book but we will go through a few of the basics in order that you may get it set up and working efficiently with in your Moodle instance. We'll start by building on the minor display customization we did in the previous chapter. Our current Xataface application is set to display only the user's table in Moodle but we don't need to see all of the fields in that table, so let's hide all but the fields we want to have access to. Follow these simple steps to clean up the table display:

1. Log in to your Xataface application at www.yourmoodlesite/cims and click on the **Users** tab to view the user's table.

2. Leave your browser for now and navigate to your Xataface directory, which should be located in your Moodle root directory and titled cims, if you have followed all of the tutorials thus far.

3. Navigate to the tables directory found inside the cims directory. There should be one directory inside the tables directory, the dataface__users directory.

4. Create a directory in the tables directory titled mdl_user. This directory represents the user's table in Moodle.

5. Open your text editor and type the following for each field in the user's table that you do not want to have displayed through Xataface:

```
[id]
visibility:browse=hidden
visibility:list=hidden
visibility:find=hidden
```

6. The preceding example starts with the ID field used in the user's table. Save the file with the fields.ini filename inside the mdl_user directory.

7. Go ahead and type the code from step 5, save the file and go back to your browser and refresh the page. Notice that the ID field, on the far left of the screen, disappears when you refresh the screen. This is because we have told Xataface to hide this field from display.

8. Return to the fields.ini file you saved in the mdl_user directory and type the code from step 5 for each field in the table. Copy the three visibility statements and then just paste them after typing in each field name enclosed in brackets to be more efficient. For this tutorial, let's keep only the following fields: username, firstname, and lastname. It's a little tedious to enter the code for all of the fields that you don't want to have displayed, but you only have to do it once. Format the file, as shown in the following screenshot, to make it easy to read later:

```
[id]
visibility:browse=hidden
visibility:list=hidden
visibility:find=hidden

[auth]
visibility:browse=hidden
visibility:list=hidden
visibility:find=hidden

[confirmed]
visibility:browse=hidden
visibility:list=hidden
visibility:find=hidden
```

9. When you've finished entering all of the information into the `fields.ini` file, save the file and refresh your browser window. Your **Users** table display should now look like the following screenshot:

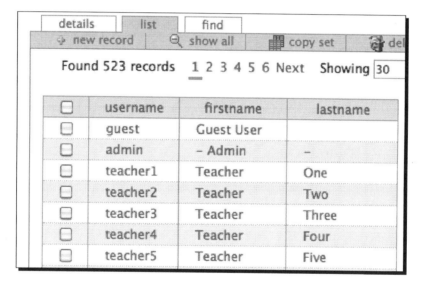

10. Now, before we finish this task, click on the name of one of the users, **teacher5** for example, under the **username** heading to show the **details** view for that user. In the `fields.ini` file, this view is controlled via the **browse** setting.

11. From your Moodle site, find the user you have selected in the previous step using the **User Administration** block, edit the profile and enter a short description in the description field window. For this example, we are using **Teacher Five** so we'll enter "`Hi, my name is Teacher Five.`"

12. Go back to your `fields.ini` file and remove the `visibility:browse` line for the **description** field. Save the file and refresh your browser window. The description line will appear in the details window with the description we just added, as shown in the screenshot displayed after step 15.

13. And, for one last customization, open a new text file with your text editor and type the following code:

```php
<?php
class tables_mdl_user {
function getTitle(&$record){
return $record->display(<firstname>) . « « . $record-
>display(<lastname>);
} }
?>
```

14. Save the file with the filename `mdl_user.php` in the `mdl_user` directory that is located in your `tables` directory inside your `cims` directory.

15. Refresh your browser window and notice that the **Current Record** title changes from **manual** to the name of the user, as shown in the following screenshot:

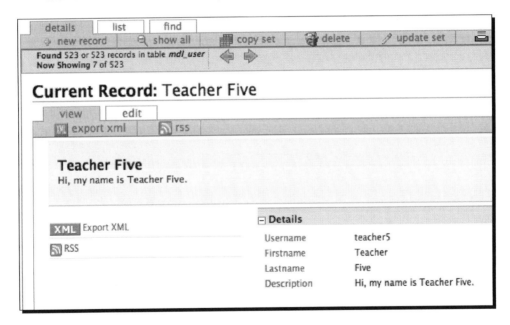

What just happened?

We have just refined our Xataface application by hiding most of the fields in the Moodle user table so that only the username, first name, and last name fields appear in the list view. We then changed one setting to display the **Description** field in the details, or browsed, viewed and finally modified the settings for the table view via a simple PHP file in order to change the record title to the name of the user. These are only a few of the many modifications that can be made in Xataface. Visit the Xataface website forums or documentation wiki found at www.xataface.com for more tips and explanations.

Time for action – setting up relationships in Xataface

Next, let's set up some relationships in Xataface so that we can see all of the values in the profile fields when we click on a user from the list view to view the details window. This will involve setting up several relationships, but once we are finished we'll have a nice interface that allows us to toggle through the profile field information. Follow these steps to get it set up:

1. In the `tables` directory located in your Xataface `cims` directory, create the following two directories:

  □ `mdl_user_info_data`

  □ `mdl_user_field`

2. These represent the two tables that contain profile field information.

3. In the `conf.ini` file, located in the `Xataface` root, titled `cims`, remove the two lines under the `disallowed_tables` list for the `mdl_user_info_data` and `mdl_user_field` tables and save the `conf.ini` file.

4. With your text editor, create a file that contains the following code:

```
[Profile Fields]
mdl_user_info_data.userid = mdl_user.id
```

5. Then save the file with the filename `relationships.ini` in your `mdl_user` directory located in the `tables` directory of your Xataface application.

6. Again, with your text editor, create a new file and type the following code:

```
[Profile Field Titles]
mdl_user_info_data.fieldid = mdl_user_info_field.id
```

7. Save the file with the filename `relationships.ini` in your `mdl_user_info_data` directory located in the `tables` directory of your Xataface application.

8. Once you have created and saved all of these files, navigate to your Xataface application, log in as admin, and view one of the student accounts from the list view of the **Users** table. We will use `Student4001` for this example.

9. In the upper-left portion of the window, you will see a block titled **this record**. Click on the plus sign next to the **Profile Fields** heading to expand the window and display the profile field records. Click on the plus sign next to one of the fields to further expand that field. You should see a display similar to the one shown in the following screenshot:

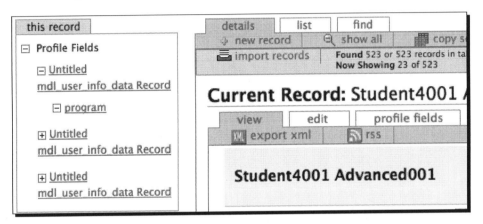

10. This display isn't very helpful because Xataface is not displaying a title for each record. We can remedy this easily by adding two simple PHP files, one to each of the table directories. In the `mdl_user_info_data` directory, located in the `tables` directory, create a file with the following contents:

```php
<?php
class tables_mdl_user_info_data {
function getTitle(&$record){
return $record->display(<data>);
} }
?>
```

11. Then save the file as `mdl_user_info_data.php`.

12. Create another file with the following contents:

```php
<?php
class tables_mdl_user_info_field {
function getTitle(&$record){
return $record->display(<name>);
} }
?>
```

13. Then save the file as `mdl_user_info_field.php` in the `mdl_user_field` directory.

14. After creating and saving the files in their appropriate locations, refresh your browser window and notice that you now have field information followed by field titles, as shown in the following screenshot:

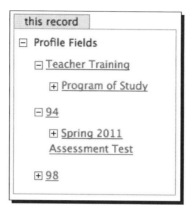

What just happened?

We just added relationships to the directories of three tables in order to be able to view the profile fields associated with a user when viewing the details window for a user. We also added some very simple PHP files in order to change the field used for the record title. This was a very simple introduction to how Xataface can be set up to display data from multiple tables used by Moodle.

Have a go hero

As I mentioned earlier, there are a wealth of customization possibilities with Xataface. Try and change the settings that we just walked through and have the profile fields displayed within each user's details view. If you succeed, remove the **this record** box that is displayed on the left side of the window as you won't need it. For help with this, visit the Xataface forums; specifically, the following forum thread, where I worked through this exact process together with the Xataface head developer: `http://xataface.com/forum/viewtopic.php?f=4&t=4765`.

Time for action – using Xataface to modify core Moodle data

Now that we have worked a little on modifying the display settings in Xataface, we should briefly discuss and experiment with actually making changes to a Moodle table via the Xataface interface. Remember, we are going to be making changes to data that is used by Moodle, so don't practice on a live site. The experimental site we have set up is the perfect environment to get some hands on experience in order to get used to the tools and processes and to also give you some time to think about how, and if, you want to use them. We'll start by enabling the history function within Xataface and then walk through editing some fields in the Moodle mdl_user table. Follow these steps:

1. First, to enable the history function, open the conf.ini file located in your Xataface root directory, titled cims in our case, and add the following two lines below the [_auth] heading and before the [_allowed_tables] heading:

   ```
   [history]
   enabled = 1
   ```

2. Save the file.

3. Log in to your Xataface application located at www.yourmoodlesite/cims, click on the **Users** tab and then on a single user to view the details window. We'll use **Student4001** for this example.

4. Notice the **history** tab that is now displayed, as shown in the following screenshot. Clicking on the **history** tab will result in a message that there is no history yet. This is because we have not yet edited a record via the Xataface interface.

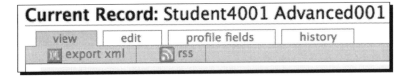

5. Click on the **edit** tab to open the editing window for the selected user. Note that all of the fields for the mdl_user table appear in the **editing** window. We need to make some setting changes to make sure that the fields we hid via the fields.ini file are not editable via the Xataface interface.

6. Open the fields.ini file located in the mdl_user directory, which is in the tables directory. Below each table heading, add the following line for each table:

   ```
   widget:type=hidden
   ```

as shown in the following screenshot. This will completely prevent access to the field. We could have used this setting earlier when we hid the fields but waiting until now allowed for the introduction of both the **visibility** and **widget** settings.

```
[auth]
widget:type=hidden
visibility:browse=hidden
visibility:list=hidden
visibility:find=hidden
```

7. Refresh the browser window and note that you are now presented with only three fields in the editing window for the user's table, as shown in the following screenshot:

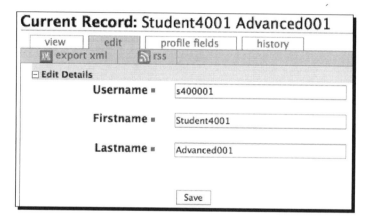

8. Change the **Firstname** to Student Four Thousand And One and click on the **Save** button.

9. Here you will get an error stating that invalid information has been entered for a long list of fields. This is because many of the fields in the `mdl_user` table have been created, by Moodle, with the **Null** setting set to **NO** but are then allowed to be left empty by Moodle. When Xataface opens the table for editing it is in a sense opening all of the fields in a row, even the ones we have hidden, and attempting to save them with the values they contain. For the empty fields, this is generating an error because the database setting is not allowing them to be empty. To correct this, you will need to use PHPMyAdmin, by clicking on **Server** and then **Database** from within the **Site Administration** block from the front page of your Moodle site, to view the table and change the field **Null** settings, on the `mdl_user` table, from **not null** to **null**. Make a note of the fields listed in the error message, as shown in the following screenshot, and change the setting for these fields. Note, the list of fields that need to be set to null may differ depending upon how you populated the user profile fields. For example, I have entered an institution name for all users so, even though that field is not allowed to be null, I am not getting an error because all fields contain information and are thus not null.

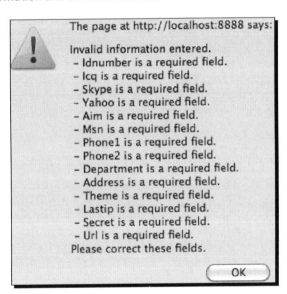

The page at http://localhost:8888 says:

Invalid information entered.
- Idnumber is a required field.
- Icq is a required field.
- Skype is a required field.
- Yahoo is a required field.
- Aim is a required field.
- Msn is a required field.
- Phone1 is a required field.
- Phone2 is a required field.
- Department is a required field.
- Address is a required field.
- Theme is a required field.
- Lastip is a required field.
- Secret is a required field.
- Url is a required field.
Please correct these fields.

OK

10. Once you have changed all of the null settings, try again to change the name of the user, to Student Four Thousand And One, via the editing page. You will see a message at the top of the window indicating that the record was saved successfully.

11. Find this student from within Moodle using the **User Administration** block with the search string **Four Thousand**. Click on the name to view the profile and note that the name change is, naturally, visible via the Moodle interface, as shown in the following screenshot:

Student Four Thousand And One Advanced001

Profile | Edit profile | Forum posts | Blog | Notes | Activity reports | Roles

12. Go back to the Xataface application and click on the **history** tab to view the history information that is now available. The **history** tab allows you to view changes made and revert to a previous setting. This is only possible however, for changes made via the Xataface interface.

What just happened?

We have just briefly introduced how to make changes to information in the Moodle database with the Xataface application. We started by enabling the history function in Xataface and then by hiding fields that we did not want to be edited and then made changes to some of the fields in the `mdl_user` table in order to allow Xataface to save rows to the table with empty, or null, values. After making all of the necessary changes, we experimented with a name change and observed the change via both Xataface and Moodle. We also confirmed that the history function in Xataface maintains a record of changes made via the tool.

Pop quiz

1. How can data modified via the Xataface application easily be monitored and fixed in the case of mistakes?

   a. By making sure that users who are given access to the Xataface application make notes of all the changes they make.

   b. By turning on the history function in Xataface that will record, in the database, a record of all changes made.

   c. Once changes have been made to the database, they cannot be reversed so it is important to be careful when working with Xataface.

   d. Records can be downloaded to CSV files daily and kept as backup copies to reference when a mistake is suspected.

2. What important change must be made to the Moodle database to allow Xataface to change only selected fields in the `mdl_user` table?

   a. Fields that you don't want to use must be deleted from the Moodle database.

   b. The settings in the database for fields that you will not access via Xataface must be set such that they are allowed to be NULL.

    c.   The Xataface tool must be set to display on the fields that you want users to be able to change.

    d.   The values that you want to control should be changed via the PhpMyAdmin tool.

Time for action – Xataface as an enrollment table maintenance tool

One last task Xataface can be used for, that we'll explore in this book, is as a tool to maintain a table in the database to be used by the Moodle enrollment tool. In *Chapter 3*, *Student Account Creation and Enrollment*, we explored the various enrollment options available in Moodle and referred forward to this chapter in stating that we would explore the external database enrollment plugin here. Actually, what I propose is to use the Xataface tool to maintain a table, added to the Moodle database, that will be used by the external database plugin. As such, it won't be an external database but Moodle doesn't care. To set up the table, follow these steps:

1.   Navigate to the Enrolments settings window of your Moodle site from the **Site Administration** block by clicking the **Courses** link and then on the **Enrolments** link.

2.   Click on the **Edit** link for the **External Database** settings. For the **External Database Server Settings**, shown in the following screenshot, use the database settings from your `config.php` file found in your Moodle root. For the **enrol_dtable** field, use the name of the table you intend to use for the enrollment plugin. For this example, I am using **enrolltable**.

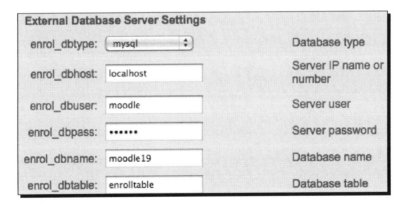

External Database Server Settings		
enrol_dbtype:	mysql	Database type
enrol_dbhost:	localhost	Server IP name or number
enrol_dbuser:	moodle	Server user
enrol_dbpass:	••••••	Server password
enrol_dbname:	moodle19	Database name
enrol_dbtable:	enrolltable	Database table

3. Scroll down and fill the remaining fields with the field values you intend to use. For this example, I will use the following fields and settings:

- ❏ `enrol_localcoursefield`: shortname
- ❏ `enrol_localuserfield`: idnumber
- ❏ `enrol_db_localrolefield`: role
- ❏ `enrol_remotecoursefield`: course
- ❏ `enrol_remoteuserfield`: enrolled
- ❏ `enrol_db_remoterolefield`: role
- ❏ `enrol_db_defaultcourseroleid`: Student (Use pull down menu)
- ❏ `enrol_db_autocreate`: No (Use pull down menu)
- ❏ `enrol_db_category`: Ignore this if the above setting is No
- ❏ `enrol_db_template`: leave blank
- ❏ `enrol_db_ignorehiddencourse`: No
- ❏ `enrol_db_disableunenrole`: No

4. Click **Save changes** after all of the settings have been entered.

5. Use PHPMyAdmin, click on **Database** from the **Site Administration** block under **Server**, to create a new table called **enrolltable**. Create the table with four fields. Use the following:

- ❏ id – BIGINT – 10 – Not Null – Auto Increment – Key
- ❏ userid – VARCHAR – 20 – utf8_general_ci – Not Null
- ❏ role – VARCHAR – 20 – utf8_general_ci – Not Null
- ❏ course – VARCHAR – 50 – utf8_general_ci – Not Null

6. Save the table.

7. Add the table to the list of tables in your Xataface application by adding the following line to your `config.ini` file found in your `Xataface` root directory, titled `cims` in our case:

```
enrolltable = "Enrollment"
```

8. Save the file and log in to your Xataface application found at `www.yourmoodlesite.com/cims` as admin.

9. You will see the **Enrollment** tab, as shown in the following screenshot, but there will be no records in the table yet.

10. Click on the new record link, shown in the following screenshot, to add a new record to the table:

11. Use `1234` for the **Userid** field, `Student` for the **Role** field, and `AdvList1` for the **Course** field, as shown in the following screenshot:

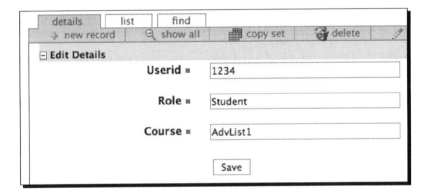

12. From your Moodle site, use the **User Administration** block to locate a user, we will use **Teacher Twenty** for this example. Click on the username and then on **edit profile** to edit Teacher Twenty's profile.

13. Click on **Show advanced** to show the **Optional** profile fields and add **1234** as the **ID Number**. Click **Update profile** to make the changes.

14. Finally, go back to the **Enrolments** window found by clicking on **Courses** and then **Enrolments** from the **Site Administration** block and click once on the tickbox under **Enable** and then on **Save changes** to enable the **External Database** plugin.

15. Now, log out of your Moodle site and back in as Teacher Twenty with the username: **teacher20** and password: **1234**. Teacher Twenty is immediately, upon logging in, enrolled in the AdvList1 course as a student as evidenced by the appearance of the **AdvList1** course in the **My Courses** block.

What just happened?

We just set up a table in the Moodle database to be used by the external database enrollment plugin. We entered all of the appropriate settings to allow the external database plugin to access the table we created and match values with values in the Moodle tables associated with course enrollments. We then changed the settings in our Xataface application to allow it to access the table and created a record in the table. Finally, we added an ID Number to a user, a teacher to match the number used in the record created in the enrollment table, and then logged in as that teacher to confirm that the plugin would enroll the teacher in the specified course, and was thus functioning correctly.

Have a go hero

The use of this external database enrollment setup can enable you to provide enrollment control to an education administrator without the need to allow them access to the Moodle system. A feature of Xataface, that unfortunately cannot be covered here, is its ability to accommodate customized import filters, which allow you to upload records to a table in bulk. Explore the Xataface forums and documentation that can be found from the Xataface website located at `www.xataface.com` and try to set up an import filter that will allow you to upload CSV, Excel, or other file formats into the enrollment table.

Summary

In this chapter, we started by exploring how to set up an SIS via the use of user profile fields. We set up three fields and populated each with information and data for all of our student accounts and then explored various techniques for aggregating the information. In the second half of the chapter, we explored further customization of the Xataface database administration tool and demonstrated how Xataface can be used to modify information stored in tables in the Moodle database. We finished up with a basic demonstration of how the Xataface tool can also be used to function as an interface for a table in the Moodle database that is set up to function as a table used by the external database enrollment plugin. With some experimentation and imagination, the Xataface tool can serve as an important tool, that functions to greatly expand the CIMS capabilities of your Moodle site, by providing a useful backside access portal for educational administrators working in your program.

Promoting Efficient Communication

A key component of any quality educational program is its ability to facilitate communication among all of the parties involved in the program. Communication and the subsequent relaying of information and knowledge between instructional faculty, administrators, students, and support personnel must be concise, efficient, and, when so desired, as transparent as possible. Moodle is designed specifically to function as a tool that allows individuals to communicate and share knowledge and it is thus the perfect system for streamlining your various program-related communication needs.

In this chapter, we will introduce and explain the following strategies for establishing an efficient communication portal through your Moodle CIMS:

◆ Set up and use of communication and information exchange portal courses for intra- and inter-departmental or program communication

◆ Building a mentor/homeroom/advisor/counselor system

◆ Feedback systems (using the questionnaire module)

Using Moodle as a hub for internal information distribution, collaboration, and communication

Up to this point in this book, we have explored Moodle's ability to function as an information portal only from the perspective of Moodle functioning as a tool to provide information to prospective students and stakeholders who are, in a sense, external to your Moodle site. Moodle's ability to facilitate information flow and communication among users within the system, who are registered users such as students and teachers, is a capability that has been a core function of Moodle since its inception. The module most often used to facilitate communication and information flow is the *forum* and we will thus focus primarily on creative uses of forums for communication within an educational program.

Facilitating intra- or inter-departmental or program communication, collaboration, and information flow

Many educational programs comprise sub-units such as departments or programs. These units usually consist of students, teachers, and administrators who interact with one another at varying levels in terms of the type of communication, its frequency, and content. The following example will demonstrate how a sub-unit—the reading program within our language program example—might set up a communication system, using a meta course in Moodle, that accomplishes the following:

- ◆ Allows the program to disseminate information to all students, teachers, and administrators involved in the program. The system must, of course, allow for settings enabling dissemination to only selected groups or to the entire group, if so desired.

- ◆ Establishes a forum for communication between and among teachers, students, and administrators. Again, this system must be fine-tunable such that communication can be limited to specific parties within the program.

The example will also demonstrate, indirectly, how a meta course could be set up to facilitate communication and collaboration between individuals from different programs or sub-units. In such a case, the meta course would function as an inter-departmental communication and collaboration system.

Time for action – setting up the meta course

To set up a communication system that can be finely tuned to allow specific groups of users to interact with each other, follow these steps:

1. We are going to set up a communication system using a meta course. Log in to your site as admin and click on the **Show all courses** link found at the bottom of your **MyCourses** block on the front page of your site.

2. At the bottom of the subsequent **Course Categories** screen, click on the **Add a new course** button.

3. Change the category from **Miscellaneous** to **Reading** and enter a **Full name** and **Short name** such as **Reading Program** and **ReadProg**. Enter a short description explaining that the course is to function as a communication area for the reading program.

4. Use the drop-down menu next to the meta course heading, shown in the following screenshot, to select **Yes** in order to make this course a meta course:

5. Change the **Start date** as you see fit. You don't need to add an **Enrollment key** under the **Availability** heading to prevent users who are not eligible to enter the course because the enrollment for meta courses is taken from child courses. If you've gotten into the habit of entering enrollment keys just to be safe however, doing so here won't cause any problems.

6. Change the group setting, found under the **Groups** heading, to **Separate**. Do not force this setting however, in order to allow it to be set on an individual activity basis. This will allow us to set up forums that are only accessible to teachers and/or administrators. Other forums can be set up to allow only student and teacher access, for example.

7. Click on the **Save changes** button found at the bottom of the screen and on the next screen, which will be the **Child courses** screen, search for all reading courses by entering **Reading** in the search field. After clicking on the **Search** button to initiate the search, you will see all of the reading courses, including the meta course we have just created. Add all of the courses, except the meta course, as shown in the following screenshot. There will be twenty courses if you have set up the site outlined in this book.

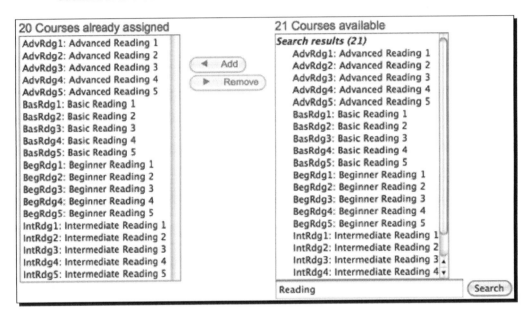

8. Use the short name link found in the breadcrumb path at the top-left of the window, shown in the following screenshot, to navigate to the course after you have added all of the reading child courses:

CIMS ▶ ReadingProg ▶ **Assign courses**

What just happened?

We just created a meta course and included all of the reading courses as child courses of the meta course. This means that all of the users enrolled in the reading child courses have been automatically enrolled in the meta course with the same roles that they have in the child courses. It should be noted here that enrollments in meta courses are controlled via the enrollments in each of the child courses. If you wish to unenroll a user from a meta course, he or she must be unenrolled from the respective child course. In the next step, we'll create the groups within the meta course that will allow us to create targeted forums.

Time for action – creating a group inside the meta course

We are now going to create groups within our meta course in order to allow us to specify which users will be allowed to participate in, and view, the forums we set up later. This will allow us to control which sets of users have access to the information and communication that will be contained in each forum. Follow these steps to set up the forums:

1. Log in to your Moodle site as admin and navigate to the meta course we just created. It will be located under the **Reading** heading from the **MyCourses** block and titled **Reading Program** if you followed the steps outlined earlier in this chapter.

2. Click on the **Groups** link found inside the **Administration** block.

3. The subsequent screen will be titled **ReadingProg Groups**. The **ReadingProg** portion of the title is from the short name of our course. From this screen, click on the **Create group** button. Title the group **Teachers** and write a short description for the group. Ignore the enrollment key option as enrollments for meta courses are controlled by the child course enrollments. Leave the picture field blank unless you would like to designate a picture for this group. Click on the **Save changes** button to create the group.

4. You will now see the **ReadingProg Groups** screen again and it will now contain the **Teachers** group, we just created. Click once on the group name to enable the **Add/remove users** button.

5. Click on the **Add/remove users** button to open the **Add/remove users** window. From this window, enter the word **Teacher** in the search window and click on the **Search** button. Select all of the teachers by clicking once on the first teacher and then scrolling to the last teacher and, while holding down the shift button on your keyboard, click on the last teacher. This will highlight all of the teachers in the list. Click on the **Add** button to add the selected teachers to the **Existing members** list on the left.

6. Click on the **Back to groups** button to return to the **ReadingProg Groups** screen. The Teachers group will now appear as **Teachers(20)** and, when selected, the list of teachers will appear in the **Members of:** list found on the right side of the screen, as shown in the following screenshot:

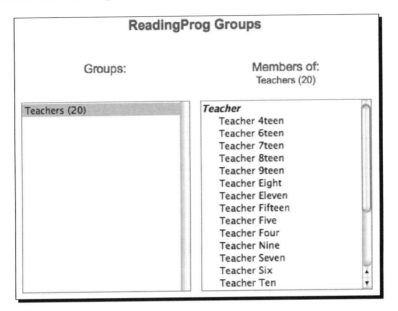

7. Next, navigate to the front page of your site and from the **Site Administration** block, click on the **Miscellaneous** heading link and then on the **Experimental** link.

8. Scroll down to the **Enable groupings** setting and click the tickbox to enable this setting. This setting enables you to group multiple groups together and also to make activities exclusively available to specific groupings. We'll need this capability when we set up the forums later. For a more detailed explanation of the groupings feature, visit the associated Moodle Docs page at: `http://docs.moodle.org/en/Groupings`.

What just happened?

We just created a group, within our Reading Program meta course, for all of the teachers enrolled in the course. Because the enrollments for a meta course are pulled from the child courses associated with a meta course, the teachers are all teachers who are teaching reading courses in our program. Later in this chapter, we'll see how we can use this group when we set up forums that we only want our teachers to have access to.

Have a go hero

We need to set up at least two more groups within our meta course. One of the groups will be for the students and the other for some educational program administrators. Try to accomplish the following tasks on your own:

1. Create a group titled **Students** and add all of the students enrolled in the meta course to the group. Follow the previous steps used for creating the **Teachers** group to accomplish this task.

2. Do the following in order to be able to create an administrators group (note this is for educational program administrators, not technical site administrators):

    ❑ Create 10 new administrator accounts

    ❑ Create a course for administrators and enroll the 10 users you created in the previous step, in the course (Enroll these users as students of the course)

    ❑ Add the administrator course, as a child course, to the Reading Program meta course

    ❑ In the meta course, create the **Administrator** group and add the administrators to it

3. Download the following files from the Packt website and follow the steps introduced in *Chapter 2, Building the Foundation—Creating Categories and Courses* and *Chapter 3, Student Account Creation and Enrollment* to upload the administrator user accounts, create the course, and enroll the administrators in the course. Note, you'll use the files in the order they are listed below:

    ❑ CIMS-CH9-adminusers.csv

    ❑ CIMS-CH9-admincourse.csv

    ❑ CIMS-CH9-adminenroll.csv

4. When you've completed these steps, your **ReadingProg Groups** window in your meta course should look like the following screenshot:

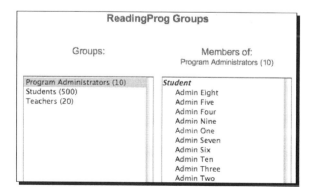

Time for action – setting up the forums inside the meta course

We are going to use this meta course as a communication and collaboration area for all users, students, teachers, and administrators, involved with the reading program, so now we need to set up some forums. We'll set up the following forums:

- A forum for all users in the course
- A forum for teachers
- A forum for teachers and administrators

To set up each of these forums follow these simple steps:

1. Log in to your site as admin and navigate to the **Reading Program** meta course.

2. Turn editing on by clicking on the **Turn editing on** button.

3. In the section numbered 1, just below the top section containing the **News** forum, use the **Add an activity** pull down menu to select and set up a **Forum**.

4. Title the forum **Reading Program**, use the **Standard forum** type, enter a short description, and use the following settings:

   - **Force everyone to be subscribed**: Yes, forever
   - **Read tracking**: On
   - **Maximum attachment size**: Increase to accommodate for files that may be uploaded in your forum
   - **Aggregate type**: No ratings
   - **Time period for blocking**: Don't block
   - **Group mode**: No groups

5. Click **Save and return to course** to finish the forum creation process and return to the course.

6. Before we create the next two forums, we need to create a couple of groupings in order to allow us to make the forums exclusive. Click on the **Groups** link found in the **Administration** block of your **Reading Program** course.

7. As we turned on the **Grouping** function in the previous section, you will now see the **Groupings** tab in between the **Groups** and **Overview** tabs, as shown in the following screenshot:

8. Click on the **Groupings** tab and add the following two groups by clicking on the **Create grouping** button:

   - Teachers
   - Program Administration

9. After creating the groupings, use the **Show groups in grouping** icon link found to the right of the **delete** link under the **Edit** heading, shown in the following screenshot, to open the **Add/remove groups** window and add the appropriate group to each grouping. Note, add both the administrator's and teacher's group to the Program Administration grouping. This will allow us to create a forum to be used exclusively by members of those two groups.

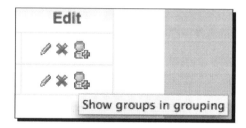

10. Now that the groupings have been specified, use the **Add an activity** pull down menu to select and set up another forum.

11. Title the forum **Teachers**, enter a short description and use all of the same settings as the **Reading Program** forum except for the settings under the **Common module settings** heading related to the group mode settings. Click the **Show Advanced** button that now appears as a result of turning on the grouping function. Use the pull down menus to select **Separate groups** for the **Group mode**, and **Teachers** for the **Grouping**. Tick the box next to the **Available for group members only** setting, make sure **Visible** is set to **Show,** and click on **Save and return to course**. The following screenshot is an example of these settings:

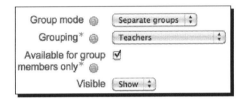

12. Once again, use the pull down menu to create another forum.

13. Title this forum **Reading Program Administration** and use all of the same settings as those used when setting up the **Teachers** forum with the exception of the **Grouping** setting, which should be set to **Program Administration**.

14. Once the three forums have been created and correctly assigned to a grouping, they should appear in your course, as shown in the following screenshot:

What just happened?

We just created three forums, each to be used by specific groups of users involved in the reading program. The first forum is a general communication forum to be used by all users enrolled in the meta course, which includes students, teachers, and program administrators. The second and third forums were set up to be exclusively available to specific groups. We set up the **Teachers** forum to be only accessible to the teachers and the **Reading Program Administration** forum to be available to only teachers and program administrators. This means that we now have forums for communication and collaboration within one course that are each accessible only to specific groups of users. The following screenshot shows the section containing these forums as viewed by a teacher, then by a student, and lastly by a program administrator. This is a graphic demonstration of which forums are visible to members of each group or grouping. Note that the groupings title (**Teachers** and **Program Administration**) is only visible to users with the teacher role.

```
Viewed by Teacher
    Reading Program
    Teachers (Teachers)
    Reading Program Administration (Program Administration)
Viewed by Student
    Reading Program
Viewed by Program Administrator
    Reading Program
    Reading Program Administration
```

Have a go hero

To confirm the functionality of the forums we've just created, log in to your site as a student to verify that the only forum visible to students in the Reading Program meta course is the **Reading Program** forum. Also, log in using one of the program administrator accounts to confirm that both the **Reading Program** forum and the **Program Administration** forum are visible. This is one of the many ways in which you can set up communication and collaboration forums within a course. Fine tuning the access privileges allows you to organize communication forums within course-and context-specific locations. Once you are comfortable with this method, explore other options for setting up communication and collaboration forums. For example, if your desire is to set up an inter-departmental communication portal, you may choose to set up a meta course that pulls its enrollment from various administrator courses situated within departments that have been set up as categories within Moodle. This will, of course, depend entirely upon how you choose to organize your educational program within the Moodle framework.

Building a mentor, homeroom, advisor, or counselor system

The mentees block, introduced in *Chapter 7, Advanced Data Access and Display* allows for some simple access to users assigned to a mentor but it is somewhat limited in its capabilities in terms of interaction between the mentee and the mentor and thus provides mainly a monitoring function. Many educational programs have mentoring or advising systems in place in which students are assigned to a mentor, advisor, or counselor. Often students are asked to visit their counselor at specific times and they are also almost always encouraged to see their advisor if they have questions or problems. Setting up a system within Moodle that allows students to interact with their mentors, advisors, counselors, or homeroom teachers, can improve access to these personnel and thereby improve the overall experience each student enjoys.

Time for action – setting up a mentor, advisor, or counseling system

In order to simplify the discussion here, I will use the term advising system for the remainder of this explanation. Remember that the system could, of course, be used as a mentoring, counseling, or homeroom system with little to no modification. Additionally, many of the ideas for this set up resemble those used in setting up the communication and collaboration system explained earlier in this chapter, so explanations will be somewhat abbreviated when deemed appropriate. To set up your advising system, follow these steps:

1. Log in to your site as admin and click on the **Show all courses** link found at the bottom of your **MyCourses** block on the front page of your site.

2. At the bottom of the subsequent **Course Categories** screen, click on the **Add a new course** button.

3. Leave the category set to **Miscellaneous** and enter a **Full name** and **Short name** such as **Advising Center** and **Advising**. Enter a short description explaining that the course is to function as an area where students may contact and interact with their advisors.

4. The only other settings that should be modified are those listed under the **Groups** heading. Change the **Group mode** to **Separate groups** and **Force** to **Yes**.

5. Set an **enrollment key** if you want to prevent users who are not enrolled in the course from accessing it. We will set up the course such that users not assigned to a group have very limited access however, so you may choose to not use an enrollment key and allow all students to access the course. One option may be to post a message in the top section of the course directing students who are not assigned to an advisor to send a message to the course director requesting an advisor. For this example, we will set up the system on the assumption that all students are enrolled by a program or system administrator and are assigned an advisor.

6. Click the **Save changes** button to create the course.

7. From the subsequent **Assign roles** page, assign one of the program administrator users, created earlier in this chapter, as **Teacher**, and five of the teachers in the system as **Non-editing teacher**. The setup for this example is shown in the following screenshot:

| Teacher | Teachers can do anything within a course, including changing the activities and grading students. | 1 | Admin One |
| Non-editing teacher | Non-editing teachers can teach in courses and grade students, but may not alter activities. | 5 | Teacher Five
Teacher Four
Teacher One
Teacher Three
Teacher Two |

8. For this example, we will enroll 50 students in this course. You may select 50 users randomly or use the file downloadable from the Packt website titled `CIMS-CH9-advisingenroll.csv`. Follow the process, explained in *Chapter 2, Building the Foundation—Creating Categories and Courses* for enrolling students in courses using the **Upload users** function found under **Users|Accounts** headings in the **Site Administration** block.

9. Once you have enrolled the students in the Advising course, navigate to the course and click on the **Groups** link found in the **Administration** block.

10. Click on the **Auto-create groups** button found at the bottom of the window.

11. Use the following settings for the auto group creation:

   - **Select members from role**: Student
   - **Specify**: Number of groups
   - **Group/member count**: 50 (the number of students enrolled in the course)
   - **Naming scheme**: Student #
   - **Create in grouping**: No
   - **Grouping name**: leave blank

12. Click on the **Submit** button to create the groups. You will see that 50 groups, each containing one student, have been created as evidenced by the long list of groups under the **Groups:** list.

13. Next, click on the **Groupings** tab and create five groupings, one for each of the five teachers we have enrolled in the course as non-editing teachers. It is recommended that you title the grouping with the name of the teacher that will be assigned to the grouping. There is unfortunately, no auto-grouping feature like the auto-creation feature for groups, so you will need to create each grouping individually.

14. After creating the groupings, click on the **Show groups** in the grouping icon to open the **Add/remove groups** window and add 10 groups—each is an individual student in our case—to each grouping, which designates a teacher or advisor in our case. When you have finished, your **Groupings** window will look something like the following screenshot:

Grouping	Groups	Activities	Edit
Teacher Five	Group 1, Group 10, Group 2, Group 3, Group 4, Group 5, Group 6, Group 7, Group 8, Group 9	0	✐ ✖ 👥
Teacher Four	Group 11, Group 12, Group 13, Group 14, Group 15, Group 16, Group 17, Group 18, Group 19, Group 20	0	✐ ✖ 👥
Teacher One	Group 21, Group 22, Group 23, Group 24, Group 25, Group 26, Group 27, Group 28, Group 29, Group 30	0	✐ ✖ 👥
Teacher Three	Group 31, Group 32, Group 33, Group 34, Group 35, Group 36, Group 37, Group 38, Group 39, Group 40	0	✐ ✖ 👥
Teacher Two	Group 41, Group 42, Group 43, Group 44, Group 45, Group 46, Group 47, Group 48, Group 49, Group 50	0	✐ ✖ 👥

15. Finally, we need to create forums for each of the five teachers who will serve as advisors. Navigate to the Advising course and use the **Add an activity** pull down menu to create five forums. Change the name of each forum to coincide with the name of the advisor. Other than that, the only settings that must be changed for each forum are the **Grouping** setting, which must be set to each respective teacher, and the **Available for group members only** setting, which must be ticked. For Teacher One, the settings will look like the following screenshot:

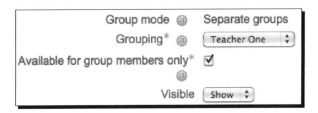

16. When you create a forum and assign a grouping, the name of the grouping is listed after the forum title in parentheses. After you have created all five forums, and if you placed them all in the same section, they should appear like the following screenshot:

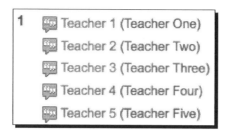

What just happened?

We just created a course to be used to house the advising program run by our imaginary school. We enrolled 50 students and five teachers, who will be our advisors, in the course and then used the **Auto-create groups** feature in Moodle to create 50 groups, one for each student. After creating the groups, we created five groupings, one for each teacher that will function as an advisor. We then assigned 10 students to each grouping, thereby assigning them to an advisor. Finally, we created a forum for each teacher/advisor and set the forum to use the grouping affiliated with one of the teacher/advisors. We also selected the setting that makes the forum available to group members only in order to prevent other group members from seeing the forum.

This setup allows each teacher to navigate to the advising course and view student posts in their respective forums. When a teacher navigates to the advising course and selects his or her advising forum, the advisor should be instructed to use the pull down menu, shown in the following screenshot, to select the group prior to viewing a post and responding to it. If the advisor posts a message when **All participants** is selected, the posted message will be visible to all of the members of the group.

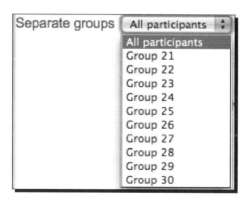

Note also, that from within the advising course, each advisor teacher may view and interact in a different teacher's advising forum. See the following *Have a go hero* section for instructions on how to prevent this type of access.

Once the advising system is set up, it can be a very powerful communication tool that allows advisors, counselors, mentors, and the like, to interact with their advisees. As you probably noticed, however, setting up the system is somewhat complicated and tedious. You'll probably want to use student names or ID numbers for group titles to make assigning students to advisors easier. The problem is however, you cannot specify student names or ID numbers for group titles when auto-creating groups. Additionally, the auto-creation feature that is available for groups is not currently available for groupings. As Moodle evolves, improvements to the grouping feature will likely include auto-creation of groupings, which, if the Moodle CIMS is used as the default grouping assignment tool, will significantly increase the time required for setting up this type of advising system. If your institution allocates students to advisors through some process external to Moodle, the difficulties mentioned here will remain and may prompt you to have custom development work done for your Moodle CIMS such as the development of a group and groupings upload tool.

Have a go hero

The advising system we have set up thus far is one that will enable your advisors, and the students who utilize them, to access each other more efficiently and, at the same time, to better archive the content of communications. You may desire to have your system more tightly regulated such that advisors are only able to view their own advising forums. This will provide for a higher level of security and privacy by ensuring that the content of communications between advisors and their advisees is kept confidential. Modifying the advising system we set up to effectively lock out advisors from other advising forums is a fairly straightforward, but somewhat tedious, process. It involves the following two steps:

1. Modify the permissions via the **Override Permissions** tab accessible from the **Assign roles** link found in the **Administration** block of the advising course. You should modify one permission setting for **Non-editing teachers**, which is the role used for the advisors. The setting is: **Access all groups** and is found under the **Course** heading. Change this setting to **Prevent**.

2. Next, to each group, you must add the teacher who is functioning as the advisor. If you do not add the teacher to each group, not grouping, he or she will not be able to see any groups as the permission setting change we made earlier prevents the non-editing teacher from viewing forums he or she is not a member of. In the future, a permission setting that allows locking out access to all groupings, except for those that a user is assigned to, will make this an easier process.

Completion of these two steps will allow your advising forums to be accessible only to the advisors, students assigned to that advisor, and the advising director to whom you assigned the role of teacher, **Admin One** in our example. Note that after completing the steps, when you log in as one of the advisor teachers, the drop-down menu—containing all of the advisees—no longer contains an **All participants** heading. While not intentional, this will prevent the advisor from accidentally posting a message that will be visible to all advisees because he or she will always be viewing, and thus interacting with, a specific advisee.

Feedback systems—using the questionnaire module

In addition to the various methods for promoting, mediating, and controlling communication and collaboration systems within Moodle, there are also various tools available to the Moodle user that allow for polling or surveying to obtain opinions and other forms of feedback from users of the system. Surveying students and teachers in order to obtain information about attitudes and opinions as well as background information is a practice common to many educational institutions. The results of this type of information gathering allows institutions to adapt to their students and teachers as well as to conduct research that, for example, may help to inform them about the effectiveness of their programs. Traditionally, surveys and questionnaires have been conducted via paper-based systems but with the advent of computers and the Internet, electronic polling has become a commonplace practice that allows for extremely efficient data gathering. One Moodle module that can be used for this type of data collection is the Questionnaire module. For the final section of this chapter, we will look briefly at the installation and use of the questionnaire module.

Time for action – installing and using the questionnaire module

Installing the Questionnaire module is a straightforward process that involves a few simple steps. Once you have installed the module, you can begin the slightly more involved process of creating your first questionnaire. We'll walk through the installation and creation of a simple questionnaire in the following steps:

1. Download the **Questionnaire** module from `www.moodle.org` by clicking on the **Modules and Plugins** link found in the drop-down menu under the **Downloads** heading in the menu bar. Use the search string **Questionnaire** to locate the module. Click on the **Download latest version** link to download the ZIP package to your hard drive.

2. Expand the compressed package and place the subsequent folder, which should be titled `Questionnaire`, in the `mod` directory, which is located in your `Moodle` root directory.

3. Log in to your Moodle site as admin and click on the **Notifications** link found at the top of the **Site Administration** block on the front page of your site.

4. You will then see a long series of messages informing you about tables being set up in the Moodle database that will finish with a **Success** message, shown in the following screenshot. Click on the **Continue** button and then navigate back to the front page of your course.

5. For this example, we will create a questionnaire, with three questions, in the **Reading Program** course, we worked with earlier. Go to the **Reading Program** course by clicking on the plus sign next to the **Reading** category folder from the **MyCourses** block and then on the **ReadingProg** course link.

6. From within the **Reading Program** course, click on the **Turn editing on** button and then use the **Add an activity** pull down menu bar to insert a **Questionnaire** into section two below the forums we created earlier in this chapter, as shown in the following screenshot:

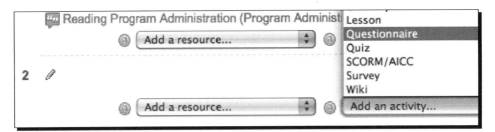

7. The first screen you will see is the **Adding a new Questionnaire** screen. This is where you enter details about your questionnaire and determine some of the settings that will control how the questionnaire is delivered and when it is available. Enter a title and description for your questionnaire and make necessary and desired adjustments to the other settings presented. All of the settings are well-documented via the question mark icon links. The following are a few of the noteworthy settings:

    □ **Response options (Type):** Here you can set your questionnaire to be accessible to a student only once, many times, or at regular intervals. In most cases, allowing a questionnaire to be completed only once is the standard approach. If you wish to poll students over a period of time however, you may opt to use the regular intervals or multiple access approach.

- ❑ **Response options (Respondent type)**: This setting allows you to deliver a questionnaire anonymously, which may be desirable depending on the content and planned use for the data that is obtained.

- ❑ **Content options**: After you have created one or more questionnaires, you will have the option here to reuse a questionnaire. As we have not yet created a questionnaire, **Create new** will be the only option.

8. Once you have selected your description and delivery options, click the **Save and display** button to view the questionnaire content window, shown in the following screenshot:

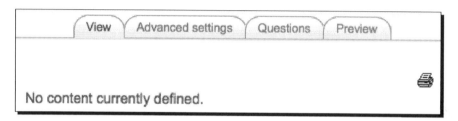

9. Click on the **Questions** tab to view the **Questions** page, shown in the following screenshot, and use the pull down menu, labeled ---**page break**--- by default, to select a question type. We will use the **Dropdown box** type for the first question in this example.

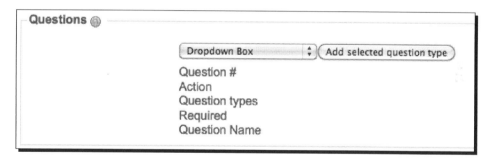

10. Click on the **Add selected question type** button to view the question settings window. Enter the name of the question, use the radio button options to make response to the question required or optional, enter the text you want to display with the question, and then list your possible answers at the bottom of the screen. Enter each possible answer on a new line. For this example, we are going to be asking students to select the name of their reading teacher. We would thus set up our question, as shown in the following screenshot :

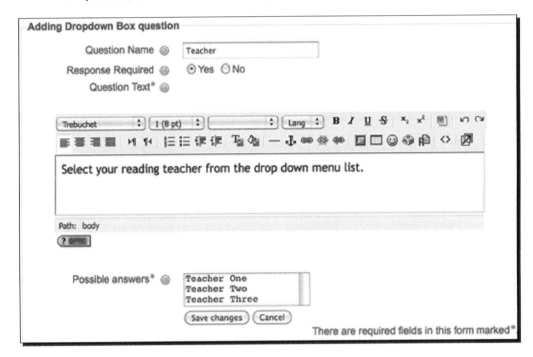

11. Click on the **Save changes** button to create the question. Note that the subsequent **Questions** window now displays the question that was just created and lists a few lines of information about its type and settings. Click on the **Preview** tab to preview the question. Once you have finished previewing the question, click on the **Questions** tab again and then add a question using the **Rate (scale 1...5)** question type.

12. Create a required response question that asks students how well they like to read in a foreign language. You'll need to direct them in the body of the question to use a **1**, if they don't like it and a **5**, if they love it. Although the information popup window for the **Possible answers** field will direct you to leave it blank for single line questions, leaving this box blank will generate an error. As an option, you can enter titles for the scale in the **Possible answers** box using the following formatting:

- **1** = I don't like it
- **2** = It's ok
- **3** = Average
- **4** = I like it a little
- **5** = I love it

13. If you use this style, you won't need to direct students about the scale in the body of the question text.

14. For the last question, create a **Yes/No** type question and use it to ask students if they plan to take more reading classes.

15. Once you have created all three questions, preview your questionnaire, using the **Preview** tab, to make sure it appears as you have planned.

16. Let's now quickly test the questionnaire to see how it appears to students and also from a teacher or administrator's perspective, once the questionnaire contains response data. Return to the front page of the **Reading Program** course, click on the **Participants** link and then randomly select a student from the list by clicking on the name link.

17. Use the **Login as** feature, found at the bottom of the profile page, shown in the following screenshot, to log in as that student and take the questionnaire. When you have finished you can scroll to the bottom of the course window and click on the **-Admin-** link located to the left of the **You are logged in as** message. Repeat the process for five or six different students.

18. Note that depending on the settings you choose for how the questionnaire is delivered, students may or may not be able to review their responses after completing the questionnaire. After you have completed the questionnaire as five or more students, return to your admin role and view the questionnaire. Notice that there is now an **All responses** tab with the total number of responses listed in parenthesis. Click on the **All responses** tab to view the responses and the various display methods available, as shown in the following screenshot, and experiment with the various onscreen and downloadable formats:

View	All responses (5)	Advanced settings	Questions	Preview

View All Responses	View By Response

View Default order	Ascending order	Descending order	Delete ALL Responses	Download in text format

What just happened?

We just created a very simple questionnaire that contains three questions and then logged in as different students to take the questionnaire. After populating the questionnaire with response data, we logged back into our site and viewed the contents of the questionnaire to see how the data can be displayed and downloaded. The clean and easy-to-read aggregated results display, shown in the following screenshot, makes for very easy initial interpretation of results, and the ability to download the results in a variety of formats makes further data analysis with advanced statistics software possible. As you can see, the Questionnaire module can function as a valuable tool for obtaining information and data from users in your Moodle CIMS.

Reading Program Survey

1. Select your reading teacher from the drop down menu list.

Response	Average	Total
teacher one	40%	2
teacher two	20%	1
teacher three	20%	1
teacher five	20%	1
Total	100%	5/5

Have a go hero

To get a better idea of how you might use the Questionnaire module, try creating a longer questionnaire using some, or all, of the other question formats. Try also answering the questionnaire with more student accounts to see how the graphic representation of the results shifts as the number of respondents increase. Also, try using the anonymous questionnaire and viewing the responses to that questionnaire, after it has been completed by one or more students, to see how Moodle protects the identity of the respondents when the anonymous option is used. Finally, try installing and using the Feedback module, available on the `Moodle.org` Modules and Plugins page. The Feedback module is very similar to the Questionnaire module and is scheduled to be a core module for Moodle 2.0. Both the Questionnaire module and the Feedback module are very similar but Moodle users often prefer one over the other based upon the appearance and ease-of-use of the interface. Experiment with both and see which one you prefer.

Summary

In this chapter, we have explored several methods of expanding our Moodle CIMS into a tool that facilitates efficient communication between the various users of the system. We started with the creation of a meta course that was assigned all of the courses in our reading program as child courses. Within this course we set up three groups: teachers, students, and educational administrators. We then created a special course to house our educational administrators and also assigned that course as a child course to our meta course and then created various forums for our groups. One forum was set up for all members to participate in, one for only teachers, and a third for only teachers and administrators. This was one example of how Forums, combined with the use of groups, can be set up to facilitate communication and collaboration.

Next we built an advising system, using some of the concepts we learned in setting up our communication forums, by creating groups and groupings within our Reading Program course. Each student was assigned to a group and then we assigned 10 groups each to an advisor, teachers functioning as advisors with the role of non-editing teacher, by using the grouping feature available in Moodle. Finally, to make our advising forums as private as possible, we removed a permission from the non-editing teacher role and then added each teacher to each single student group within his or her advising grouping. This process, while a bit tedious, enabled us to set up an advising system using forums that keeps communication between advisors and advisees confidential, but that is still easily navigable for advisors and program supervisors.

In the last section of the chapter, we explored the use of the Questionnaire module and experimented with a short questionnaire. We looked at how the results of a questionnaire are tabulated within Moodle. This module is a wonderful addition to a program that wishes to obtain aggregated data from a group of students or teachers that can be used for statistical analysis as well as for program improvement efforts.

This chapter provided several concrete examples of how Moodle can function to improve the efficiency of communication between all parties involved in an educational program. Use of the tools presented here can help your organization to communicate more effectively and efficiently, to disseminate information in a more transparent fashion, and to interact with students as individuals with unique questions, concerns, and needs. In the next, and final chapter, we will explore how Moodle can be set up to help deliver a curriculum based upon a fine-tuned set of rules and regulations via a third-party enrollment plugin.

10
Advanced Enrollment Plugin

Almost all educational programs that organize a series, or set of courses into a curriculum, also establish and enforce rules about how a student may matriculate through the courses. Colleges and universities, for example, design a curriculum such that more advanced level courses are taken by students who are in their junior and senior years and who have already completed more basic prerequisite courses in their earlier years. Likewise, programs within an educational institution, such as language education programs, dictate which courses students may take based upon the students' levels. For example, a student who is studying Spanish for the first time would take an entry level course while a different student, who has mastered the basics and even studied abroad in a Spanish-speaking country, would take a more advanced level Spanish course. Additionally, most educational institutions set course capacity limits, especially for courses that include an interactive component, in order to ensure that teachers are able to provide adequate attention to each student in his or her classroom.

The final step in adapting your Moodle instance into a full-fledged CIMS, that will be covered in this book, is to enable your site to function as a registration and enrollment system that will allow you to regulate how students matriculate through the set of courses that make up your curriculum.

In this chapter, we will walk through the following in order to help you get your registration system installed and set up in your Moodle CIMS:

- Download and install the Registration Enrollment plugin
- Enable and set up the Registration Enrollment plugin to control enrollment for selected courses
- Test the Registration Enrollment plugin to confirm its functionality

Introducing the Registration Enrollment plugin

The Registration Enrollment plugin that will be introduced in this chapter was developed through a Nihon University Individual Research Grant for 2009 that was awarded to the author of this book and the plugin was donated to the public under the same GNU Public License used by Moodle. Developmental work, in the form of programming and design collaboration, was performed by the Moodle Partner, MoodleRooms.

This plugin uses values stored in the custom user profile fields that were discussed in *Chapter 8, Setting Up a Mini SIS* and it will allow you to control all of the following when students register for courses within your Moodle CIMS:

   ◆ Set a maximum number of students that may enroll in a course

   ◆ Set up multiple priority enrollment periods in order to allow specific groups
      of students to register for courses before they are open to all students

   ◆ Control enrollment in a course based upon a value stored in a user profile field

   ◆ Specify the number of courses in which a student is allowed to enroll in
      a given period

Additionally, the following capabilities have been incorporated into the future development plan for the plugin in the form of filters internal to the plugin:

   ◆ Ability to select multiple user profile fields when specifying the necessary criteria
      for course enrollment

   ◆ The ability to chain together a series of logical elements, or statements, in order
      to fine-tune the conditions used for determining whether a student can enroll in a
      course or not

As additional funding becomes available, or if another developer wishes to add to the functionality, this plugin will evolve with more features and capabilities. Please consider contributing to the development of this and other publicly available plugins as your Moodle CIMS site takes hold and you discover a need for specific capabilities and functionality.

Time for action – installing the Registration Enrollment plugin

Installation of the Registration Enrollment plugin is the same as for other blocks, modules, and plugins. To download and install the plugin follow these steps:

1. From the Moodle **Modules and Plugins** page search for and download the
     registration system.

2. Expand the `registration_system` folder that is downloaded to your hard drive.

3. Inside the folder will be a `blocks` directory and an `enrol` directory. Copy the contents of each to the respective directories located in your Moodle root directory. There are two directories (folders) in the `blocks` directory and one in the `enrol` directory.

4. After you have placed all of the components of the plugin in their correct locations, log in to your site as admin and click on the **Notifications** link found in the **Site Administration** block on the front page of your site.

5. You will see a short series of messages indicating that the tables for the registration system have been set up correctly. Click the **Continue** button found at the bottom of the screen below the **Success** message, as shown in the following screenshot:

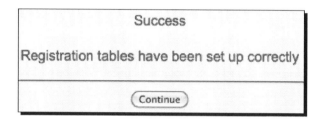

What just happened?

We just downloaded and installed the Registration Enrollment plugin in the same fashion that almost all Moodle plugins (blocks, modules, and other plugins) are installed. This has set up the tables in the Moodle database that will be used by the system, as well as placed all of the PHP files that are a part of the system, in their correct locations. Next, we will enable the Registration Enrollment plugin and start working with the various settings it contains.

Time for action – creating and populating the user profile fields

We are going to set up our registration enrollment system to use two user profile fields, the Program of Study field we created in *Chapter 8*, *Setting Up a Mini SIS* and a new field to house information about students' proficiency levels. The registration enrollment system uses user profile fields, and their values, to establish criteria that control whether a user is allowed to enroll in a course or not, so we thus need to create and populate the new user profile field before we may proceed with the Registration Enrollment plugin setup. Follow these steps to create and populate the new field:

1. Log in to your Moodle site as admin and, from the **Site Administration** block, click on **Users**, then **Accounts**, and then **User profile fields**.

2. Use the pull down menu to create a new **text input** user profile field.

3. We are going to create a user profile field titled "level" and use the field to store proficiency level information such as Advanced, Intermediate, and Beginner. Use the following values for the field you are about to create:

   ❑ **Short name**: level

   ❑ **Name**: Proficiency level

   ❑ **Description**: Short description

   ❑ **Required**: No

   ❑ **Locked**: Yes

   ❑ **Unique**: No

   ❑ **Display on signup page**: No

   ❑ **Visible to**: Visible to user

   ❑ **Category**: Other fields

   ❑ **Default value**: None

   ❑ **Display size**: 15

   ❑ **Maximum length**: 15

   ❑ **Password field**: No

4. The following screenshot is of the **Creating a new "Text input" profile field** screen with all of these settings entered and selected:

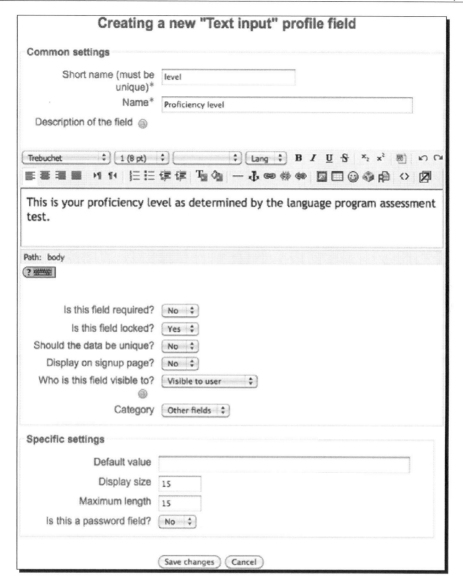

5. After you have entered all of the settings, click on the **Save changes** button to create the field.

6. Next, we will populate the field for 60 students. This will be more than sufficient to allow us to test the registration enrollment system after we have finished setting it up. Use the CIMS-CH10-ProfileFields.csv file found at the Packt website and the procedure outlined in *Chapter 8, Setting Up a Mini SIS* to populate the fields for these 60 students. Note that 15 students from each of the four levels of students we have set up in our site (Advanced, Intermediate, Beginner, and Basic) were selected randomly and those are the levels that are being used to populate the field we have just created.

What just happened?

We have just created and populated an additional user profile field, called "level", to be used by our registration enrollment system. Note that the fields that were just populated will be visible to users when they log in and view their profiles as well as to users of the Xataface system we set up in *Chapter 7, Advanced Data Access and Display* and *Chapter 8, Setting Up a Mini SIS*. We have set up these fields such that they are locked to the user viewing his or her profile within Moodle, but these values could be accessed and edited from our backside Xataface application if we wanted educational administrators to be able to modify the information. Next, we need to set up our registration enrollment system such that it will use these fields, and their values, to control enrollment in some of our courses.

Time for action – setting up the Registration Enrollment plugin (default site-wide settings)

Now that we have installed the files that make up the Registration Enrollment plugin and have created a new user profile field to be used by the system, we need to enable the plugin and then set it up to control the enrollment for some of our courses. Follow these steps to get the system up and running:

1. Click on the **Courses** and then **Enrolment** links found in the **Site Administration** block on the front page of your Moodle site.

2. This will present the **Enrolments** window that will look like the following screenshot. Tick the **Enable** box found to the right of the **Registration Enrolment** line, as shown in the following screenshot, and then click on the **Save changes** button:

Name	Enable	Default	Settings
Authorize.net Payment Gateway	☐	○	Edit
External Database	☑		Edit
Flat file	☐		Edit
IMS Enterprise file	☐		Edit
Internal Enrolment	☑	⊙	Edit
LDAP	☐		Edit
Moodle Networking	☐		Edit
PayPal	☐	○	Edit
Registration Enrolment	☑	○	Edit

Save changes

3. Next, click on the **Edit** link to access the plugin settings.

4. The **Registration Enrolment** window that will appear, shown in the following screenshot, presents a **Save changes** button but clicking on this button will merely return you to the **Enrolments** window, shown in the preceding screenshot. Instead, click on the **Main Registration Block Settings** link to access the settings.

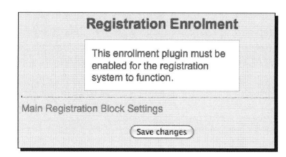

5. The **Filter Settings** window, shown in the following screenshot, will be displayed. This is the window from which settings for the registration system can be accessed. Although the **logical** filter tickbox appears on the **Filter Settings** window, programming that will allow the chaining together of logical expressions is not yet complete and this function is thus not yet available. Additionally, while the **multifield** filter is functional, it cannot be used in conjunction with the **profile plugin** and thus does not incorporate the various settings that are available when using the **profile** filter. Select the tickbox next to the **profile** filter and click the **Save** button to save the filter setting.

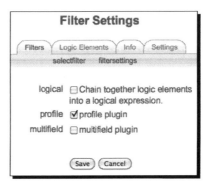

6. After you have selected the **profile plugin** and clicked the **Save** button, click the **Logical Elements** tab to access the various settings for the site-wide default settings for the registration enrollment system. The subsequent window will be the **Logical Elements Settings** window, the top portion of which is shown in the following screenshot:

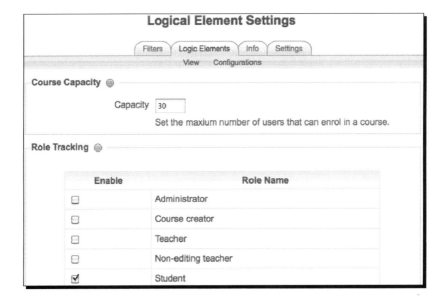

7. The following is a list, and brief description, of the settings that can be adjusted from this window. The suggested setting, for this tutorial, is listed in a subpoint after each setting description. Several of these settings can also be overridden at the individual course level. This override capability is also noted in the following list. Note also that the first two settings, **Course Capacity** and **Role Tracking**, can be seen in the preceding screenshot. The remaining settings are shown in the screenshot that follows this list:

- **Course Capacity**: Use this to set a maximum number of users allowed to enroll in a course. This setting can be overridden at the individual course level. Set this to 30 (we will override this value at the course level for our example).

- **Role Tracking**: Use this to set the roles to which you want the enrollment registration system to apply. This setting cannot be overridden at the course level. Enable **Student** by clicking in the tickbox located to the left of the **Student** role name.

- **Period**: These settings control the period of time during which users are allowed to enroll via the Registration Enrollment plugin. Note that multiple periods may be created but that they should not be overlapped. Doing so will result in unpredictable and/or inaccurate behavior. This setting cannot be overridden at the course level. Give the **Period** a name such as **Test Period**, allow only one enrollment, and set a date that is approximately one week from the time you plan to test the plugin.

- **Priority by Period Startdate**: This setting allows you to set a priority enrollment period, designated by a specific number of days and hours, prior to the **Period** start date and time, during which users with a specific value in a userfield, selected and designated by a site administrator, may enroll in the course. This may be conceptualized as an advance enrollment feature that is used for students who meet predetermined criteria for advanced enrollment. This setting can be overridden at the individual course level. Additionally, multiple instances of the **Priority by Period Startdate** may be created to accommodate various situations and conditions.

- **program Userfield**: Use this and set the **Value** to Teacher Training. Set the **Days** and **Hours** settings such that a user who meets this condition will be able to enroll when you test the system. (For example, if you have set your course to start in seven days, set this value to seven days. This will allow you to log in as a user who is enrolled in the Teacher Training program and confirm that the user is able to advance enroll in the course.)

- ❏ **Userfield Value**: This is the setting that must be used to specify what condition needs to be met for users to enroll in the course. For our example, we will create a new course that is available only to advanced level students, so use the **level Userfield** that we created earlier and set the **Value** to Advanced.

- ❏ **Send iCalendar Event on Enrol**: Although this setting appears on the **Logical Elements Settings** page, this feature has not yet been added to the Registration Enrollment plugin and is thus not yet selectable. Settings listed here from **Period** to **Send iCalendar Event on Enrol** can be seen in the following screenshot:

Period

Name	Test Period
Allowed Enrollments	1
Start Date	1 October 2010 10 45
End Date	7 October 2010 10 45

The period in which these settings will apply.

(Add Instance)

Priority by Period Startdate

Userfield	program
Value	Teacher Training
Days	7
Hours	0

Users that have matching fields with the value will be able to enrol X days before the current period's enrollment start date.

(Add Instance)

Userfield Value

Userfield	level
Value	Advanced

Users whom have this user field matching this value can enrol

Send iCalendar Event on Enrol

Email an iCal event for course start time upon a user's successful enrollment.

(Save) (Cancel)

8. Click the **Save** button, shown in the preceding screenshot, to save all of the settings that you have just entered.

What just happened?

We have now enabled the Registration Enrollment plugin and set the default settings to be used by the plugin. Some of these settings, such as **Role Tracking** and the **Period**, are settings that can only be modified from this site-wide setting area while others, such as **Course Capacity** and **Priority Period**, are settings that serve as site-wide default settings but can be overridden from within each individual course. One note of caution here is to remember that while multiple enrollment periods can be created, they must not overlap. Future versions of this plugin may allow for the creation of multiple enrollment periods, that may be selected from within each individual course, but this initial version is equipped only to utilize one period at a time. It is thus important to be careful when creating additional enrollment periods to make sure that they do not overlap.

Time for action – registration enrollment system settings (course level)

In addition to the site-wide settings used by the registration enrollment system, there is also a block that is used at the course level to override values and add additional priority periods to those set at the site-wide level. As we have already enrolled users in the courses we have created on our test site, we will create a new course, set it up to use the registration enrollment plugin, and use the **Course Registration** block to override some of the site-wide default values. Follow these steps to create the course and get it set up to use the Registration Enrollment plugin:

1. Log in to your Moodle site as admin and click on the **Show all courses** link found at the bottom of the **MyCourses** block.

2. From the subsequent **Course Categories** window, click on the **Add a new course** button found at the bottom of the page.

3. Using the pull down menu, set the **Category** to **Listening** and give the course a **Full name** of Special Listening and a **Short name** of SP-List. Enter a short **Summary** and leave the remaining **General** settings at their defaults.

4. Scroll down to the **Enrolments** heading and use the **Enrolment Plugins** pull down menu to select the **Registration Enrolment** plugin, as shown in the following screenshot. Make sure the **Yes** button, next to the **Course enrollable** heading, is selected but leave the **Start date** and **End date** disabled. Additionally, the **Enrollment duration** can be left as **Unlimited**.

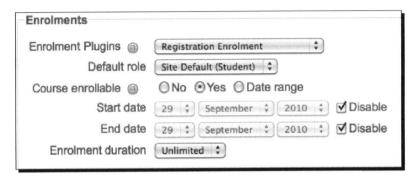

5. For this example case, use the default values for the remainder of the course settings. Scroll to the bottom of the page and click on the **Save changes** button to create the course.

6. On the subsequent **Assign roles** page, you may assign a teacher but we will not be using a teacher account for this example, so it is unnecessary. Click the **Click here to enter your course** button to enter the course.

7. From within the course, click the **Turn editing on** button.

8. With editing turned on, use the **Blocks** drop-down menu to find and select the **Course Registration** block.

9. Once you have added the **Course Registration** block, and with editing turned on, several icons will appear below the **Course Registration** block title, as shown in the following screenshot:

10. The first icon from the left allows you to assign roles that will have access to the block. If no roles are assigned here, the only user able to access this block is the admin. The second icon, the visibility setting, will most likely not be used because access can be controlled via the role setting. The third icon, the Configuration icon, will present a window that allows for setting the maximum capacity. It is recommended that you use the Logical elements link—explained next—instead of the Configuration setting, in order to avoid confusion. The last three icons, the delete and move icons, perform the same actions as on all other blocks.

11. Turn off editing in your course and then click on the **Logic Elements** link to access the course level settings for the Registration Enrollment plugin. Notice that all of the headings that appeared in the site-wide settings window, explained earlier in this chapter, are visible here, and that those that cannot be overridden at the course level, cannot be selected or modified. Those that can be overridden contain an **Override** link to the right of the heading title, as shown in the following screenshot:

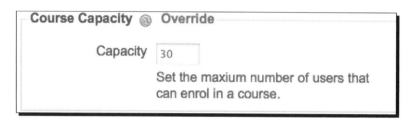

12. Also note the **Add Instance** button located within the **Priority by Period Startdate** setting box, shown in the following screenshot. This allows for adding additional priority enrollment periods.

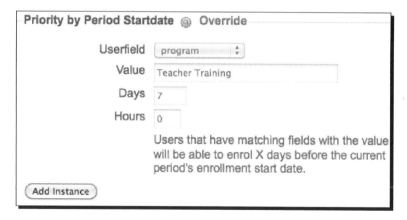

13. Click on the **Override** link located on the right of the **Course Capacity** heading and change the value from 30 to 5, as shown in the following screenshot:

14. For this example, we will not override or add any other settings, so scroll down to the bottom of the page and click on the **Save** button to save the **Course Capacity** override setting.

What just happened?

We have just created a new course for the purpose of testing the Registration Enrollment plugin and set the course to use the Registration Enrollment plugin. We then created an instance of the Course Registration block from within the course and modified the site-wide Course Capacity settings by applying an Override and changing the maximum capacity from 30 to 5. As a result of both the site-wide settings we have chosen for the registration enrollment system and the settings we have dictated from within the course we set to use the plugin, we now have a course in which five students, who must be designated as Advanced level students, may enroll. Additionally, students in the Teacher Training program, who are Advanced level students, will be able to enroll seven days prior to the beginning of the enrollment period. Next, we need to test the system to make sure that it will perform as desired.

Testing the Registration Enrollment plugin

In order to understand how the registration enrollment system responds to both students who are eligible to enroll in a course and to those who are not, we will walk through some simple test enrollment scenarios using the course we have just created and some of the student accounts to which we assigned the **level** User profile fields earlier in this chapter.

Time for action – testing the priority enrollment period setting for an eligible student

We will now set up a scenario that will allow us to test the functionality of the priority enrollment period feature. Follow these steps to test the priority enrollment period setting:

1. First, in order to test the priority enrollment setting, please make sure that your current time is within the priority enrollment period window of time. In other words, if you have set the course enrollment period to start seven days from today, you will need to also have your priority enrollment period set to at least seven days in order to make it possible for the student accounts that meet the criteria to be able to enroll.

2. Once you are sure that the current time, the time you intend to test the system, is within the priority period, use the **Bulk user actions** filter feature found in the **Site Administration** block by clicking on the **Users** and then the **Accounts** link, to select a user who is designated as an advanced user.

3. Click on the **Show Advanced** button from within the **Filter** heading and create a filter that will return only students with the value **Teacher Training** in their **program userfield**, as shown in the following screenshot:

4. After clicking on the **Add filter** button to add the first filter, create a second filter, that will be applied to the group of students returned by the first filter, to select only those students with the value **Advanced** in their **level userfield**. The settings for the second filter are shown in the following screenshot:

5. If you have created the CIMS Moodle site outlined in this book to this point, applying these two filters will result in five students being displayed, as shown in the following screenshot:

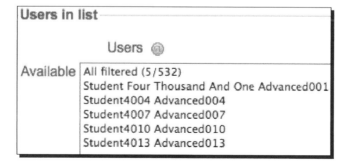

6. Note the students who meet the criteria for priority enrollment (students 4004, 4007, 4010, and 4013) and use the following three usernames and log in passwords for testing the system, as explained in the following steps. Note you can also obtain this information by referring to the file we used to create these accounts, introduced in *Chapter 3, Student Account Creation and Enrollment* to find the log in username and password for each student.

  ❑ Student4001—Username = S400001 and Password = S4001

  ❑ Student4004—Username = S400004 and Password = S4004

  ❑ Student4007—Username = S400007 and Password = S4007

7. Now, log out of the site and then log back in using the account information, as listed in step 6, for Student4001.

8. After logging in as Student4001, click on the **Show all courses** link found at the bottom of the **MyCourses** block.

9. From the subsequent **Course Categories** page, click on the **Listening** category link. On the resulting page the **Special Listening** course will be listed below the **Listening Sub-categories**.

10. Click on the **Special Listening** course link to attempt to enroll in the course. As this student meets the criteria for registering in this course (he or she is an **Advanced** level student and is also enrolled in the **Teacher Training** program and thus eligible for advanced enrollment), the **Would you like to enroll in this course?** message will appear, as shown in the following screenshot. Click on the **Yes** button to enroll this student.

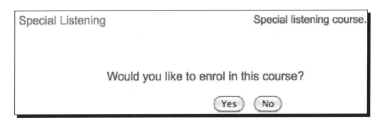

11. You are then taken to the front page of the course as the student is enrolled in the course. Log out of the site and follow the same process for the other two students listed in the previous steps (S400004 and S400007).

What just happened?

We just enrolled a student in a course that is set to use the Registration Enrollment plugin. The student was able to enroll in the course because he or she met all of the criteria we set up via the Registration Enrollment plugin site-wide and course specific settings, which are:

♦ The student is an Advanced level student

♦ The student is enrolled in the Teacher Training program, which makes him/her eligible to enroll ahead of the enrollment period

♦ The student is not yet enrolled in any courses that use the Registration Enrollment plugin and thus does not yet exceed the number of courses allowed, which we have set at one

Time for action – testing the priority enrollment period for an ineligible student

Follow these steps to see how the Registration Enrollment plugin will handle a student who meets the criteria set for enrollment in the course, but who does not meet the priority enrollment period criteria.

1. Log out of the site and log back in as Student4002.

2. Student4002 is an **Advanced** level student, which is the criteria for enrolling in the class, but is not enrolled in the **Teacher Training** program, the criteria for advanced enrollment. Use the **username S400002 and password S4002** to log in as this student.

3. Navigate to the course using the **Show all courses** link found in the **MyCourses** block and click on the course link to attempt to enroll in the course.

4. You will receive a message informing you that the enrollment period has not yet begun for the course with a message about when the period will begin, as shown in the following screenshot. The time remaining until the enrollment period starts will, of course, depend upon the time you have entered for the enrollment period to begin.

Special Listening   Special listening course.

You may not enrol in this course.

You can not enrol until the enrollment period begins on Thursday, 7 October 2010, 10:45 am (1 day 20 hours)

What just happened?

We just tried to enroll a student who met the criteria for enrolling in the course, which is being in the Advanced level. The student however, did not meet the priority enrollment criteria and was thus not allowed to enroll in the course. The student was thus presented with an on-screen message informing him or her that enrollment would be possible once the enrollment period begins. We saw that the message presented to such students also provides information about the enrollment period start date and time as well as how much time remains before the said period is to begin.

Time for action – testing the Registration Enrollment plugin for a non-eligible student

Follow these steps to see how the Registration Enrollment plugin will handle a student who does not meet any of the criteria for enrolling in the course. Note, this example is also applicable to students who meet the priority enrollment period criteria but do not meet the primary requirement, which is defined from within the plugin using the **Userfield Value** setting. Users who may, incidentally, meet the priority enrollment period requirements, are not allowed to enroll in a course if the primary requirement has not been fulfilled.

1. Use the following account to log in to the course: Student3001 – Username = S300001 **and Password =** S3001.

2. Again, navigate to the **SP-List** course and click on the course link to attempt to enroll in the course.

3. This time you will see an error message informing the student that he or she is not eligible to enroll in the course, as shown in the following screenshot. Note, you can change the text of the error message that appears via the language block_ registration.php file located at the following path in your Moodle directory yourmoodledirectory/lang/en_utf8/block_registration.php. **Open** the file with your text editor and change only the text in between the single quotes.

Special Listening   Special listening course.

You may not enrol in this course.

User profile field does not match course field.

You are logged in as Student3001 Intermediate001 (Logout)

What just happened?

We just tried to enroll a student who did not meet the Advanced level criteria we set for the course. The student was informed, via an enrollment error message, that he or she was not eligible to enroll in the course.

Have a go hero

You will probably want to customize the message that appears when students are not allowed to enroll in a course. Open the file that contains the language strings, mentioned in the previous step, and change the text to something that is appropriate to your institution or program, then retry the enrollment and verify that the message appears as desired.

Time for action – testing the course capacity setting of the Registration Enrollment plugin

Let's now test the course capacity setting to make sure that the Registration Enrollment plugin will prevent users from enrolling in a course once its capacity has been met. Follow these steps to test this feature:

1. As we currently only have five students in our system who are eligible to enroll in the course and the course maximum is set to five, we will have to change a setting to create the scenario. There are several ways this can be achieved. The easiest is to navigate to the **SP-List** course and change the course capacity setting via the **Course Registration** block.

2. We earlier overrode the site-wide setting of 30 and set the capacity of this course to 5. We currently have three students enrolled in this course, so change this number to 3, as shown in the following screenshot, and click on the **Save** button at the bottom of the page:

3. Now, log out of the site and back in as Student4010, one of the students that is eligible to enroll in the course, and one who is eligible to advance enroll. The user information for this student is Username = **S400010** and Password = **S4010**.

4. Navigate to the **SP-List** course and click on the course link to attempt to enroll in the course. The student will be displayed with an error message informing him or her that the course has reached its capacity, as shown in the following screenshot. Note that students may still be enrolled via the **Assign roles** function found in the **Administration** block of the course by a teacher or administrator. This allows for special enrollments through the use of a system that, for example, requires students to consult with instructors personally and be approved for enrollment by the teacher after the maximum capacity has been met.

Special Listening   Special listening course.

You may not enrol in this course.

The number of students who have enrolled in this course is already equal to the maxium allowed.

You are logged in as Student4010 Advanced010 (Logout)

What just happened?

We just tried to enroll a student in our course who met both the base enrollment criteria and the priority enrollment period criteria. The student was however, not allowed to enroll in the course because the course capacity, that we set to three, had been met. The student thus received an error informing him or her that the course was at its maximum enrollment.

Have a go hero

Many institutions allow students to enroll in courses that are already at their max only after they have talked with the instructor in person and received permission to enroll in the course. Edit the error message students see when the course has "filled" to reflect this policy and instruct students to see the instructor of the course to request permission for enrollment.

Time for action – testing the Registration Enrollment plugin base criteria

Follow these steps to confirm that the plugin will allow a student, who meets the base criteria, to enroll in a course once the enrollment period has begun:

1. Navigate to the site-wide settings for the Registration Enrollment system and change the enrollment date from seven days in the future, to today. This will allow all users who meet the enrollment criteria to enroll today, the day you are testing the plugin.

2. Also, navigate back to the **SP-List** course and change the capacity setting that we changed to 3 back to 10, in order to allow more enrollments.

3. Next, log out of the site and back in as an eligible student. We'll use **Student4015** for this example. While this student is not enrolled in the Teacher Training program, he or she is in the **Advanced** level and thus meets the criteria for enrollment in the course now that we have changed the enrollment period to start today.

4. Navigate to the **SP-List** course and attempt to enroll in the course by clicking on the course link. The **Would you like to enroll in this course?** message will appear and clicking on the **Yes** button will enroll this student in the course, which confirms that the plugin is allowing eligible students to enroll once the enrollment period has begun.

What just happened?

This simple test allowed us to confirm that students who meet the base criteria, but do not meet the priority enrollment criteria, may enroll in the course once the enrollment period has begun.

Time for action – testing the Registration Enrollment plugin after the period has ended

In order to make sure that the plugin will not allow students to enroll in a course once the enrollment period has ended, follow these test steps:

1. First, change the enrollment period via the site-wide settings. These settings are accessed via the **Site Administration** block by clicking on the **Courses** and then **Enrolments** links.

2. Click on the **Edit** link to the right of the **Registration Enrollment** plugin name and then on the **Main Registration Block Settings** link to access the plugins settings, which are then found by clicking on the **Logic Elements** tab.

3. Change the **Period** such that the end date and time has passed. For example, change the period end date to yesterday's date. This will close the enrollment period for all students. Note, also make sure to change the start date and time to some time that occurs before the end date and time.

4. Log out of the site and then back in using the following account: **Student4011—Username = S400011** and **Password = S4011**. This student is an Advanced level student but is not in the Teacher Training program.

5. Attempt to enroll in the course by navigating to and clicking on the **SP-List** course link. This time the error message informs the student that the enrollment period for this course has ended and that he or she may thus not enroll in the course, as shown in the following screenshot:

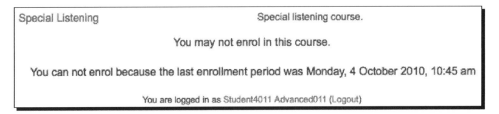

Special Listening   Special listening course.

You may not enrol in this course.

You can not enrol because the last enrollment period was Monday, 4 October 2010, 10:45 am

You are logged in as Student4011 Advanced011 (Logout)

What just happened?

We just attempted to enroll a student, who met the enrollment criteria, in the course but the student was not allowed to enroll because the enrollment period had ended. We saw that the student receives an error informing him or her that the enrollment period ended and is given information about when the period ended.

Time for action – testing the Registration Enrollment plugin Allowed Enrollments setting

In order to confirm that the Allowed Enrollments setting will limit the number of courses a student is allowed to enroll in, follow these steps. Also, remember that this setting will only control the number of enrollments in courses that are set to use the Registration Enrollment plugin.

1. From the site-wide settings for the **Registration Enrollment** plugin, scroll down to the **Period** heading and change the **Allowed Enrollments** setting to 1, as shown in the following screenshot:

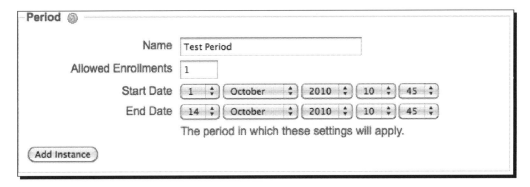

2. The setting of 1 will mean that students can only enroll in one course that uses the Registration Enrollment plugin and as we currently only have one such course in our test site, we will need to create one more course that uses the Registration Enrollment plugin.

3. Also, change the enrollment period that we "closed" for the previous test, back to a time frame that includes your current time in order to "open" the enrollment period.

4. Create a new course that uses the Registration Enrollment plugin, as explained earlier in this chapter.

5. Add the **Course Registration** block to the course.

6. Now, log in as one of the advanced level users that we enrolled in our **SP-List** course and attempt to enroll in the newly created course.

7. You will receive an error explaining that the student has reached his or her maximum enrollments and may not enroll in any more courses, as shown in the following screenshot:

Test Max Enrollments   Test course to make sure max enrollments works.

You may not enrol in this course.

Max Allowed Enrollments for this period have been reached.

You are logged in as Student Four Thousand And One Advanced001 (Logout)

What just happened?

We have just tested the allowed enrollment setting by trying to enroll a student that is already enrolled in the maximum number of courses allowed by the plugin. We were able to confirm the functionality of the plugin by observing that the student was not allowed to enroll in the course and was issued a message informing him or her of the reason.

Pop Quiz

1. Which of the following would you use to allow users to enroll in a course three days prior to the official enrollment period?

   a. The Max Allowed Enrollments setting.

   b. The Course Capacity setting.

   c. The User Field Value setting.

   d. The Priority by Period Startdate setting.

2. Which of the following would allow you to use the registration enrollment plugin to limit enrollment in one course to 15 and in another course to 50?

   a. The site-wide Course Capacity setting.

   b. An Override on the Course Capacity from within each individual course.

   c. Manually closing enrollment once the capacity has been met.

   d. Use of multiple site-wide Period settings.

Testing the Registration Enrollment Plugin—a review

We have successfully tested various scenarios to verify that the Registration Enrollment plugin will control enrollments in our courses as per the conditions we dictated when we set up the plugin. We tested and were able to verify the functionality of the following scenarios:

- That the system prevents a user who does not meet the criteria for enrollment from enrolling in the course.

- That the system prevents a user who is eligible to enroll in the course from enrolling prior to the enrollment period start date and time.

- That the system will allow a user who meets the enrollment criteria and who also meets the criteria for priority enrollment to advance enroll in the course.

- That the system will not allow any users, eligible or ineligible, to enroll in the course once the course capacity has been met.

- That the system will not allow any users to enroll in the course once the enrollment period has ended.

- That the system will allow users who meet the criteria to enroll in the course during the enrollment period.

- That the system will prevent users from enrolling in more courses than are allowed via the **Allowed Enrollments** setting.

This system provides crucial functionality for educational programs that wish to position Moodle as a CIMS within their institution. Hopefully, additional funding and/or volunteer development efforts for refinements to the system will enable it to evolve into an even more advanced enrollment management tool. One such feature, mentioned earlier in this chapter, is the ability to apply enrollment condition rules via the use of multiple user profile fields.

Have a go hero

The current 1.0 version of the Registration Enrollment plugin, while still slightly rough around the edges, allows for a wide variety of uses through the use of the user profile fields and the priority enrollment settings. Try experimenting with the plugin and setting up multiple enrollment periods, that do not overlap, each with its own conditions for enrollment. Inversely, experiment with multiple priority enrollment settings, which may occupy the same time frame, to accommodate for different enrollment conditions. The flexibility built into these two settings will allow you to work many scenarios into your enrollment settings.

A note on Moodle customization

The registration enrollment system introduced in this chapter was developed through a Nihon University Individual Research Grant for 2009 and is an example of how Moodle can be customized to meet the needs of a particular institution or program. Once the initial design and conceptualization phase of the project was approved and funding was granted, MoodleRooms, a Moodle Partner in the U.S., was contracted to carry out the programming and testing of the plugin. The development of even a seemingly simple plugin was a project that spanned the course of over one year and involved many e-mails and testing sessions. If you plan to undertake the development of a customized Moodle Block, Module, or Plugin, it would invariably be beneficial to work on the following at the outset of the project:

- ◆ Establish a detailed specification outline that explains the functionality and logic behind the planned development.

- ◆ Choose a developer, if the project is going to be contracted out, and make sure that the developer is confident that the proposed functionality can be accomplished.

- ◆ Seriously consider Moodle Partners for any development you have done as they are the most intimately familiar with the Moodle system and also channel a portion of their income back to Moodle headquarters, which means you are also supporting Moodle financially when you use a Partner.

- ◆ Make sure that you are involved in the testing process and that the plugin being developed is tested rigorously to ensure that all bugs have been worked out of the final product.

- ◆ Establish a communication channel with the individuals involved in the programming and testing of the plugin and utilize it as frequently as possible.

In the end, you will have a customized plugin, which adds functionality to Moodle and that enables it to further meet the needs of your institution and, hopefully, you will consider contributing the development to the Moodle community via the `Moodle.org` website. Contributions of this type can be made via the CONTRIB Coordinator, *Anthony Borrow*, by following the instructions outlined at the following address on the `Moodle.org` website: `http://docs.moodle.org/en/Development` (Guidelines_for_contributed_code).

Note also that your participation in the forums in the **Using Moodle** course found on the `Moodle.org` website is one very easy way that you can contribute to Moodle's development and evolution.

Summary

In this chapter, you were introduced to the Registration Enrollment plugin and we then walked through the download and installation process for the plugin. We enabled the plugin and worked through the set up by entering the settings we planned to use. Next, we created a course in which we specified the registration enrollment plugin as the enrollment method and then added the Course Registration block to the course. We used the block to override some of the site-wide settings and then tested the system by logging in as various users to see how the plugin would perform. We observed how the plugin allows eligible users to enroll in courses as well as how it prevents ineligible users from enrolling and how it informs these users that they may not enroll in the course.

The Registration Enrollment plugin can be used in conjunction with other enrollment plugins to manage enrollment on your Moodle site, but if you are working to establish your Moodle site as a Curriculum and Information Management System, you may opt to use it as the sole enrollment plugin and thus position your Moodle site as the portal through which students must register for their courses. Institutions or programs choosing this route will need to consider how course enrollment data, stored in the Moodle database, will be utilized for various administrative tasks such as transcript creation, but remember that Moodle is an open and flexible system that can accommodate most all educational environments as well as interact with various external data management systems, and it is thus highly likely you'll be able to figure out a way to position your Moodle site as your own CIMS.

Pop Quiz Answers

Chapter 3

Student Account Creation and Enrollment

1	B

Chapter 5

Enabling your Moodle Site to Function as an Information Portal

1	B

Chapter 6

Customized Roles

1	B
2	D
3	D

Chapter 7

Advanced Data Access and Display

First pop quiz:

1	B
2	B
3	B

Second pop quiz:

1	B

Chapter 8

Setting Up a Mini SIS

First pop quiz:

1	D

Second pop quiz:

1	B
2	D

Chapter 10

Advanced Enrollment Plugin

1	D
2	B

Index

Main Menu block, adding to 26, 27
Front Page settings window
  about 20
  settings 20, 21

G

Gradebook template
  creating 100-103
  importing 104, 105
grade retrieval
  courses, locking for 107, 108
grading standards
  about 98
  Gradebook template, creating 100-103
  Gradebook template, importing 104, 105
  standard grading scale, creating 98, 100
  target course, preparing 103, 104
groups
  creating, within meta course 231, 232

I

IMS Enterprise plugin 83
installation, Aardvark Pro original theme 34-37
installation, Attendance package 31-33
installation, Bulk Course Upload tool 53
installation, Content Pages block 122-126
installation, Custom SQL query tool 176, 177
installation, Enhanced User Administration block 168, 169
installation, Mac OS X package 8-10
installation, mentees block 161, 162
installation, Moodle 7
installation, My Courses block 28-31
installation, PHPMyAdmin 173-175
installation, questionnaire module 243, 244
installation, Registration Enrollment plugin 252, 253
installation, themes 34
installation, third party contributions 27
installation, Windows package 10-18
installation, Xataface 181-186
installing
  Aardvark Pro original theme 34-37
  attendance package 31-33
  Bulk Course Upload tool 53
  Content Pages block 122-126

Custom SQL query tool 176, 177
Enhanced User Administration block 168, 169
Mac OS X package 8-10
MAMP package, for Mac OS X 8-10
mentees block 161, 162
Moodle 7
My Courses block 28-31
PHPMyAdmin 173-175
questionnaire module 243, 244
Registration Enrollment plugin 252, 253
themes 34
third party contributions 27
Windows package 10-18
XAMPP package, for Windows 10-18
Xataface 181-186
Internal Enrollment plugin 81

L

label area
  customizing, on front page 23-25
language program 40
LDAP 83
Learning Management System. *See* **LMS**
Lightweight Directory Access Protocol. *See* **LDAP**
links
  adding, to submenu items 132, 134
LMS 6
logo
  customizing 136, 137

M

Mac OS X
  MAMP package, installing for 8-10
Mac OS X package
  installing 8-10
Main Menu block
  adding, to front page 26, 27
MAMP package
  about 7
  installing, for Mac OS X 8-10
mentees block
  about 237
  installing 161, 162
menu bar
  customizing 129
  foreign language fonts, using 129

profile field

creating, for program enrollment information 201, 202

program enrollment information

profile field, creating for 201, 202

Q

questionnaire module

about 243

installing 243, 244

using 244-248

R

Registration Enrollment plugin

about 252

benefits 252

capabilities 252

default site-wide settings 256-261

installing 252, 253

registration enrollment system settings 261-264

setting up 256-261

testing 264

testing, for non-eligible student 268, 269

user profile fields, creating 253, 256

user profile fields, populating 253, 256

Registration Enrollment plugin, testing

about 264

allowed enrollments setting 272, 273

base criteria 270, 271

course capacity setting 269, 270

for ineligible student 268, 269

priority enrollment period, for ineligible student 267, 268

priority enrollment period setting, for eligible student 264-267

relationships

setting up, in Xataface 215-217

roles

about 140

administrative monitor role 152-156

assistant administrator role 146-152

censored student role 142-145

default roles 140, 141

parental Monitor role 157-161

S

security measure, Xataface 192-194

SIS 7, 197

Site Administration block 140, 198

site, Moodle

about 85

advising system, setting up 238-242

attendance policy 86

attendance standards, for students 86

basic customization 19-23

blocks 27

final grade submission process, implementing 105, 106

forums, creating inside meta course 234-237

front page 18

grading standards, for students 98

groups, creating inside meta course 231, 232

label area, customizing on front page 23-25

main menu block, adding to front page 26, 27

meta course, setting up 229, 230

modules 27

permissions 141

roles 140, 141

setting up 18

standard policies, implementing 85, 86

standard procedures, implementing 85, 86

URL 8

SQL queries

about 178

writing 178-180

standard grading scale

creating 98, 100

standardized test

administering, for students 109-113

standard policies

implementing, in Moodle site 85, 86

standard procedures

implementing, in Moodle site 85, 86

Student Information Systems. *See* **SIS**

students

about 140

account, creating for 64-70

enrolling, for course 64-70

standardized test, administering for 109-113

Thank you for buying
Moodle as a Curriculum and Information Management System

About Packt Publishing

Packt, pronounced 'packed', published its first book "*Mastering phpMyAdmin for Effective MySQL Management*" in April 2004 and subsequently continued to specialize in publishing highly focused books on specific technologies and solutions.

Our books and publications share the experiences of your fellow IT professionals in adapting and customizing today's systems, applications, and frameworks. Our solution based books give you the knowledge and power to customize the software and technologies you're using to get the job done. Packt books are more specific and less general than the IT books you have seen in the past. Our unique business model allows us to bring you more focused information, giving you more of what you need to know, and less of what you don't.

Packt is a modern, yet unique publishing company, which focuses on producing quality, cutting-edge books for communities of developers, administrators, and newbies alike. For more information, please visit our website: www.packtpub.com.

About Packt Open Source

In 2010, Packt launched two new brands, Packt Open Source and Packt Enterprise, in order to continue its focus on specialization. This book is part of the Packt Open Source brand, home to books published on software built around Open Source licences, and offering information to anybody from advanced developers to budding web designers. The Open Source brand also runs Packt's Open Source Royalty Scheme, by which Packt gives a royalty to each Open Source project about whose software a book is sold.

Writing for Packt

We welcome all inquiries from people who are interested in authoring. Book proposals should be sent to author@packtpub.com. If your book idea is still at an early stage and you would like to discuss it first before writing a formal book proposal, contact us; one of our commissioning editors will get in touch with you.

We're not just looking for published authors; if you have strong technical skills but no writing experience, our experienced editors can help you develop a writing career, or simply get some additional reward for your expertise.

Moodle 1.9 Teaching Techniques

ISBN: 978-1-849510-06-6   Paperback: 216 pages

Creative ways to build powerful and effective online courses

1. Motivate students from all backgrounds, generations, and learning styles

2. When and how to apply the different learning solutions with workarounds, providing alternative solutions

3. Easy-to-follow, step-by-step instructions with screenshots and examples for Moodle's powerful features

Moodle 1.9 Testing and Assessment

ISBN: 978-1-84951-234-3   Paperback: 392 pages

Develop and evaluate quizzes and tests using Moodle modules

1. Create and evaluate interesting and interactive tests using a variety of Moodle modules

2. Create simple vocabulary or flash card tests and complex tests by setting up a Lesson module

3. Motivate your students to excel through feedback and by keeping their grades online

Please check **www.PacktPub.com** for information on our titles

[PACKT] open source ✤
PUBLISHING
community experience distilled

Moodle 1.9
English Teacher's Cookbook

Silvina P. Hillar

Moodle 1.9 English Teacher's Cookbook

ISBN: 978-1-849510-88-2   Paperback: 304 pages

80 simple but incredibly effective recipes for teaching reading comprehension, writing, and composing using Moodle 1.9

1. Packed with recipes to help you use Moodle effectively to teach English

2. Create a different atmosphere to help students improve their writing skills using Moodle

3. Implement different techniques in the teaching of reading comprehension, writing, and composition using a variety of resources from the free and open source software available

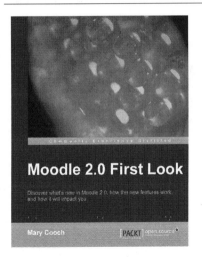

Moodle 2.0 First Look

Mary Cooch

Moodle 2.0 First Look

ISBN: 978-1-849511-94-0   Paperback: 272 pages

Discover what's new in Moodle 2.0, how the new features work, and how it will impact you

1. Get an insight into the new features of Moodle 2.0

2. Discover the benefits of brand new additions such as Comments and Conditional Activities

3. Master the changes in administration with Moodle 2.0

4. The first and only book that covers all of the fantastic new features of Moodle 2.0

Please check **www.PacktPub.com** for information on our titles

Moodle 1.9 Multimedia

ISBN: 978-1-847195-90-6   Paperback: 272 pages

Create and share multimedia learning materials in your Moodle courses.

1. Ideas and best practices for teachers and trainers on using multimedia effectively in Moodle

2. Ample screenshots and clear explanations to facilitate learning

3. Covers working with TeacherTube, embedding interactive Flash games, podcasting, and more

Moodle 1.9 Math

ISBN: 978-1-847196-44-6   Paperback: 276 pages

Integrate interactive math presentations, build feature-rich quizzes, set online quizzes and tests, incorporate Flash games, and monitor student progress using the Moodle e-learning platform

1. Get to grips with converting your mathematics teaching over to Moodle

2. Engage and motivate your students with exciting, interactive, and engaging online math courses with Moodle, which include mathematical notation, graphs, images, video, audio, and more

3. Integrate multimedia elements in math courses to make learning math interactive and fun

Please check **www.PacktPub.com** for information on our titles

17577574R00164

Made in the USA
Lexington, KY
18 September 2012